MINNEAPOLIS/ST. PAUL
SAGINAW/BAY CITY/MIDLAND
ROCHESTER
BOSTON
HARTFORD/SPRINGFIELD
MUSKEGON
FLINT
BUFFALO
ELMIRA/CORNING
MILWAUKEE
LANSING
PROVIDENCE
DETROIT
GRAND RAPIDS
WILLIAMSPORT
NEW YORK
CLEVELAND
NEWARK
TOLEDO
YOUNGSTOWN/WARREN
SOUTH BEND
AKRON/CANTON
SHARON
ALLENTOWN/BETHLEHEM/EASTON
CEDAR RAPIDS
CHICAGO
FORT WAYNE
PITTSBURGH
HARRISBURG
PHILADELPHIA
DES MOINES
OMAHA
MOLINE/ROCK ISLAND/DAVENPORT
DAYTON
BALTIMORE
COLUMBUS
WASHINGTON
LINCOLN
NEWPORT NEWS
HAMPTON/WILLIAMSBURG
CHARLESTON
RICHMOND
NORFOLK/PORTSMOUTH
BRISTOL/JOHNSON CITY/KINGSPORT
KANSAS CITY
GREENSBORO/HIGH POINT
WINSTON-SALEM
RALEIGH/DURHAM
KNOXVILLE
ASHEVILLE/HENDERSONVILLE
CHATTANOOGA
CHARLOTTE
MEMPHIS
HUNTSVILLE/DECATUR
ATLANTA
BIRMINGHAM
JACKSONVILLE
MOBILE
NEW ORLEANS
TAMPA
ST. PETERSBURG
CLEARWATER
WEST PALM BEACH
FORT LAUDERDALE
MIAMI

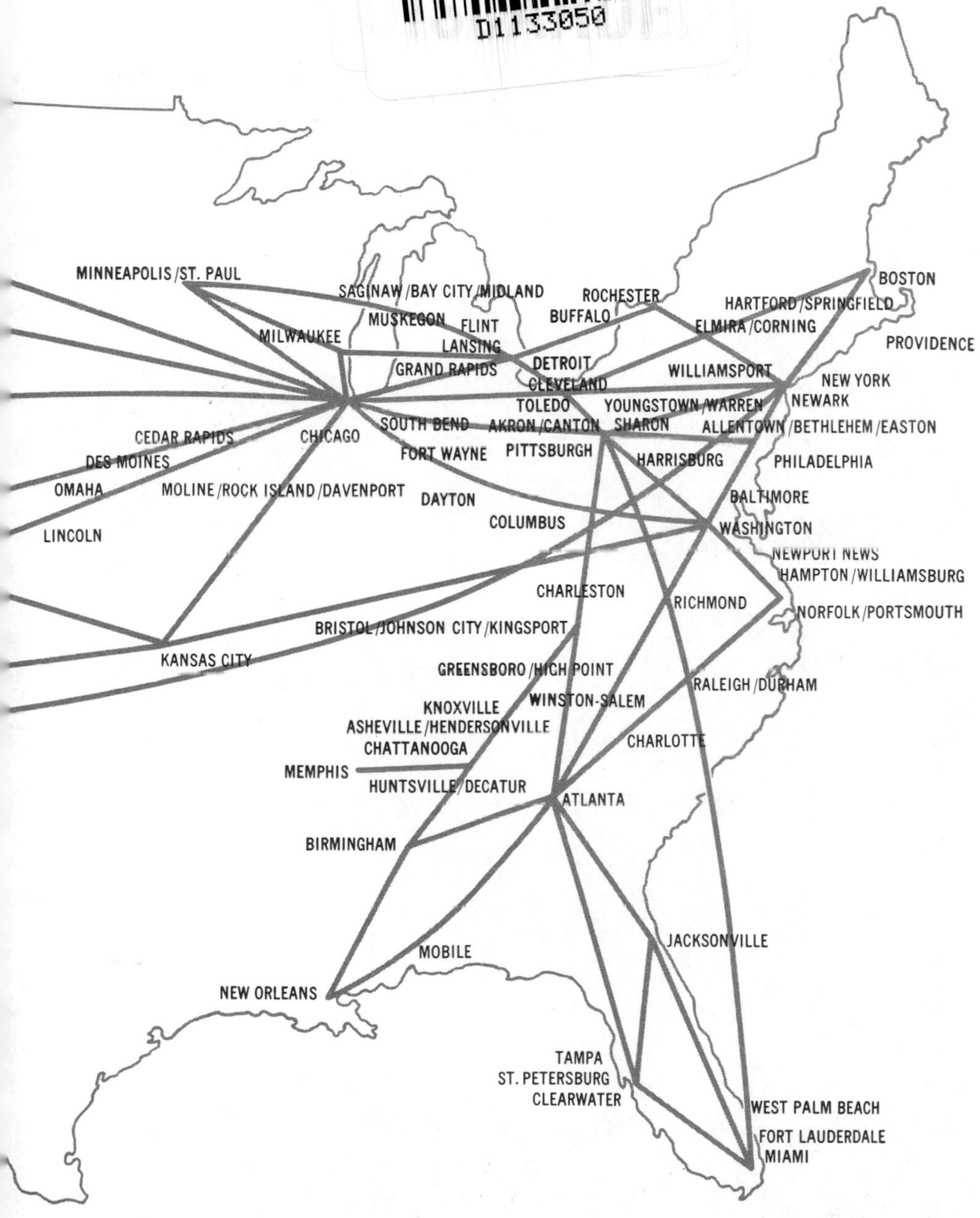

High Horizons

High Horizons

DAREDEVIL FLYING POSTMEN TO MODERN MAGIC CARPET— THE UNITED AIR LINES STORY

By Frank J. Taylor

NEW REVISED EDITION

McGRAW-HILL BOOK COMPANY, INC.

NEW YORK · LONDON · TORONTO

HIGH HORIZONS

Library of Congress Catalog Card Number: 61-14687

NEW REVISED EDITION, 1962

63159

TO THE FAR-SEEING POST OFFICE PIONEERS, WHO BLAZED THESE SKY TRAILS TO THE HIGH HORIZONS

PREFACE

Looking Skyward

> For I dipt into the future, far as human eye could see,
> Saw the Vision of the world, and all the wonder that would be;
> Saw the heavens fill with commerce, argosies of magic sails,
> Pilots of the purple twilight, dropping down with costly bales.
>
> —ALFRED TENNYSON

When this story began some four decades back, most men and women were still earthbound, looking skyward. The high horizons were reached only by the tedious ups and downs of ground transport. A few adventurous souls had soared on wings, risking their necks in the flimsy kites of the barnstormers. The aeroplane *was a recognized military vehicle, but even pioneers in commercial aviation insisted that planes would never carry mail over the mountainous ramparts of the Pacific Coast. Others contended that it was foolhardy and dangerous to try to fly passengers over the Alleghenies, nightmare of the early Post Office air mail pilots. But in the Pacific Northwest and along the Pacific Coast, men who were too inexperienced to recognize the impossible made their bids for air mail routes and flew them, thus launching airways that in time were to become vital parts of the U.S. air network. Daring fliers soon proved that the Alleghenies were no barrier to planes; the route over them became the most heavily traveled airway in the nation.*

There were numerous other forecasts about what the airplane would never do, but events proved that in the fast-moving air transport industry almost anything could happen. The only safe forecast an aviation prophet could make was that today's best, no matter how good, would be outdated by tomorrow. The skeptics who said the Oregon-California Siskiyou mountains were too dangerous to fly over did not know about the lightweight new engines soon to be installed on planes—engines so radical in design and so reliable in performance that they revolutionized air transport. They had no inkling of the embryo airliners taking shape in the dreams of designers. They did not know that shortly pilots would talk with airways stations as easily as people on the ground telephoned each other, or that electronic beams would make paths through space as dependable as highways or railroad tracks.

Nobody had heard of radar, hence no one could foresee devices which would enable pilots to see through fogs, storms, and darkness, or dispatchers to scan the sky for planes invisible to the eye. The doubters could not foresee the day when airliners would make their own atmosphere, in which crews and passengers could exist at six-mile-high altitudes as comfortably as on the ground. Nobody knew that balloon-borne gadgets would take the guesswork out of weather everywhere, so that airliners could fly easily over or around storms. The idea that blasts from jets would blow airliners across the continent in four hours was a far-fetched dream.

Which explains why this story of United Air Lines' first thirty-five years is called HIGH HORIZONS. No matter what horizon had been conquered, next year's horizon was sure to be still higher. The year 1926 is a good time to start the story, with flash backs to the feats of the intrepid Post Office air mail pioneers, whose daring made possible the free-enterprise air transport system unique to this country. That was the year the first small airlines later to be merged into the United system were born.

While the United story typifies the saga of the spectacular growth of air transport in the United States and other lands, this book does not attempt to cover air transport as a whole. The United story is simpler to tell. It is a tale of scientific conquest of the unknown unparalleled in history, the story of a group of entrepreneurs who never realized what couldn't be done and who, therefore, like the aerodynamically unsound bumblebee, went ahead and flew anyway.

CONTENTS

High Horizons

CHAPTER I

The Daredevil Flying Postmen

Shortly after midnight of Washington's Birthday, February 22, 1921, occurred a great crisis in the infancy of American commercial aviation. The scene was the chilly, primitive Omaha airport. At 1:10 A.M. a little group of anxious listeners, after waiting far into the night, heard a welcome sound, the gunning of a Liberty motor in the overcast that hung above the air strip. Guided by impromptu lighting from blazing drums of gasoline, a cumbersome De Haviland plane dropped smoothly to the ground and taxied to the hangar. Out stepped pilot James H. Knight, better known as Jack "Skinny" Knight, slapping his cold gloved hands to start his sluggish corpuscles circulating. After shaking hands with the reception committee, Knight looked around apprehensively.

"Who's going to take her on from here?" he asked.

"Nobody," replied Airport Manager Bill Votaw. "Your relief man washed out at Chicago. It looks like the flight's off."

Nobody said anything for a moment that seemed like a fateful hour—which it was. Finally Knight pulled out his big watch and studied it.

"It's too damn bad to get halfway across the continent and have the flight fizzle out," he said. "I'm going to take this mail on to Chicago."

"Jack, you've never flown the Omaha-Chicago leg, even in daylight," protested Votaw.

"I know, but I can make it, if they'll keep on lighting bonfires."

While he warmed his chilled bones and sipped black coffee in the all-night beanery across from the hangar, Jack Knight studied a Rand McNally road map, the next best excuse for an airway map anyone could find at the airport. In fact, there were no airway maps because there were no airways in that cold, blustery winter night of 1921. That was the reason Jack Knight and nine other daredevil flying postmen were voluntarily flying the air mail by night as well as by day across the continent from San Francisco to New York, and vice versa, guided only by beacon fires lighted by enthusiastic farmers and chambers of commerce across the prairies. By their reckless demonstration the flying postmen hoped to persuade Congress that, with lighted airways, they could cut coast-to-coast mail time in half.

The intrepid winged postmen, most of them World War I veterans, had been flying the mail over stretches of the Post Office coast-to-coast route, the same main line across the country covered by the overland stage, the pony express, the pioneer transcontinental railroads, and the earliest motor highways, since May 15, 1919. On that date they had inaugurated the Chicago-Cleveland run; then followed by flying the "hell stretch" from Cleveland to New York. Gradually, the route was extended to Omaha and San Francisco. In less than two years, flying the mail by day and putting it on trains by night, they had cut the New York–San Francisco mail time from ninety hours, all rail, to seventy-two hours by plane and rail together. One in four of the forty pilots who pioneered the air mail lost his life in a crash, and thirty out of the original forty were to die flying the post.

But as of the tail end of Washington's Birthday, 1921, while Jack Knight sipped his coffee and pored over his map, the United States government had concluded that air mail was a failure, except for a few die-hard enthusiasts. Nowhere on earth was there successful day-and-night air mail operation. The Wilson administration, which had pioneered the idea of flying the mail, was going out of office, come March 4. The incoming Harding administration was committed to a return to normalcy, including less expenditure of public funds. As a last-gasp effort to save civil aeronautics, the postal authorities, under hard-driving Assistant Postmaster General Otto Praeger, and the volunteer flying postmen had decided to fly the mail for one night without beacons or landing lights or navigational aids other than bonfires. They picked Washington's Birthday, at the tag-end of winter, as the last possible moment to arouse popular enthusiasm and spur the outgoing Congress to action.

Bad luck plagued the crucial demonstration from the start. The two westbound flights washed out because of unflyable weather over the graveyard run between New York and Cleveland. One eastbound flight ended in a crash in Nevada, but in the predawn darkness Pilot Farr Nutter climbed from San Francisco's Crissey Field, alongside the Golden Gate, to 12,000 feet and cleared the Sierra Nevada about daylight. At Reno, Pilot Jack Eaton took over and winged the load of mail to Salt Lake City, where Pilot Jimmy Murray picked it up. Murray, pulling into Cheyenne Field at 4:57 that afternoon, turned the mail over to Pilot Frank Yaeger, who winged it to North Platte, Nebraska. There he found Jack Knight, just out of a hospital after suffering a broken nose a week before in a rough landing, waiting to fly the Omaha leg in the historic flight. Knight was held up three hours until 10:45, while mechanics repaired a broken tail skid on his plane. Bonfires, kept blazing by impromptu ground crews at several Nebraska cities, guided him on the nonexistent beam, but he was long overdue when the watchers at Omaha heard his motor.

About 2 A.M., after waiting for the snowstorm to ease up, Knight took off from Omaha on the flight that was to make him a legendary hero of civilian aviation. He flew a compass course for Des Moines, but a strong crosswind from the north made navigation difficult, and he had to pilot the bulky De Haviland with its whining struts crabwise to hold his course. Every few minutes he studied the road map on his knees with the aid of a flashlight. Then he peered over the side of the cockpit for a railroad or a highway to check his course. Each time he used the flashlight, it blinded his eyes for seeing through the darkness. Then low clouds hit the earth and he bumped along, buffeted by the winds, flying by dead reckoning. No longer were there bonfires to reassure him. It was one man, two wings, and a Liberty motor against the night, the weather, and the hazard of finding a place to land.

Knight flew for what seemed an eternity, watching the fuel gauge swinging ominously. He caught the twinkle of lights through a hole in the clouds, dropped down to catch a glimpse of the dome of the capital at Des Moines. There was too much snow on the ground to risk a landing, so he cut in his emergency tank of fuel and followed a railroad track to Iowa City, one of the emergency stops for the flight, with barely enough gas for twenty minutes' flying. At Iowa City he could see no lights marking the landing field. He gunned his Liberty to waken the sleeping town. Suddenly a red flare burst in a field, and Knight pulled his plane alongside it. A sleepy old Swede greeted him. He was the night watchman.

"Everybody goes home when they hear the flight is off," he told Knight, "but I hear your engine and I light a fuse anyway."

"It's a good thing you did," said Knight. "My gas tank is dry. Got any gas?"

Together they rolled out a drum of fuel and poured the gas into the plane's tanks. Knight taxied to the end of the field and took off with the aid of a brace of flares marking the end of the runway, and pointed toward Chicago. He soared above the clouds with only the stars to keep him company, until dawn tinged over the eastern horizon. The fog broke and he saw underneath him a welcome sight, Maywood Field, the Chicago air strip used by the flying postmen. For the first time the faithful Liberty coughed and faltered, after pounding through the long night on all twelve cylinders.

"Go ahead and quit, we'll make it anyhow," said Knight aloud to the engine as he glided down to the field.

Pulling his creaking limbs out of the cockpit, Knight found himself the center of a jubilant, excited throng of people. Women in evening gowns kissed him and men in dinner jackets wrung his hand. News wires had flashed the story of his thrilling flight, and word had spread through Chicago's night clubs. Hundreds of patrons, instead of going home, had taxied out to the airport to greet him. Newspapers headlined him as a hero. In a plane already warmed up, Pilot Webster flew the mail to Cleveland, where Pilot Ernie Allison picked it up and soared over the hell stretch to Hazelhurst Field on Long Island. Letters that had left San Francisco the day before were in New York in 33 hours and 20 minutes, cutting the transcontinental time to less than half.

The headlines that screamed from the newspapers that afternoon continued to heroize Knight. Read one—"Jack Knight, ace of

U.S. air mail service got its start in May, 1918, when Post Office Department pilots began flights between New York, Philadelphia, and Washington, D.C. On hand at the latter city to welcome first inbound flight were (from left) Otto Praeger, Asst. Postmaster General, who directed the new service; M. O. Chance, postmaster of Washington, D.C.; A. L. Burleson, Postmaster General, and President Woodrow Wilson. (U.S. Air Force photo.)

Legendary hero of air transport is Jack Knight, savior of the air mail in the memorable flight of February 22, 1921, when the flying postmen volunteered to wing the mail from coast to coast with only bonfires to guide them at night.

Memorable occasion—Varney Air Lines' first flight on April 6, 1926, which marked true beginning of commercial air transportation in the United States and start of what eventually became United Air Lines. Above: Take-off of Swallow biplane from Pasco, Washington, on 460-mile flight to Boise and Elko. Below: Boise's Mayor E. M. Eagleson and Postmaster Lou Thraikill hand mail to Leon Cuddeback, who piloted history-making flight.

Workhorse of the airways in the period 1947–1957 was the DC-6 Mainliner, which carried 50 or more passengers and 5,500 pounds of baggage and cargo at 300 miles per hour.

Its predecessor was an open-cockpit, single-engine biplane such as this Varney Air Lines' Swallow which carried its pilot and 600 pounds of mail, at around 90 miles per hour.

mail service, hailed." Another proclaimed the "conquest of the air; night-rider's story of perils he meets in the sky." "A daring flight by night keeps air mail going," announced another prophetically. The daring flight of one pilot had caught the public's fancy and dramatized air transport as no other advance did, until even Jack Knight's feat was eclipsed by another daredevil flying postman who had bailed out of mail planes twice, Charles A. Lindbergh, in his epic solo flight across the Atlantic six years later.

More important, the new Congress sensed this popular appeal. Prodded by President Harding a month after he took office, Congress got busy on laws authorizing Federal regulation of civil aviation and appropriated $1,250,000 for continuing and expanding air mail service and lighting the airways. Though it took four years after Knight's epic flight to complete the beacon system, the toddling civilian aviation industry survived a real crisis that night and began to grow.

It gained strength in many ways, some even more important than the public pressure which led Congress to authorize the country's network of lighted—and, later, beamed—airways. A still greater contribution was the know-how gained by the flying postmen at the risk of their necks. Their flying feats in the stick and wire crates became not only legend but were the basis for flying techniques that eventually made United States air transport the pace setter for the world. Too many postal pilots paid for this learning with their lives, yet out of nearly every crash it was learned how to avoid a similar accident in the future, with the result that plane transport, in a short quarter of a century, became as routine as travel by rail or by water.

Air transport's incalculable debt to the flying postmen is based largely on daredevil exploits and flying feats that no pilot in his right mind would have thought of attempting a decade later. Another of Jack Knight's adventures, this time as a beginner on the then dangerous New York–Cleveland leg over the Alleghenies, illustrates the hazards of the early seat-of-the-pants flying era. Like other pilots on this run, Knight kept a notebook of names of farmers with phones along the route. Sometimes the numbers were useful to call after a crash; more often they proved helpful when the ceiling closed down around Bellefonte, Pennsylvania, and a pilot had to telephone ahead to ask how far a farmer could see through the rain or the fog. A typical "weather report" was:

"Well, I can see Slocum's barn."

"How far is that?"

"Oh, just across the east forty."

That meant visibility fair, go ahead and fly.

The early airmen flew the highways, the railroads, and even telephone lines through the Alleghenies. They wanted to be sure they could see the sides of the canyons, or that they could see the tunnels through which a railroad sometimes ducked, in time to pull up over the hill and pick up the rails on the other side. Pilot "Pop" Anglim was following a railroad track near Bellefonte one day when the road dove into a tunnel. Anglim was a wartime flier and promptly did an Immelmann turn, which sent him back up the railroad the way he came, but upside down. Straightening out, he decided he was taking the wrong railroad, so he returned to the next junction and changed to the right one.

A postman could have flown above the overcast, but with no radio beam to check his flight and no accurate way to measure ground speed, he never knew exactly where he was or when to come down. Also, the postmen were afraid of ice on the wings, which added weight and taxed the underpowered engines beyond their capacity. Out west, there were peaks high enough to serve as landmarks above the overcast, but over the Alleghenies a pilot who flew above the fog was flying blind. Postman J. Dean Hill, when he left Bellefonte, invariably lighted a long cigar and puffed leisurely as he flew. When the stogie burned down to two inches in length, he figured it was time to come down over the Jersey meadows. Hill always claimed that his stogie was the first instrument to aid commercial fliers.

Jack Knight belonged to the opposite school, a pilot who stayed below the clouds where he could check landmarks. Leaving Cleveland for Bellefonte, as a dense fog dropped over Ohio one day, he hugged the highway to keep on course. When the houses and trees began clipping by him, he knew he was only forty feet off the ground. Too low! Pulling up, he found a power line and flew it east, so close he barely missed the tops of the poles. When the hills of western Pennsylvania rose beside his plane, he climbed to 8000 feet and followed a compass course for Bellefonte. He flew for two hours on top without finding a hole through which to come down. Then he nosed down through the thick soup.

Suddenly Knight thought of Charlie Lambert, who had crashed into a hillside only three days before while dropping through the clouds like that. He pulled up on top again, considered bailing out, as "Slim" Lindbergh had done twice, parachuting down safely. Instead, Knight pulled out a notebook and jotted down his last will and testament. Slipping the notebook into his jacket pocket, he pointed the plane down through the overcast. At 3000 feet he leveled off. He knew that the peaks around Bellefonte rose 2600 feet, and that Bellefonte Field was in the 1200-foot elevation. There was nothing in sight but the thick, soupy fog, so he dropped down to 2500 feet. Still no mountainside rose up to slap him. He nosed down slowly until he reached 1500 feet. Nothing but fog. Lost completely, he eased down gingerly to 1200, then 1100 feet. Suddenly a concrete road loomed out of the mist 100 feet below.

He followed the road in a course as crooked as a snake's backbone. Eventually it ran through a town. Knight circled around the water tank and read the sign on it—"Mifflinburg Carriage Works." That stood his hair on end. He had dropped into one of the wildest, narrowest canyons in the Alleghenies, where a mile either way meant a crash into a hillside. But at least he knew where he was and could follow the road into Bellefonte, which lay smothered in fog. When the ground crew heard his motor droning over the airport, they ignited the drum of gasoline to send up a column of smoke, around which Knight spiraled to a safe landing.

Years later in 1942, when Jack Knight had retired from active flying to become director of public education for United Air Lines, he came across the old notebook and did some figuring. He had flown almost 2,000,000 miles since writing the last will and testament at 8000 feet above the clouds without making any use of it. But he and hundreds of other pilots had use for a lot of the other ideas jotted down in the little black book while he was flying by the seat of his pants for tough old Uncle Sam, personified by hard-hitting Otto Praeger, Assistant Postmaster General in charge of the air mail, and to many an early pilot a relentless driver of men.

Actually Praeger, a fearless, determined man, was only living up to the traditions of the Post Office Department, which had pioneered post roads, river steamer routes, the overland stage, pony express, the railroads, and even motor transports for mail routes during the century past. The Post Office heads accepted it as a departmental duty to give a lift to the airplane, the newest and fastest means of transporting the mail. Luckily for United States commercial aviation, these Post Office Department officials believed that air transport should eventually be freed from the military branches of the government, and likewise that it should be a commercial rather than a state venture as soon as the airplane could pay its own way. By pioneering air mail in its infancy, they hoped merely to put a weak, young industry on its feet.

The air mail service was incubated with planes and pilots borrowed from the United States Army Signal Corps. By the middle of 1918, the Post Office had shaken loose from the Army and owned seventeen planes in its own right. They were open cockpit affairs, but they made such a good showing on the experimental Washington–Philadelphia–New York run that by the end of the year the irrepressible Otto Praeger was ready to launch the beginnings of coast-to-coast service, despite the lack of emergency fields and navigation aids. Postmaster General Burleson gave the project his blessing, provided Praeger's pilots could fly in any kind of weather. Praeger promised they would, and picked November 12, 1918, as the day to open the New York–Chicago route. Weatherwise it was one of the worst days of the winter, and the flimsy planes that took to the air from both ends of the run were batted down by storms soon after they took off. Undefeated, Praeger tried again on January 2, 1919. Again storms forced the planes down.

Somewhat jolted but not discouraged, Praeger promoted two emergency landing fields at Bellefonte and Lehighton, both in Pennsylvania. On their third try, Praeger's pilots launched first the Chicago-Cleveland leg, then in midsummer added service over the Alleghenies to New York. This time the mail planes stayed in the air, though two pilots lost their lives in 1919 and five in 1920 as a result of crashes. The following year, twelve gave their lives pioneering a technique for a transportation system for which there existed no rules or know-how. The early pilots called their underpowered wood and canvas crates "flying bricks." Most of them were Army De Havilands, rebuilt by the Post Office at the cost of $2000 per plane.

The Post Office tradition that "the mail must go through" led Praeger to discharge two pilots who refused to take off one day with zero ceilings. Both were fliers known for their courage, one being E. Hamilton Lee, who until he retired in 1949 was United's senior pilot with more than 4,400,000 flying miles without an accident. When authorities refused to reinstate them, on the grounds that postal service demanded unquestioning discipline to orders, all the flying postmen quit their planes in the first air mail pilots' strike on record. The strike started on July 25, 1919, and lasted two days, the pilots holding out for the right to make the final decision as to whether the weather was flyable or not, a principle later firmly established on the airlines. The first pilots' strike ended in a compromise; the discharged pilots got their risky jobs back, and both pilots and postal authorities agreed to let the airport managers decide if planes and weather were flyable.

Nevertheless and in spite of the magnificent showing of the pioneers, who demonstrated that air mail could be flown from coast to coast in 33 hours, morale of the pioneer airmen was low when the Harding administration took over on March 4, 1921. Otto Praeger, whose ruthless drive had made the United States air mail service the world's best, gave way to Colonel E. H. Shaughnessy, who, after a quick survey of the situation, took drastic steps to restore the spirit of the pilots. One step was to assign each pilot his own plane. Another was to cancel night flying until beacons and radio beams could be installed to guide pilots on their courses. The flying postmen were granted more say-so as to whether the weather was flyable or not. Morale rebounded, but unfortunately before he could carry out his whole program Colonel Shaughnessy was killed in the collapse of the roof of the Washington Theater.

The new boss of the growing air mail service was Colonel Paul Henderson of Chicago, son-in-law of Representative Martin B. Madden of Illinois, chairman of the all-important House Ways and Means Committee. This connection gave the air mail pioneers a voice in Congress, where they needed it. Henderson, destined to be a potent figure in air transport, both in and out of the Post Office, believed that to become an important factor in American life and business, air mail had to fly around the clock.

Henderson pushed the building of beacons every 25 miles along the main line from New York to San Francisco, which the Post Office called its Columbia Route. Near each beacon Henderson wanted an emergency landing strip, known to the pilots as "crack-up fields." On the eastern leg, Charlie Stanton, hard-hitting test pilot, sloshed the muddy roads of Ohio into Indiana and Pennsylvania, looking for sites for emergency landing fields and beacons. Stanton sold the idea not only to farmers but to their wives and their youngsters. When he found a farmer worried about having planes fly over his home and his barn, Stanton argued that the safest place to have a beacon was on the barn, because pilots always flew half a mile to the right.

"By cracky, that's so," was the usual answer, and the Post Office had another beacon location.

Out west, Jack Knight and Slim Lewis sold the same idea to farmers on the plains and the prairies. Thus on a shoestring and at remarkably small cost the Post Office got scores of landing strips and beacons installed to serve for emergency landings. These were fitted with blinker lights to inform the night flier where he was. Henderson himself stumped the country, prodding the pride of local towns and cities and talking them into building airports, which the Post Office had no funds to construct. Later there was much misunderstanding, because many of the cities thought that the Federal government was to reimburse them. But Henderson got his airports and left behind a legacy of local politics that long was to plague the air transport industry. Most remarkable of all, by July 1, 1924, when enough beacons were installed to guide pilots in night mail flights across the country, Henderson had promoted 1886 miles of lighted airways with emergency landing facilities at the amazingly low cost to the Post Office of half a million dollars.

The flying postmen were getting other aids, some of them inside the cockpits. Some planes carried one-way radios, usually because the pilot was a Handy Andy interested in experimenting. Many of the air mail pilots preferred seat-of-the-pants flying and distrusted the new gadgets and instruments—and not without reason.

Pilot Charlie Ames, watching a standard Army altimeter as he snaked up a canyon in the Alleghenies near Bellefonte, pulled up to clear a peak as he had done many times before. He failed to clear the crest of Litney Range, 6 miles from Bellefonte Field, and crashed. When Ames's altimeter was checked, it was found to be 50 feet off, the barometric pressure having changed since he left an elevation not much above sea level.

"Well, that's how we learned to use altimeters," explained Slim Lewis, who was Ames's roommate. "Charlie lost his life to progress, and they named a field for him."

Slim Lewis, World War I test pilot, was luckier in his adventures. Slim was flying the mail over Pennsylvania one day when the wind swept a piece of the tail off his plane. Lewis could neither climb nor descend nor turn, and he was too low to bail out. So he kept on flying until the engine stopped. The plane dropped slowly onto a baseball diamond and rolled into a tea house in a nearby park.

"Where am I?" asked Lewis, when rescuers pulled him out of the wreckage unhurt.

"Tyrone, Pennsylvania."

"What will you take for this place?" he asked, surveying the wrecked tea house.

Lewis promised, on behalf of the Postmaster General, to rebuild the tea house. Soon afterward, when night flying was launched, the Post Office granted his request for transfer out west. That was the night-flying end of the airway. One day, following a route east of Cheyenne beneath low clouds, Slim was forced to the ground when the ceiling closed down. Before his plane rolled to a stop, it hit a bull. The bull knocked off one wing of the plane. Climbing out of the cockpit, Lewis discovered that the impact had broken the bull's leg. To put the animal out of its misery, Lewis got a revolver out of the cockpit and shot the bull, just as the owner of the ranch appeared. Angrily, the latter explained that the dead animal was the prize Hereford bull of the area. So Slim had to pay for the dead bull. The deal involved the equivalent of 6500 air mail stamps. Years later, after serving as superintendent of United's western division, Slim Lewis retired to a ranch life in almost the identical spot where he bought his first prize Hereford bull for the Postmaster General.

Through these years of trial-and-error operation, with little to guide them but resourceful intuition, the flying postmen hung up an enviable record for living up to the Post Office motto. They did it largely by a performance in excess of duty, as was demonstrated when Pilot Frank Yaeger was forced down by a closing-in fog near North Platte. With the ceiling too low to permit flying, Yaeger discovered that he could taxi across the prairie, bumping along on the ground until he came to a fence. When a fence interrupted his taxiing, he took off, flew a few hundred feet, cleared the obstruction, then taxied again on the ground. Thus Yaeger covered the last 50 miles into North Platte and delivered his mail to the postmaster.

Or it was dramatized by Paul Scott, who cracked up trying to negotiate Little Lake Pass, near the eastern border of Nevada. Scott pulled himself out of the wreckage with a dislocated shoulder. Salvaging the registered mail pouch, he staggered down the snowy mountainside, slipped and rolled to the bottom. When he picked himself up, his shoulder was back in place again. He trudged into Shafter emergency field and delivered the registered mail.

Another time, over Saltair, Utah, in midsummer, Scott looked back to see the fuselage of his plane burst into flames. He landed in a hurry on the desert, yanked out the mail and stacked it well away from the burning plane. Then he sat down to wait for the gas tanks to explode. It was a short wait. When the flames hit the tanks, the explosion aimed a stream of burning gasoline at the one spot in a million acres of sagebrush where Scott had stacked the United States mail.

Some of the postmen equipped themselves for extended stays in the mountains or desert in case they were forced down. One of the foresighted air mail pilots was Werner O. Bunge. He was forced down one day by minor engine trouble in the Idaho desert. Bunge made repairs, then looked around for room to take off. Everywhere he looked, there was sagebrush as far as the eye could see. Getting out his ax, Bunge began to chop. It took a day and a half to clear a strip long enough for a take-off. By this time his hands were raw as beefsteaks. To make sure of getting off the ground, he lightened his load by stacking half his mail bags alongside the improvised runway. Gunning his engine, he lifted the plane out of the sage, found the nearest emergency field, unloaded the half load, flew back to his desert air strip, made an emergency landing, and brought out the rest of the mail.

Then there was Clair Vance, forced down at a mining camp known as "Last Camp" in the Sierra Nevada west of Reno. When search parties failed to find him in the first forty-eight hours, Vance was given up for lost. The following day he walked into Reno, leading a string of burros. On each burro was a sack of mail. Vance turned the mail over to the postmaster and started off with his animals.

"Where are you going?" they asked him.

"To the grocery store," he replied. "I promised the old prospector who lent me these donkeys that I would bring them back loaded with grub."

Trouble was more or less routine with the flying postmen. Thanks to trouble, they were acquiring technique. Winging the mail from coast to coast was becoming such a dependable operation that air mail users gradually quit sending carbon copies of their air mail letters by rail post. By 1923, the air mail project was living up to the claim that Postmaster Burleson had made for it two years before, when the enthusiastic Texan wrote in his last annual report, "The air mail service of the United States is the only practical commercial airplane service in the world. No service in foreign countries compares with it in magnitude, in continuous dependability, and in benefits to commerce."

Pilots no longer considered four years their average life expectancy. In fact, along about 1924 Jack Knight wrote, for the *U.S. Air Mail Pilot*, "We of the western division know how the riders of the Pony Express, the drivers of Ben Holiday's overland stage line, and the freighters of the fifties legged it and fought it out down there below. What's a crash or a forced landing to that? All we have to do is fly."

But there was still plenty of daredevil adventure in flying the mail for the Post Office, and down in their hearts the pilots knew it, as was revealed by a farewell greeting found in an envelope in the pocket of Captain Hyde Pearson, who crashed in the Pennsylvania hills. It read, "To my beloved brother pilots and pals—I go West, but with a cheerful heart. I hope what small sacrifice I have made may be of use to the cause. When we fly, we are damned fools, they say. When we are dead, we weren't half bad fellows. But everyone in this wonderful aviation service is doing the world more good than the public can appreciate. We risk our necks; we give our lives; we perfect a service for the benefit of the world at large. They, I know, are the ones who call us fools, but stick to it, boys, I am still very much with all of you. See you all again."

CHAPTER II

The Western Pioneers

Soon after Glenn L. Martin, one of the fathers of American aviation, launched his first small factory to build aeroplanes in Santa Ana, California, two prospective customers from the Pacific Northwest turned up, bursting with yearnings for wings. They were Vern C. Gorst of North Bend, Oregon, and William E. Boeing of Seattle, Washington. Unknown to each other and as different in background and personality as two humans could possibly be, the urge to fly made them kindred spirits destined to lead roles in the slowly unfolding drama of United States air transport.

Early in 1915, while Congress was debating and rejecting the idea of allowing the Post Office to experiment with air mail service, Gorst learned to fly from Silas Christopherson, early stunt flier, while Boeing was taught to pilot a plane by Glenn Martin himself. Then, since Gorst lived on Coos Bay and Boeing lived on Puget Sound, both neophyte fliers bought Martin pontoon-equipped planes, known as "Flying Birdcages" because of the criss-cross of wires that held the wings and struts together. The pusher engines, like the seats for the pilots and passengers, hung like perches in a birdcage. Before long both birdcages cracked up. And these crackups played a part in American aviation in vastly different ways.

How Bill Boeing reacted to his crackup will come later. Gorst's crash was the greater tragedy because, although he was uninjured, he and his partner, Charles O. King, were building a chain of small Oregon bus lines on a shoestring and they were unable to spare the money to buy a new plane. For the next decade Gorst had to satisfy his urge to fly by reading everything he could lay his hands on about aviation and by watching the barnstorming stunt fliers winging overhead. Not until 1925 was Gorst able to get into the air again.

By that time he was head of six little shoestring bus lines he had promoted, operating over short routes scattered from Medford, Oregon, to Santa Monica, California. Late in 1925 a group of Oregon stage line men gathered at the Coos Bay Hotel in North Bend to talk over highway transportation problems, of which there were plenty. When they had finished, Gorst took the floor to pose a bigger problem yet, which none of the others had thought about.

"What are we going to do about airplanes?" he asked. "In a short time they will be flying right over our heads, carrying our passengers and our mail."

While devouring aviation literature, Gorst had learned that the Post Office was about to call for bids from private operators to fly the feeder lines delivering air mail to the Post Office Department's route between San Francisco and New York. The longest of these feeders was to blanket the Pacific Coast from Seattle to Los Angeles. Gorst proposed that the stage line operators join forces to land the contract which covered their territory. The suggestion aroused such enthusiasm that before the meeting broke up they raised a kitty of some $1100 to pay Gorst's expenses in making a survey of the proposed route. With the money in his pocket, Gorst hurried down to San Francisco, where he hired R. B. "Pat" Patterson, a stunt flier with a 90-horsepower Swallow plane, to fly him on a survey trip from Crissey Field by the Golden Gate to Vancouver, British Columbia, and back by an alternate route.

It was midwinter, November 21 to December 10, and the tiny plane dodged through mountain passes and storms, picking landing sites, usually pastures or fair grounds, from the air and dropping into them unannounced. Gorst and Patterson completed the trip without accident or need of repairs, at a cost of $43 for gas and $5.25 for oil. It was typical of Vern Gorst's genius for doing the impossible on a shoestring. He reported that flying the air mail from the Mexican to the Canadian border was entirely feasible and persuaded his fellow stage operators to take about $14,000 worth of stock in the proposed $500,000 Pacific Air Transport company he undertook forthwith to organize.

This was far from enough cash to start the enterprise, so Gorst hot-footed over Washington, Oregon, and California like a Fuller-brush salesman, peddling stock to anyone who would buy a share for $100. His biggest haul was $25,000 from Julius Meier, the department-store tycoon of Portland. Most of the money came in driblets, $100 to a $1000. When he couldn't get money, Gorst traded stock for anything the proposed airline might need. He swapped stock to the Standard Oil Company for gasoline. In Grass Valley he encountered a stunt pilot, Ralph "Pee Wee" Virden, who owned a plane with which he did stunt flying. Gorst lured both the pilot and the plane into the Pacific Air Transport fold. At Medford, Oregon, he needed an airfield and a manager. With stock as bait he got both, when a young automobile dealer, Seely V. Hall, later one of United Air Lines' top executives, joined the enterprise. While he peddled stock, eventually raising $175,000, including about $40,000 of his own capital garnered by selling his interests in all but one of his stage lines, Gorst hired ten pilots from two hundred barnstormers who heard about the new enterprise and tackled him for jobs. Gorst's two qualifications were that they had to be able to fly and were willing to take some of their wages in stock.

As a promoter Vern Gorst was without peer in a fledgling industry in which promoters were a dime a dozen at the time. Born at Port Orchard, Washington, not far from the town of Gorst, which was named for his family, young Gorst was lured to Alaska by the Klondike gold strike in 1894. After prospecting for a year, he returned to the University of Washington to study geology and assaying. By 1899 he was back in Alaska, hunting gold, but soon decided there was more money in transportation. Gorst first transported supplies to the sourdoughs on his back, tramping on snowshoes. Then he acquired a dog team and a sled and became a freighter.

In 1903, after marrying a girl he met in Alaska, Gorst settled in southern Oregon to try for a stake in the Josephine County gold mining boom. Again, after several backbreaking years, he concluded that the gold was in transportation. He bought an early Cadillac. His friend, Charley King, owned one of the first Packards in Oregon. Forming the partnership of Gorst & King, they started a 5½-mile stage line between Jacksonville and Medford. The partners packed the passengers on top of each other and on the running board, and not only made money but had the distinction of forcing a competitive short-line railroad to fold up. From that time on, for the next four decades, the agile and inventive Gorst was up to his ears in promoting transportation, by auto, by boat, by sea plane, by land plane.

As the time neared for bidding on CAM-8 (Commercial Air Mail Route No. 8, as the Post Office Department designated the Pacific Coast route), competition for the dubious plum reared its head. The big wing of commercial aviation on the Pacific Coast was a well-heeled company headed by Harris M. "Pop" Hanshue, former auto racing driver and successful Los Angeles automobile dealer. Stung by the way in which the Post Office had set up the Columbia line from New York to San Francisco without taking Los Angeles into consideration, publisher Harry Chandler and real estate promoter William M. Garland had passed the hat as a gesture of civic pride and raised a quarter of a million dollars, with promise of more as needed, to put Los Angeles on the aviation map. With this capital, they organized Western Air Express, which proposed to bid on all air mail routes terminating in Southern California.

Another potential competitor shaped up in San Francisco, where an aviation enthusiast named Allan Bonnalie aroused the interest of a group of Southern Pacific executives. Bonnalie's survey of the situation persuaded them that the railroad should have a toe in the air transport business, partly to expedite its own communications, partly to get the jump on a potential competitor. Bidding for CAM-8 seemed the logical way to do this. Fortunately for Gorst and the air-minded stagecoach men, Bonnalie's program was squashed by stiff-necked President William Sproul, who doubted that the airplane would ever be an important factor in transportation.

"If it ever is, we will buy up the airlines the way we are buying up the stage lines," said Mr. Sproul, whose crystal ball was unable to foresee the day, four decades later, when airliners would replace the Southern Pacific's crack passenger trains as the routine mode of travel between cities of the Pacific slope.

Luckily, while the Southern Pacific was counting itself out, the Southern California competitors were counting themselves halfway out. Hanshue concluded that airplanes would never fly successfully over the rugged Siskiyou Range. He sent his assistant, James G. Woolley, to talk Vern Gorst into tossing Pacific Air Transport's capital in with that of Western Air Express to bid on that part of CAM-8 south of the formidable mountain barrier. When Gorst declined, Western bid on that part of the route only. Gorst bid on the entire contract, from Seattle to Los Angeles. When the postal authorities looked at PAT's shaky structure, they asked Gorst to raise his cash resources to half a million dollars. Gorst assured them that was his goal, but he had been unable to raise all of the capital as yet.

There being no other legitimate bidders, Postmaster General Harry S. New granted the contract to Gorst, who promptly traded it, on March 6, 1926, to the newly organized Pacific Air Transport in consideration of 250 shares of Class B common stock. Gorst already owned 134 shares of this stock. Since the incorporation called for issue of only 500 shares of Class B, which was the voting stock, this put Gorst in undisputed control of the new company. Outstanding were some 1700 shares of A stock of the same $100 par value, but nonvoting. Later this issue was increased to 4500 shares. But even so, by this shrewd deal, Gorst was made undisputed boss of Pacific Air Transport, one of the country's wobbliest but potentially most lucrative airlines. It grew to be one of the keys to the future United Air Lines system.

Before Pacific Air Transport could start service, Gorst had to lay out an airway. He and his pilots, a resourceful and daring group of ex-barnstormers, persuaded a score of towns along the route to establish community air strips. Gorst bought old automobile lights and rigged up makeshift beacons on high buildings, poles, and hills, and above windmills and atop barns. He talked the Standard Oil Company into painting the names of towns in huge letters on the roofs of the company's buildings, so that his fliers would know where they were without buzzing railroad stations.

Always the bargain hunter, Gorst picked up two Travelair planes, a Swallow and a Waco, and three spare motors, for little more than a song. The backbone of the PAT fleet was the new

Ryan monoplane, equipped with Wright Whirlwind engines. After Claude Ryan of San Diego flew Gorst to Seattle in the first experimental model of this sturdy little plane to prove its dependability, Gorst ordered the first ten of them to come out of the Ryan plant, at a cost of about $3700 per plane, plus $5000 more for the engines. Plane No. 16 out of the Ryan plant was sold to a former air mail pilot, "Slim" Lindbergh, who named it "The Spirit of St. Louis." Lindbergh later told Gorst that what decided him in favor of the Ryan for his hazardous solo flight across the Atlantic was the performance of the little planes over the California and Oregon mountains.

Nevertheless the new line's losses were appalling. PAT launched its service on September 15, 1926. Before the winter storms ended, three of Gorst's original ten pilots had lost their lives. Pilot Patterson, who had helped Gorst lay out the line, flew into a hill near Medford in the fog. Pilot Eddie Near dozed off and flew into the ground near Turlock, California. Later Art Starbuck crashed. It was a venture so new and untried that pilots had to fly by their wits, until Chief Pilot Grover Tyler could evolve flying rules for the line. Despite the hazards and the discomforts, there were foolhardy passengers who begged to be packed in among the mail sacks in the open cockpit. The fare for the 18½-hour flight from Seattle to Los Angeles was $132, and there are still businessmen in Pacific Coast cities who proudly display frayed bits of pasteboard, resembling movie theater tickets, to prove that they once bounced over the Siskiyous with PAT's mail bags.

In spite of PAT's surprising showing operationswise, Gorst was continuously in trouble. The mail contract provided that the airline was to receive 75 per cent of the revenues from the sale of air mail stamps. Although substantial, it was never enough to meet the overhead. Pilots, who averaged about $400 a month for risking their necks, took part of their pay in stock certificates, which they tossed into lockers and forgot. Oil companies took stock for gas, and donated oil for test purposes.

The main base of the airline was at Crissey Field at San Francisco, where Gorst made his headquarters, living in a cheap Mission Street hotel. His salary as president of the company was the same as the pilots received. A born bargain hunter, he picked up engine

Milestones in 32-year aviation career of Capt. Harry Huking, United's senior pilot until his retirement in 1956 when his logbook recorded more than 5 million miles and 29,000 hours of flying. Above: With Postmaster Austin Jackson of Reno on start of first regular day-and-night, coast-to-coast air mail service in 1924. Below: With Mrs. Huking and daughter Mary at San Francisco after his farewell flight for United.

Cargo loading in 1927, at Hadley Field, New Jersey, eastern end of National Air Transport, which merged into United Air Lines to form the first coast-to-coast airline.

Veteran flying postman, dapper E. Hamilton Lee, who had title of "world's flyingest" man prior to his retirement from United's ranks in 1949.

Close-up of a "flying brick" being christened with champagne in 1928 for a maiden voyage on the NAT end of the Main Line. The daughter of the mayor of Toledo, Ohio, does the honors as Pilot Leo McGinn stands by.

There goes the air mail—in a "flying brick," as the early Liberty-powered planes were known affectionately by pilots, who peered around windshields, struts, and cables to see where they were headed.

Evolution of Air Transport from Flying Postman to DC-7 Mainliner

1920 . . . Converted wartime "De Haviland" . . . 1 pilot, no passengers . . . 400-horsepower Liberty . . . 100 miles per hour . . . 400 pounds air mail . . . 72 hours coast-to-coast by plane-rail schedules.

1927 . . . Boeing 40 between San Francisco and Chicago . . . 1 pilot . . . 425-horsepower Wasp . . . 105 miles per hour . . . 1600 pounds payload including mail, 2 passengers and baggage . . . 32 hours coast to coast, $400.

1929 . . . Boeing tri-motor 80-A San Francisco–Chicago . . . 2 pilots and stewardess . . . three 525-horsepower Hornets . . . 120 miles per hour . . . 3800 pounds payload including 14 passengers, mail, express, baggage . . . 27¾ hours coast to coast, $[illegible]59.50.

1933 . . . Boeing 247 . . . 2 pilots and stewardess . . . two 550 horsepower Wasps . . . 171 miles per hour . . . 2500 pounds payload including 10 passengers, mail, express and baggage . . . 19½ hours coast to coast, $160.

1936 . . . Douglas DC-3 . . . 2 pilots and stewardess . . . two 1200-horsepower twin-row Wasps . . . 180 miles per hour . . . 5800 pounds payload including 21 passengers, mail, express, freight and baggage . . . 15¾ hours coast to coast . . . $160.

1954 . . . Douglas DC-7 . . . 2 pilots, flight engineer, and 2 stewardesses . . . four 3350-horsepower Curtiss-Wright turbo-compound engines . . . 365 miles per hour . . . 17,610 pounds payload including 58 passengers, baggage, mail, express, and freight . . . 7½ hours nonstop coast to coast . . . $158.85.

Western pioneer, Vern C. Gorst, who learned to fly in a "flying birdcage" and who launched Pacific Air Transport on a shoestring and a prayer to pioneer one of United's important routes.

Vern Gorst (left) got his first taste of flying in a Glenn Martin "birdcage."

Old Number One—the first Ryan monoplane to fly the Los Angeles–Seattle route.

The Seattle Daily Times

SEATTLE, WASHINGTON, THURSDAY, MARCH 18, 1926.

PLANE SETS RECORD FOR S. F. TO SEATTLE FLIGHT

Front-page stuff was this survey flight for PAT by Vern Gorst and plane builder Claude Ryan.

Air mail pioneers. Above: Postmaster C. M. Perkins of Seattle chomps cigar as he turns first pouch of southbound mail over to Chief Pilot Grover Tyler of Pacific Air Transport on September 15, 1926. Below: Pilot Leon Cuddeback, who inaugurated Varney Air Lines' service between Pasco, Boise, and Elko on April 6, 1926. He is shown beside tiny Swallow biplane of type Varney used in beating other early private contractors into the mail flying game.

and plane parts wherever he could get them cheap. One day, spurred by the prospects of a bargain but out of money, he walked into the main office of the Wells Fargo Bank in San Francisco. It was the lunch hour, and the officer on duty was a young man in his twenties, William A. Patterson. Spotting Gorst looking about uneasily, Patterson asked if he could do something for him.

"I thought you could when I came in, but I guess not," replied Gorst, edging toward the door.

Patterson, who had just been promoted to the new business department, persuaded Gorst to sit down and tell his story. He wanted to borrow a few hundred dollars to buy a new airplane engine, which unfortunately lay at the bottom of San Francisco Bay, into which one of the ill-fated planes of the Dole flight to Hawaii had plunged. Gorst thought he could get it cheap, but concluded, after Patterson asked about the effect of salt water on engines, that it wasn't much of a buy at all. Before he left, he had intrigued Patterson in PAT's problems. The young banker went out to Crissey Field to look over the line's base and see what his bank could do to bolster up the airline's financial structure. Bankerlike, he asked to see PAT's financial statement. Gorst showed it to him.

"Where is your entry for depreciation?" asked Patterson.

"I thought you'd ask that," replied Gorst. He took Patterson out into the hangar and showed him a row of bins filled with parts. "When a part is worn out, we go to the bin and get another one. That's all the depreciation we have."

Nevertheless, Patterson decided to take a chance. He loaned Gorst $5000. It was Patterson's first loan on his own responsibility. When Wells Fargo's President Frederick L. Lipman heard about it, he called his young business getter into his office.

"About that loan to the flying machine company," he began. "I don't think that the flying machine business will ever amount to much."

Patterson pointed out that one way to get new business was to help fledgling companies get on the wing. Lipman was unimpressed with the argument.

"I have only one fear," said Lipman. "If this loan turns out badly, you might lose confidence in yourself. You had better stay close to those flying machine men until we get the money back."

Patterson did, spending most of his spare time at Crissey Field talking with the pilots, learning their problems, helping Gorst and his associates put the airline on a semblance of a businesslike basis. The loan was repaid on the dot. Patterson persuaded Gorst to take his next check from the Post Office, in payment for carrying the mail, and buy $15,000 worth of government bonds, which he used as security to borrow $14,000 cash, thus establishing a line of credit. Then Ken Humphries (who later built Pacific Intermountain Express into the biggest trucking operation in the country) came in as manager, investing his entire savings, $10,000. Though the airline was short of operating capital, business looked better, especially during the summer of 1927, when flying weather was good. Gorst with his shoestring airline was almost out of the woods. There was one forbidding cloud on the horizon. That was winter with its storms. Gorst, a sensitive man and, unlike Otto Praeger, no driver of men, recoiled at the thought of the toll of pilots that the next winter might take.

Meantime other pioneers were having their troubles flying feeder lines over the mountains and deserts of the Far West. One of them was an enthusiastic World War I Army flier, Walter T. Varney, who returned to his home in San Mateo, California, with unlimited optimism about the future of aviation. Young Varney first organized a flying school at San Mateo, then launched an air ferry service across San Francisco Bay and an air express run between San Francisco and Stockton and Modesto in California's interior valley. The resourceful Varney used his instructors and advanced flying students to pilot his planes. His school mechanics serviced them. This reduced his overhead and provided his pupils with practical experience.

When the Post Office advertised for bids on feeder lines connecting with the overland air mail late in 1925, Varney decided to go after a contract. Already rated as an experienced air transport man as a result of his express flying, he looked over the list of routes open for bids and picked the 460-mile line from Elko, Nevada, to Boise, Idaho, and thence to Pasco, Washington. Although this looked like the makings of an airline that flew from practically nowhere to nowhere, Varney shrewdly chose it because he figured other operators would hesitate to fly over the hazardous desert and mountain terrain it covered.

Varney guessed right. His bid of 8 cents per ounce was the only one entered, and he was awarded the contract on October 7, 1925. The Post Office agreed to pay him 80 per cent of the air mail postal revenues. Anticipating no passengers over the rugged terrain, Varney, backed by his father, who was a partner in the billboard firm of Varney & Green, ordered six small single engine, 90-horsepower Swallow planes for his fleet.

The Swallows were little more than trainers, like the planes he used at his flying school. In fact, Varney raided his school to get the airline organized. His chief pilot was Instructor Leon D. Cuddeback, who had learned to fly at the school, and his three other pilots were advanced students. Four mechanics from the school made up his ground crew. A bookkeeper and a traffic man to promote the use of air mail rounded out Varney's airline, which began as his personal venture but was later incorporated as Varney Air Lines, Inc. At that time, Varney turned over his air mail contract and his equipment in exchange for a controlling block of the company's stock.

His Swallows were delivered early and his pilots were r'aring to go, so Walter Varney undertook to be the first western air mail contractor to get into the air. Spring was in the air and hopes were high when Chief Pilot Cuddeback took off from Pasco, Washington, on April 6, 1926, and coaxed his underpowered Swallow to Boise, then over the mountains to Elko, with the first small bag of letters. Cuddeback returned two days later. This first round trip marked the beginning of air mail service by any of the lines later merged into the United system.

Varney ran into bad luck immediately. His other pilots, less experienced than Cuddeback, were unable to nurse the underpowered Swallows over the mountains. Within a week Varney's fleet was in such bad shape mechanically that he had to appeal to the Postmaster General for sixty days of grace, during which he hoped to get delivery of several 150-horsepower Wright engines. The extension was granted. In the nick of time, he was saved by Vern Gorst, who agreed to let Varney have the first three Ryan planes scheduled for delivery to Pacific Air Transport. By June 1,

Varney was back in the air again, this time to stay and to build an airline that eventually blanketed a million square miles of the Pacific Northwest. Varney's intrepid venture was one that played an important role in drawing the airways map of the United States.

Varney's little line lost money from the start, in spite of his economical operation. His pilots were paid $250 a month, with a bonus for dependable flying. In July, the Post Office boosted his air mail pay to $3 per pound, almost twice the money brought in by the air postage. To get as much of this "gravy" as possible, Varney persuaded chambers of commerce to send greetings everywhere by air mail. He designed a Christmas card weighing exactly one ounce, and persuaded people in Boise and Pasco to air mail thousands of them.

The southern terminus of Varney Air Lines was switched from Elko to Salt Lake City, a better connection not only with the Post Office Columbia route, but also with Western Air Express, flying north from Southern California. Varney began to make some money, which he invested in a fleet of faster Stearman mail planes, capable of carrying greater payloads. In 1929, when the Post Office advertised a new air mail route, Spokane to Pasco to Portland and Seattle, Varney bagged that, too. This gave him some sizable population centers, and the short route from the east to the Pacific Northwest.

Walter Varney had grown in three years to a sizable air transport operator, big enough to attract the attention of C. M. Keys, the outstanding aviation promoter of the country. When Varney decided to incorporate his line, Keys put some money into the new Varney Air Lines, Inc., and one of his top-flight associates, Colonel Paul Henderson, then general manager of National Air Transport and Transcontinental Air Transport, became a director in the Varney company. By this time, Varney was enthusiastic about carrying passengers to and from the Pacific Northwest, connecting at Salt Lake City with Boeing Air Transport, which had meantime captured the San Francisco–Chicago air mail contract. Varney ordered nine four-place Boeing B-40s to handle the passenger traffic, which never materialized, though his air mail revenues climbed to almost $1,000,000 a year. Varney's passenger service set-up was simple—a coffee percolator at Pasco, another at Boise. Tickets were mimeographed.

But by this time, Varney's ambitions were anything but simple. With the backing of a holding company organized by the Keys interests, Aviation Corporation of California, he opened an office in San Francisco and bid unsuccessfully on feeder line air mail contracts in Colorado, Wyoming, Montana, Michigan, Texas, and even in Mexico, where he brashly tried to compete with Pan American Airways' astute Juan Trippe.

Distant horizons, rather than the high horizons over which his planes soared, proved Walter Varney's undoing. Elevating himself to Chairman of the Board of Varney Air Lines, Varney made shrewd Louis Mueller, a San Francisco attorney, president of the airline. An easy spender and generous host, Varney traveled wide, in this country and abroad, invariably taking along a party of friends as his guests. His financial ties with the Keys interests, which were intent on muscling into the Pacific Northwest, which the Boeing system regarded as its special bailiwick, eventually convinced the Boeing management that the Varney lines must be absorbed.

At this point it is appropriate to trace what became of the purchaser of Glenn Martin's second pontoon plane back in 1915. Bill Boeing, scion of a wealthy lumbering family, assembled his new toy on Lake Union back of Seattle. Yale-trained, a shy introvert who avoided people, Boeing spent much of his time hunting and fishing. The compelling motive for buying the pontoon plane was to get to lakes and rivers in British Columbia quickly and easily. Boeing's flying crony was a retired Navy officer, Commander Westervelt. There was also a flying Chinese named Wong, whom Boeing had brought back from Southern California to service the plane. Like Gorst, Bill Boeing soon cracked up the flying birdcage. Unlike Gorst, he immediately ordered replacements. When Glenn Martin wired that it would take six months to supply them, hot-tempered Bill Boeing blew up.

"By God, we can build a better airplane ourselves, and do it faster," he told Westervelt, who thought so, too. With Wong, they went to work on a craft from the pontoons up, in a small hangar by the lake, and completed it in less than six months. A stick and wire job known as the B & W Flying Boat, it flew so well that Boeing decided to go into the plane building business. Both the Army and the Navy, with an eye to the way the war in Europe was taking to air, were looking for planes. Bill Boeing bought an old boat building works on the Duwamish River, just west of Seattle, for his plant.

The year before he had donated a sizable sum to the University of Washington to launch a study of aeronautics, a gift that paid prompt dividends. When he called Washington's President Suzzalo for some engineering and drafting talent, the University sent over three bright young engineers just graduated. They were Philip G. Johnson, who had worked his way through college driving a laundry wagon, Clair L. Egtvedt, a young Norseman who had worked west from Minnesota to study at the University of Washington, and Roland Mayer, later an outstanding lighter-than-air naval flier.

Jim Foley, boss of the boat plant, signed all three on at $90 per month. Johnson and Egtvedt, who stayed with Boeing, made an unbeatable team. Phil Johnson, the rough, likable extrovert, was a driver of men, a production man, and a salesman. Egtvedt, shy dreamer, was a master of design. Bill Boeing provided the backing and gave them full range. He rarely came to the plant. Johnson and Egtvedt were soon running it. Out of the ever-expanding little factory came a steady flow of revolutionary Army, Navy, and commercial planes that won for Seattle worldwide fame as an aircraft center. It was a distinction that culminated in the fleets of heavy bombers that turned the tide of World War II. It might be said that all this aeronautics came about indirectly because of Bill Boeing's wrath over a six-month delay in getting parts for his original flying birdcage.

One of Boeing's few cronies was a World War I flier named Edward Hubbard. Sensing an opportunity to do more flying and for a profit, Hubbard persuaded Canadian postal authorities to let him fly Orient-bound mail from Seattle to Victoria on steamer days and pick up mail bound for the United States from Canadian Pacific liners just in from the Orient. This short flight across Puget Sound saved the day. Boeing liked the idea. He and Hubbard formed a partnership, Boeing furnishing the flying boat and Eddie Hubbard serving as pilot. Occasionally, to relieve Hubbard, Bill Boeing flew the mail over to Victoria himself. The service started on March 3, 1919, six years before the United States Post Office signed its first contract with the private operators of feeder lines. Thus the Hubbard-Boeing operation might be considered the first private enterprise air mail operation in the country.

Hubbard also served as a test pilot for the Boeing Aircraft plant. Late in 1926, through his postal acquaintances, Hubbard got wind of the plan of the United States Postmaster General to call for bids from private operators for flying the mail over the Columbia Route across the country. The route was to be split into two operations, New York to Chicago and Chicago to San Francisco. When Congress passed the Kelly Act, the Postmaster General did call for bids. Phil Johnson was out of town selling Boeing airplanes to the Navy at the time, so Eddie Hubbard came over to talk with Clair Egtvedt, who was in charge at the Boeing plant. Hubbard said he thought Boeing should submit a bid for the San Francisco–Chicago route.

"Let's take a good look at this proposition," said Egtvedt. "It is an entirely new problem."

They decided that Hubbard should find out how much air mail revenue might be expected, and how much it would cost to operate the line, while Egtvedt concentrated on the design of a more economical and reliable mail plane. Within two days both men had their answers. It looked like too little business to operate an airline. However, Eddie Hubbard thought that with some well-directed publicity and advertising, the air mail business would be doubled, and on that basis the deal looked better. Hubbard worked out in more detail how many pilots and planes he would need and dug deeper into operations costs. Egtvedt went back to his drafting board to dream up a plane that would fly the Sierra Nevada and the Rockies with two passengers in addition to the mail load.

Concluding that they could fly the mail profitably for $1.50 per pound per 1000 miles, Hubbard and Egtvedt hustled uptown to put the proposition up to Bill Boeing, who would have to put up the money, a lot of it. Boeing listened with interest, particularly when Egtvedt pointed out that the airline would be a fine new market for planes, and when Hubbard emphasized that they had made money from the start on the little Seattle-Victoria air mail line. Boeing asked a lot of questions, but showed no particular enthusiasm. After the pair left Boeing's office Hubbard and Egtvedt had a feeling that he and they were not going into the air transportation business.

Next morning, when Egtvedt came to work at 8 A.M., he learned to his surprise that Bill Boeing had been trying to reach him for an hour. By the time Egtvedt and Hubbard got uptown, Boeing was excitedly pacing the floor. Explaining that he had talked over the airline business with Mrs. Boeing, who urged him to go into it, he said that he hadn't been able to sleep all night because the more he thought about the idea, the more promising it looked. He asked them for detailed figures, then called Phil Johnson long distance. Johnson was only mildly enthusiastic; but by the time he returned to Seattle, he, too, had caught the spirit of the new venture. Hubbard was given the job of setting up Boeing Air Transport. Johnson was president, with Hubbard as executive vice-president and general manager.

When the bids were opened in Washington on January 15, 1927, Boeing's was so much lower than that of Harris Hanshue's Western Air Express that it caused a furor in the industry. The Boeing bid was $1.50 per pound for the first 1000 miles, and 15 cents per pound for each additional 100 miles, or $2.98 per pound to fly the mail from San Francisco to Chicago. Western Air's bid was $2.24 and 24 cents per pound, respectively. Western was already receiving $3 per pound for flying the Los Angeles–Salt Lake run. The aviation industry predicted that Bill Boeing would squander his fortune carrying air mail at the ridiculously low rate. The Post Office heads evidently thought so, too. They ruled that Boeing must post an $800,000 bond to guarantee operations, and United States Senator Wesley Jones of Washington had to call on the Postmaster General to assure him that William E. Boeing of Seattle was a responsible citizen.

As manager of the new airline, Eddie Hubbard set up headquarters in Salt Lake City, junction point with Western Air Express operations from Southern California and Varney Air Lines from the Pacific Northwest. One of Hubbard's first moves was to hire

D. B. Colyer, ex-schoolteacher and Army flier who had been Second Assistant Postmaster General in charge of air mail. He became Boeing Air Transport's superintendent of operations. Colyer knew all of the Post Office pilots, and hired the veterans who had been flying the route by day and by night for the past three years.

As soon as Egtvedt could deliver the first of the fleet of twenty-five Boeing 40-A mail planes, the flying postmen were checked out on them. Though the pilots rode in open cockpits, there was a tiny cabin between the wings into which first two, and then, in later designs, four passengers were packed like sardines. The vast improvement in speed and power over the old converted De Havilands enabled the fleet of new planes, costing $25,000 apiece, to mark a milestone in air transportation history. BAT started service without a hitch on July 1, 1927, less than six months after the awarding of the mail contract. Instead of going broke, the new airline made money from the start and became the key link in the future United Air Lines system.

Late in 1928 when the Boeing 40s had demonstrated their earning capacity, Vern Gorst, head of PAT, and Grover Tyler, his chief pilot, called at the Boeing plant to see about buying some of the new planes for their line. The B-40s cost $25,000, an unheard-of price for planes at the time. Gorst, still struggling to finance his line, was unable to raise the money for the planes. Competition had developed on the California end of the PAT line, notably from Maddux Air Lines, flying Ford Tri-motor planes, and West Coast Air Transport, using Tri-motor Fokkers, the latter owned by Western Air Express. They carried passengers only, because Gorst had the mail contract. To get the air mail business, Harris Hanshue offered to buy Gorst's controlling B Stock for $250 per share. Ken Humphries, who had become general manager, and W. A. Patterson, serving as the line's voluntary financial adviser, opposed the deal, which would have left hundreds of holders of nonvoting stock out in the cold. Patterson finally suggested to Boeing that BAT buy all of PAT stock, voting and nonvoting alike, and merge the two airlines. Bill Boeing finally offered $200 a share for the stock, and Gorst accepted, mainly because Boeing agreed to keep all of PAT's employes on the payroll and to buy all of the stock held by the other shareholders on the same or better terms. When Bill Boeing handed Gorst a $94,000 check for his stock to close the deal, Gorst looked at it and said:

"Well, a fool and his money are soon parted. I want to spend $30,000 of this on a Boeing Flying Boat to open a Seattle-Alaska airline."

Gorst launched the farthest-north airline and ran it for five years, hoping the Post Office would accept his offer to fly mail to Alaska for $450 per flight. When the air mail service to Alaska was finally authorized, it was not Gorst but smooth Juan Trippe of Pan-American Airways who bagged the contract—for $4000 per flight. Defeated at last, Gorst folded his airline and operated a flying service for sportsmen and also a water transportation system on Puget Sound. A quarter of a century later, still lean and leathery and spry, Gorst was operating one of his original stage lines between North Bend and Marshfield, Oregon. When Vern Gorst died on October 18, 1953, one of air transport's most colorful pioneers became a legend.

Shortly after Boeing acquired PAT, W. A. Patterson, the young banker who had befriended Gorst in his hour of financial trouble, had a long distance call from Seattle. It was Phil Johnson, asking if Patterson would fly to Los Angeles to check the offer of a group of Mexican officials, who had said that Boeing could have a license to fly the air mail south of the border. Patterson accepted the assignment as a favor to a depositor. He reported back from Los Angeles that a license to fly air mail in Mexico was not a contract. Johnson asked him to catch the next plane to Seattle, which Patterson did, arriving on Saturday afternoon. Johnson took Patterson over to Bill Boeing's home for dinner. Not a word was said about the Mexico air mail proposition. Finally Johnson asked, "When are you going back?"

"Tomorrow morning," said Patterson.

"I wish you would stay over until Monday. I want to show you something tomorrow," said Johnson.

Patterson agreed. The next day Johnson took his puzzled young guest down to the Boeing plant. It was Sunday, and the only sign of life was the watchman. Johnson pointed out the rows of planes being built, then opened doors marked "Secret—Military work—

Stay out." Finally he led Patterson to his own office. Through an open door they entered a brand new office, equipped with new furniture.

"This is your office," said Johnson.

"What do you mean?" asked Patterson.

"I need an assistant," said Johnson. "You're just the fellow we need to bring some order into this business." Patterson protested that he had just bought a new house in Berkeley and was doing well at the Wells Fargo Bank.

"You'll do better up here," predicted Johnson. "Call up your wife and see what she says."

Patterson did. Mrs. Patterson said that they could sell the house, and she knew that Patterson would never be happy until he had a fling in the air transportation business. Patterson flew back Monday to tell his employers what had happened. President Lipman still took a dim view of the future in the flying machine business.

"Maybe you're right. But I will never be satisfied until I try it," insisted Patterson.

"Well, any time within the next three years that you want to come back, your desk will be waiting," said Lipman.

Thus there came into the air transport scene one of its most dynamic and influential figures. Born in Honolulu, the son of a sugar plantation superintendent who died when the boy was a youngster, Patterson was enrolled in a military school just outside Honolulu while his mother returned to the mainland to be with her relatives and to find work. The lad hated the school and ran away. Caught the first time, he made it to the Honolulu waterfront on his second try a few days later, and signed on as a cabin boy on a sailing ship. Seasick for twenty-four harrowing days, he reached the mainland, joined his mother, worked as an office boy in the bank while he completed his schooling and three years of college at night classes. He had climbed up the rungs to become a junior officer at twenty-nine, when Phil Johnson lured him into the air transportation game.

When Patterson reported for work a week later, he found Johnson away on a trip. Before leaving, Johnson had taken all the letters and memoranda needing attention from his desk and dumped them on Patterson's new desk, with a note that Patterson was to decide matters as he saw fit. One of Patterson's first jobs was to round up all of the outstanding PAT stock that Vern Gorst had peddled from Los Angeles to Seattle. Patterson began buying it at $200. Pilots who thought the stock was no good began shaking certificates out of their old jackets and digging them out of lockers. The price began to climb when word spread that Bill Boeing wanted to buy in every share of PAT. A Portland attorney, Phil Grossmayer, organized a syndicate of stockholders to bid up the stock. Prices skyrocketed to $666 per share, for the once-worthless $100 par value certificates. At this price the Grossmayer syndicate sold out. Patterson picked up the last two shares outstanding from a North Bend prostitute who exercised astute business acumen by holding out for $666 per share.

In the meantime, in the winter of 1929, Eddie Hubbard, who had dreamed up the airline, collapsed and died suddenly after strenuously shoveling snow in front of his house. This left BAT without an operating head. Although Phil Johnson was head of the airline, his interest lay in building planes and selling them rather than in flying them. When Johnson looked around for a man to run the airline, his eye fell on his man Friday. He dumped the airline into Patterson's lap. It was Patterson who saw the high horizons of the future and who equipped and stabilized the airline to spread its wings over them.

CHAPTER III

West Meets East at Chicago

Henry Ford, eccentric founder of the Ford automobile empire, remained to the end of his days a man of simple tastes with a hankering for the company of low-pressure cronies he had known in his early struggling days. Often Ford's important decisions were influenced indirectly by these associations. One such was his decision to enter the growing aviation field.

Among the old friends whom Ford liked to slip off and visit occasionally was Joe Brooks of Dearborn. Brooks was Henry Ford's fiddling crony. As Ford became one of the world's richest men, Joe Brooks somehow never prospered much, but remained, in Ford's opinion, an outstanding fiddler. This might seem irrelevant to aviation history except that Joe Brooks had a son, Harry, who spent so much time fooling around with an old World War I surplus Jenny that Joe told Henry Ford one day that the boy was a no-account ne'er-do-well.

"Send him over and let me see what I can do with him," suggested Ford.

Harry Brooks came over, bringing with him an idea for a better airplane that intrigued Henry Ford tremendously. Ford ordered one of them built. By the time they had completed it, young Brooks's enthusiasm had whetted Ford's interest in aviation, a brand-new horizon for the unpredictable automobile genius. The enthusiasm was shared by William B. Mayo, chief engineer for the Ford Motor Company, and to a certain extent by Ford's son, Edsel, who had taken over general management of the company. Soon Harry Brooks became a sort of adopted Ford son, with the run of the Ford plant. Henry Ford encouraged him to spark the company's new aviation division.

Meantime another flying machine man moved into the Ford aura. He was William B. Stout, a mechanical genius in his own right and an inventor of repute. Stout had an idea that the airplane of the future would be built entirely of metal instead of spruce and canvas. He also designed a radically new cantilever wing that eliminated the cables with which early airplane builders braced the wings to the fuselage.

Stout had a thoroughly practical, albeit revolutionary, idea. Running out of money to complete his all-metal plane, he addressed a unique letter to a list of leading industrialists, outlining his idea and his problem, and concluding with:

"I should like a thousand dollars—and only promise you one thing: you will never see it again, but you will get a thousand dollars' worth of education."

Many of the recipients put this down for another crackpot letter. But Henry Ford didn't, nor did his son Edsel. Each sent Stout a thousand dollars, as did enough aviation-minded industrialists to enable Bill Stout to organize the Stout Metal Airplane Company and build the first experimental model, an all-metal plane powered by a single Liberty motor. The performance of this craft soon proved the inventor's theories to be correct.

By this time—1924—young Harry Brooks's enthusiasm, plus the general mania for aviation investment at the time, persuaded Henry and Edsel Ford to buy the Stout Metal Airplane Company and make it the Ford Aviation Division with Inventor Stout as general manager. Bill Stout enlarged his one-engine plane to a tri-motor job, powered by three Wright Whirlwind engines. This was the famous Ford Tri-motor plane, known among pilots as "The Tin Goose," one of the slowest and safest planes ever designed. The Tin Goose had one great advantage: it could take off in a short space and land at a slow speed.

Just as Bill Boeing went into air transport as an outlet for his airplane factory, so Stout and the Fords decided to launch an airline with their Tin Goose. Ford's Aviation Division began flying from Dearborn to Chicago and Cleveland on April 3, 1925. At first the Ford Tri-motors carried only company cargo and personnel, but the airline operated on schedule and with amazing dependability. In February, 1925, a bill sponsored by Representative Clyde Kelly, entitled "An Act to Encourage Commercial Aviation and to Authorize the Postmaster General to Contract for Air Mail Service," was passed by Congress. By the time contracts were ready to be let, Ford already had an efficiently operated airline with well-trained personnel. The Ford line was awarded the Dearborn-Cleveland and the Dearborn-Chicago air mail contracts in October. Though several other feeder line contracts had been awarded already, Ford's group beat the other pioneers into the air with the mail by starting daily service on February 15, 1926. Eddie Hubbard and Bill Boeing had flown the Seattle-Victoria air mail service in 1919, but this was a foreign postal deal and the Ford line actually carried the first air mail on contract within the United States.

Though the Fords lost money on cargo, passengers, and mail, the airline hung up a phenomenal record for safety and on-time flying, operating for the next three years without a single fatality. In fact, this record made the slow and noisy Ford Tri-motor a popular plane with early airlines seeking to lure timid passengers into the sky. Though the prestige of the Ford name had contributed immeasurably to growing public confidence in the idea that the airplane was here to stay, Henry Ford himself refused to fly. Then young Harry Brooks, trying for a Detroit–New York nonstop record in a souped-up midget plane, overshot his goal and landed in the sea and was drowned. Ford abruptly ceased building and operating planes.

Meanwhile, Bill Stout had organized Stout Air Services which inaugurated an experimental airline between Detroit and Grand Rapids in mid-1926, receiving an air mail contract for the route in July of that year. Unlike the other feeder line operators, the Fords and Bill Stout, who was an independent thinker on his own, had no wish to prosper at the government air mail feed bag. When the volume of air mail proved negligible between Detroit and Grand Rapids, Stout petitioned the Post Office in July, 1927 to cancel the route. The plea was granted and Stout discontinued flying the mail. However, two months later, the company began passenger operations between Detroit and Cleveland, then between Detroit and Chicago.

Before this happened, Stout Air Services enjoyed a dizzy whirl in the public spotlight. Organizing as not only an airline but a holding company, with William B. Stout as president and William B. Mayo as vice-president and director, Stout sold ownership to the public and, free from the restraint of the conservative Fords, laid ambitious plans to build an aviation empire. Stout's associates surveyed routes all over the country, including the Salt Lake–Los Angeles run, the Jacksonville–Miami Beach route, airways from St. Louis as a center to Pittsburgh, Detroit, Chicago, Washington, New York, Kansas City, and Dallas, and even Boston. Stout even planned to capture the Chicago–San Francisco leg of the Columbia Route of the Post Office, and did underbid the "Los Angeles crowd" headed by Harris Hanshue, only to be underbid in turn by Eddie Hubbard and Bill Boeing of Seattle. To popularize flying, Stout started sightseeing flights over several cities, and carried more than 15,000 passengers over Detroit in the summer of 1927.

Stimulated by the sale of the popular Ford Tri-motor planes and by the ambitious Stout expansion program, sale of stock in the Stout line boomed. The ride that Bill Stout promised his backers looked so promising that in November, 1927 he was able to send them another letter in which he said, "You not only got the education, but doubled your money."

Meantime the automobile capital of the world was plunging into another air transport project, the joint brainchild of Carl B. Fritsche of Detroit and Clement M. Keys of New York City. Fritsche was general manager of the Aircraft Development Corporation, one of the numerous investment groups springing up like toadstools at the time to cash in on the aviation bonanza. Fritsche and his automotive-minded colleagues dreamed of making Detroit the air transportation hub of the country, just as Chicago had become the railroad mecca. How close they came to succeeding in stealing the airline show from Chicago, whose patriarchal fathers saw little future in the air, is revealed in the birth of National Air Transport, which eventually emerged out of the dreams of Fritsche and Keys.

Early in 1925, these two effervescent promoters decided to raise

Airline founder Walter T. Varney (fifth from left), with his wife and father, who backed him, and Leon Cuddeback, Varney chief pilot (seventh from left), snapped before Varney mail plane in 1926.

Trail blazers in a new industry. Walter Varney (right), founder of Varney Air Lines, snapped in 1946 with C. T. Wrightson, United's oldest employe in seniority, now station manager at Fresno.

The first civilian mail carriers in the country were William E. Boeing (holding mail sack) and Edward Hubbard, who later inspired Boeing Air Transport. In this home-built seaplane, Hubbard and Boeing launched a Seattle-Victoria international mail service on March 3, 1919, to save a day in handling mail carried by trans-Pacific ocean liners.

Master minds of the Boeing group and founders of Boeing Air Transport, largest of United Air Lines' predecessors. Standing: Clair Egtvedt, Edward Hubbard, William Herron and O. W. Tupper. Seated: Philip G. Johnson and William E. Boeing.

Plane that revolutionized air transport in 1927, the Boeing 40, powered by new Wasp air-cooled engine from Pratt & Whitney plant, conquered mountains and space, set new records for performance and cut cost of carrying mail, cargo, and passengers in half. Famed Boeing 40 could carry two passengers plus mail. Such planes were introduced by Boeing Air Transport on San Francisco–Chicago run.

C. M. Keys, promoting genius of the aviation boom period in the twenties, and head of the so-called Keys group. Keys was the moving spirit in the founding of National Air Transport, eventually the eastern leg of United Air Lines, and of Transcontinental Air Transport, which grew into rival TWA.

John J. Mitchell, Jr., secretary and treasurer of National Air Transport, one of the Chicago group of young men who backed NAT when their elders turned down the airline idea and who made Chicago an air transport center. Mitchell returned to the United fold later as a director.

William B. Stout, founder of Stout Air Services, who interested the Fords in backing aviation, pioneered air passenger service.

Colonel Paul Henderson, former Assistant Postmaster General, and father of the night air mail, who was one of the founders and first general manager of National Air Transport.

Stout Air Services, merged into National Air Transport, developed the art of handling passengers by air, while other airlines were interested mainly in mail. Stout built and used the sturdy "tin goose," popular name for Ford Tri-motor planes.

Mail being loaded aboard a National Air Transport plane at Cleveland in 1928 while air transport still was in the open-cockpit single-engine airplane stage.

The famed Boeing 40, which proved its rugged and dependable qualities on the San Francisco–Chicago run of Boeing Air Transport, starting in 1927. BAT's fleet of twenty-five such planes made money from the start, to the astonishment of other operators, who expected Bill Boeing to go broke flying the mail.

The tri-motored Boeing wasn't overly fast, but it carried substantial loads of mail, passengers, and express. Air express service was launched by contract with the Railway Express Agency in 1927.

$2,000,000 to found an airline operating between New York, Detroit, and Chicago. No shoestring operation launched by seat-of-the-pants fliers with more hopes than dollars, this was to be an amply financed airline and the nucleus of a vast system that eventually would connect the centers of population of the entire country.

Keys agreed to raise the first million in New York City, whose financiers were already air-minded and investment-wise, many of them having hit the jackpot building planes, engines, and other aeronautical equipment for the Allies during World War I. C. M. Keys was a former *Wall Street Journal* editor who, sensing the public enthusiasm for aviation, had ceased writing about financiers to become one of them and promote more than a dozen multimillion dollar aviation corporations, of which he was generally president, albeit seldom a large stockholder. Among them were the Curtiss Aeroplane and Motor Company, the North American Aviation Company, Eastern Air Transport, Inc., and others. Keys had no difficulty in raising the New York $1,000,000 from among the Wall Street men he knew so well.

Though National Air Transport was to have an authorized capital of $10,000,000, an unheard-of backlog of capital for an airline at the time, the promoters figured they could get started with $2,000,000 cash. Fritsche wanted to raise the other $1,000,000 in Detroit, largely among the automobile magnates, including Edsel Ford, who was tagged for president of the proposed new airline. He soon had to revise his ideas, because Henry Ford said that Edsel was busy enough running the other Ford interests, and Keys decreed, "No, the airline should terminate in Chicago, and we want Chicago money in it." Keys insisted that Detroit capitalists put up $500,000 and Chicago the other $500,000. Fritsche quickly raised Detroit's $500,000 without difficulty.

Then he and Keys and Colonel Paul Henderson, so-called "father of night air mail," who had resigned as Second Assistant Postmaster General to become general manager of the new airline, descended on Chicago to coax half a million dollars out of the Windy City's capitalists. Banker Rufus Dawes gave a luncheon, to which the heads of banks and large industries came. Keys, Henderson, and Fritsche outlined their plans for National Air

Transport in glowing terms. The rail-minded Chicagoans listened in stony silence. Nobody offered to risk hard money in the flying machine business.

After the dismal luncheon, Thomas Wolfe, the young promoter in charge of the Chicago Chamber of Commerce new business department, looked over the list of guests and noted that nearly every man who had come to the party had a son in his twenties who had been a World War I flier, or who had taken up flying since the war.

"Why not call a meeting of the sons and see if they won't put up the money?" he suggested.

So Dawes gave another luncheon. The guests were young John J. Mitchell, Jr., Philip K. Wrigley, Lester Armour, Phil Swift, Wayne Chatfield-Taylor, Earle Reynolds, John F. Gilkey, Jr., Marshall Field III, Robert P. Lamont, all men on the make. It took about ten minutes to raise the $500,000 that put Chicago on the air transport map. When Jack Mitchell, ex-Navy flier who became treasurer of the new airline, told his father what he had done, old John J. Mitchell, president of the Illinois Merchants Bank, said, "I never thought I'd live to see my son in a fly-by-night business."

Mitchell, Jr., argued that never in history had a faster means of transport failed to win out in competition with a slower form. Still doubtful, the older Mitchell conceded the point and granted his blessing to the fly-by-night business. The other elders did so, too, reluctantly, sensing probably but not admitting that this was the beginning of a new era in transportation, which had been the very lifeblood of their city. Largely because they were vigorous and enthusiastic, the youthful Chicagoans who came into the NAT picture by lucky default became potent factors in air transport.

National Air Transport, incorporated in Delaware, May 21, 1925, was headed by Howard E. Coffin, vice-president of the Hudson Motor Car Company of Detroit. C. M. Keys, whose investment in the company was relatively slight, was chairman of the executive committee. Other vice-presidents included Charles L. Lawrance, president of the Wright Aeronautical Corporation; Wayne Chatfield-Taylor, Chicago capitalist; Eugene W. Lewis of Detroit; with Fritsche as secretary, Mitchell as treasurer, and Colonel Henderson as general manager and later vice-president.

The airline began operations on May 12, 1926, with ten Curtiss

Carrier Pigeons and thirty-five government surplus Liberty engines to power them. The Pigeons were capable of carrying 1000 pounds of cargo. NAT started off with only eight Army-trained pilots from Kelly Field on the payroll. But the pilots and their Pigeons weren't flying the New York–Detroit–Chicago airway for which the airline was organized. Instead, they winged out of Chicago, the city that was reluctant to have anything to do with NAT in the first place, to launch a feeder service by way of Kansas City to Dallas, Texas, one that tapped a dozen population centers in the west Mississippi Valley. NAT won the bid on CAM Route 3, a 995-mile airway, and laid ambitious plans to pick up others.

Since the NAT management was more interested in mail and other cargo than in passengers, no effort was made to fly to Detroit or New York until one year later, when NAT won by a narrow squeak the contract to fly the eastern leg of the Post Office Columbia line. The NAT promoters knew there would be competition for this route, the very reason for organizing their airline, so they undertook to work some deals in advance to make their position more secure. One was with Western Air Express at Los Angeles, which seemed a cinch to win the San Francisco–Chicago end of the line. The idea was to submit a bid for the entire San Francisco–New York air mail contract jointly with the westerners. Hanshue, afraid that Western would lose its identity if merged with the big eastern company, and sure of winning the Chicago–San Francisco leg of the route, backed off and nothing came of the negotiations.

The strongest prospective rival bidder on the Chicago–New York leg was Colonial Air Transport. The NAT management carried on extended negotiations with the Colonial heads, with the view of combining their resources to bid on the route. The rivals were unable to get together, so both NAT and Colonial submitted separate bids. NAT's bid was lower than Colonial, but two other bidders were lower still. One, submitted by Earle F. Stewart of Chicago, offered to carry the mail for 35 cents per pound. It was promptly rejected by the postal authorities as too low to be considered seriously. The other was by North American Airways, Inc., which underbid NAT's $1.24 by one cent a pound.

North American Airways was the brainchild of Charles A. Levine, a New York junk dealer who had suddenly acquired fame by financing a plane and flying with Clarence C. Chamberlain on one of the first trans-Atlantic flights. Levine announced that the bid was his, and at the Postmaster General's office proposed to the NAT men that they combine with his company to operate the route jointly. The two groups adjourned to the Carlton Hotel. A postal inspector accompanied the NAT men. Levine proposed that NAT buy a half interest in his company and supply the management. In turn, he agreed to deliver not only the air mail contract but also fourteen pilots who had flown the route for the Post Office Department. Levine had a secret agreement with the flying postmen who were promised jobs and substantial stock interests in North American Airways. Levine also had an employment agreement with one other Post Office employe.

On the grounds that this was collusion, and also because Levine was president of two other companies holding salvage contracts with the War Department that were being investigated by the Department of Justice, the Postmaster General threw out the North American Airways' bid and awarded the contract to NAT. Colonel Henderson, NAT's general manager, promptly hired the veterans of the risky route over the Alleghenies, checked them out in the open-cockpit Pigeons, and began flying the Chicago–New York route, bypassing Detroit completely, on September 1, 1927.

In the light of the later scramble for the lucrative passenger business between the country's two largest population centers, the airline's lack of enthusiasm for flying passengers between Chicago and New York is little short of amazing. Passengers were something to be carried only in an emergency, at a fare of $200 between the two cities, 724 miles. Theoretically the Pigeons had room for one passenger, packed in among the mail bags with a sack or two on his lap as a rule. Tickets were sold with the proviso that the pilot could dump the passenger at any stop along the route, if the plane became overloaded with mail. At $1.24 per pound, the mail load was more profitable than a passenger, and a lot less nuisance. Any adventurous traveler taking the risk was issued a typical flying outfit, coveralls, helmet, goggles, and a parachute. Pilots seldom took the trouble to show him how to use the parachute.

Nevertheless NAT flew 168 passengers between Chicago and New York that first year, most of them being air-minded travelers delivered to it by the more passenger-conscious Boeing Air Transport from the west. NAT finally invested in a Travelair cabin job with accommodations for three passengers, but used it in the Chicago–Kansas City service, where it carried 1560 passengers in 1928. It also experimented with a Tri-motor Ford which was used for sight-seeing purposes. Eventually NAT pulled out of the passenger business entirely, as a result of a deal with a new competitor which it owned in part.

The newcomer was Transcontinental Air Transport, promoted by C. M. Keys with the backing of the Pennsylvania and Santa Fe railroads. Keys, always a promoter, decided to capitalize on the public adoration for Charles A. Lindbergh. Lindbergh was given a substantial block of stock in TAT and joined the line as technical adviser. More important, he lent it his name. TAT was known as "the Lindbergh line."

Still fearful of the risk of flying passengers after dark, particularly over the Alleghenies, TAT entrained its passengers overnight from New York to Columbus, Ohio, where they were transferred to Tri-motor Fords. The big all-metal planes winged them by day to Waynoka, Oklahoma, from which point they were taken overnight by the Santa Fe to Clovis, New Mexico. Here another Ford was waiting to pick them up and fly them on to Los Angeles.

TAT was strictly a plush operation from the start, with an aura of Hollywood glamor, including gold plates from which the passengers ate their meals and gold pens as souvenirs. They were met at the airports (palatial for those days) by teardrop Aero-cars to whisk them to their next mode of transportation. Generally there was a Hollywood movie star for a fellow passenger. But it cost $480 to plane-train from New York to Los Angeles, and it took 48 hours to make the trip. Often the big plane flew with only two or three passengers, and TAT managed to drop $2,750,000 in the first 18 months. A good share of it was NAT's money. When TAT was launched, NAT bought 50,000 shares of stock for $1,000,000, giving it a 10 per cent interest in TAT.

This interlocking interest in a competitor was nothing unusual for the day. TAT was not only an airline but a holding company. It even held blocks of stock in competitors which took air mail contracts away from its part-owner, NAT, notably Northwest Airlines, which captured the Chicago-Minneapolis run. All this went on in spite of the fact that TAT's general manager was Colonel Paul Henderson, who also managed NAT. The dynamic colonel spread himself thin over the scattered and confusing aviation empire, dominated by what was known as "the Keys Group." He probably spread himself too thin, because the men who eventually became the builders of sound air transport were the youngsters out on the line, flying the planes, fighting the weather, mastering new instruments of flight, and developing a flying technique the hard way.

Among TAT's first three employes was a round-faced young MIT engineering graduate from New Hampshire, ex-Navy flier John A. Herlihy, employed to lay out airports for the new airline. Fortunately for NAT, the TAT management dismissed Jack Herlihy in 1930, and he was hired by E. P. "Bert" Lott, superintendent of flying for NAT, as a night pilot on the New York–Cleveland run. Lott was an ex-World War I aviation mechanic who flew postwar as a barnstormer, then pioneered aerial mapping before joining NAT as chief superintendent of flying. Later he flew a United airliner as captain, then became superintendent of flying, next designed airports for United, and eventually became an assistant to the vice-president–flight operations before retiring in 1958. Herlihy soon advanced to general superintendent, then chief engineer of NAT. During this period, he acquired the nickname "Scotty" because of the sharp eye he kept on the airline's expenses. It was typical of the NAT management, which watched the corners and operated conservatively in an era of chasing rainbows. Later, Herlihy had charge of United's system-wide operations and, still later, of all engineering and maintenance activities as a senior vice-president.

Herlihy's resourceful ingenuity helped change NAT's flying from a cockpit operation to a system. So did the organizational ability of Bert Lott, whose specialty was flight dispatch, and a third newcomer, R. E. "Dick" Pfennig, a pioneer in aviation mechanics whose mania was safety.

"In the old NAT days, each pilot was his own dispatcher," recalls Herlihy. "If he thought he could make it, okay, he flew. If not, he put the mail on the train. About 1931 we hit on the idea of flight dispatch, and set it up under Dick Pfennig. The government had a weather service, and the best weather man was Henry Harrison, over in Cleveland. We would call up Henry, and if he said the airway would be open, that was good enough for us. We'd fly."

Henry T. Harrison, referred to by Herlihy, was another specialist who helped revolutionize the technique of airline operation. A meteorologist for the United States Weather Bureau since 1924, Harrison was chosen by Admiral Byrd as aerologist for the Byrd Antarctic expedition in 1928. While chasing storms across his weather chart, Harrison hit on the idea of the elastic airway that could be switched on short notice a hundred miles to the north or the south, to avoid storm fronts and also to pick up tail winds. His study of storms blossomed during World War II, when he was borrowed by the Air Force as a weather expert. Back in NAT days, when the pilots developed the habit of "calling up Henry in Cleveland," Harrison was one of the small group of studious experimenters who were working to transform air transport from a daredevil game to a precision operation.

"By 1930," continued Herlihy, "we had one-way radio to give the weather report every hour. The pilot could hear it, and also hear the radio range. But we had no ground control of planes. The pilot was boss until Boeing developed two-way radio. After that the pilot was no longer in complete control as he flew along. That took a lot of the fun out of flying for the pilots, who thought the ground guys were going to be telling them how to fly all of the time. It didn't work out that way, because two-way radio changed our whole system of operation."

Other miraculous gadgets, too, came into the life of the air mail pilot, who up to this time had been essentially a daring athlete. Suddenly he found himself a technician, flying his plane according to a flight plan and depending upon an ever-increasing array of dials, lights, and indicators on the dashboard in front of his stick, which no longer was a stick but a wheel.

"I remember putting a cardboard with two slits in it over my goggles so I couldn't see anything from my cockpit seat but the instruments and forcing myself to fly by instrument on clear days," Herlihy recalled. "One day I hit a bump over Pennsylvania. Instead of looking outside to see what I had hit I found I was looking at the instruments first. It dawned on me then that this flying business had become a scientific profession and it was going to amount to something."

Two outstanding United veterans whose careers typified the evolution of the rugged, daring, early seat-of-the-pants flier into the scientific pilot-captain of a modern Mainliner flight crew were Walt Addems of National Air Transport and Dick Petty of Boeing Air Transport. Lean, thoughtful Walt Addems built his own first plane, a glider which he converted into a flying machine by installing a 50-horsepower engine. That was at Manteno, near Chicago, just before World War I, in which Addems was an artilleryman envying the dashing aviators who winged overhead. Out of uniform, Addems became a stunt flier at state fairs, then a ferry pilot, and finally he was hired in 1927 to fly the night mail for NAT.

About the same time, Lott turned down another ambitious young candidate for a night flying job because he couldn't fiddle, it being the idea at the time that musical instrument training was a good setting-up exercise for reading airplane instruments. So D. R. Petty, a young Cornhusker who had abandoned his medical studies at the University of Nebraska, hopped out to Cheyenne and hit Boeing Air Transport for a job. Boeing didn't care whether he could fiddle or not and signed him up to fly Boeing 40-Bs.

In 1929, NAT launched instrument flying, utilizing such magic aeronautical brains as the gyroscope-turn indicator, the rate-of-climb indicator, and the first horizon guide, which told the pilot how nearly he was flying right side up. Addems took to instruments fast. When the Bureau of Aeronautics set up the first instrument rating tests in Cleveland in 1931, he was the first transport pilot to get his instrument rating, after flying in a covered cockpit guided solely by gadgets on the panel. This flair for scientific flying eventually lifted him to the top as general manager of flight operations for the entire United system—a post he held until 1951 when he returned to the cockpit as a captain on the San Francisco–Honolulu run; then retired, at age sixty, in 1959.

Addems's successor as boss of United's pilots was Dick Petty. Flying for BAT out of Omaha, Petty took to instruments quickly, was known as "a high flier," a precision pilot who preferred to fly above the clouds, utilizing the new radio beacons to keep his bearings. In 1931, when Russ Cunningham, Boeing's instrument expert and later United's communications director, was checking out

BAT pilots in blind flying, he picked up Petty in Des Moines. The two headed for Omaha, with Petty flying the plane, his side of the cockpit covered. Half way to Omaha, they hit line squalls and thunderheads. Cunningham let Petty fly through them on instruments, without telling him they had run into weather.

"Dick flew right on the beam, with only instruments to guide him," recalled Cunningham later. "I didn't tell him we'd flown through the storm until he landed at Omaha. It was the finest precision flying I had seen."

Petty had a gift for handling people as well as planes. This combination of talents won him the job of assistant superintendent of flight operations for the United system in 1937. During World War II, on leave from United, he dropped the first paratroops into Sicily, became chief of staff of the 52d Troop Carrier Command Wing, and wound up as a colonel. Later he became a brigadier general in the Air Force Reserve.

Petty was United's flight manager at Los Angeles when W. A. Patterson tagged him in 1951 for the newly created post of vice-president–flight operations, with headquarters in Denver. A man of few words, Dick Petty proved a stickler for perfection. He set up a system of rigid yearly proficiency checkups on United's pilots. Veterans as well as new co-pilots had to prove at least once a year that they were equal to any flying situation encountered along the Main Line. Those who failed were transferred to ground jobs; the rest emerged as the most carefully screened and skilled teams of pilots employed in the industry.

While the pilots were evolving their profession, the wobbly new business in which they had cast their lot was changing, too. A boom-or-bust period of air transport followed the era of the pioneer enterprisers. It soon became clear that the arbitrary decision of the postal authorities to break the transcontinental air service into two parts at Chicago, just because the railroads ended there, was a mistake. The bus lines and the truck lines had blindly followed this transportation gospel. But air speed, which soon reduced the entire country to the size of Pennsylvania timewise, knocked that conception into a cocked hat. Though West met East in Chicago, it was apparent that an airline across the country should be one continuous operation from coast to coast. Making this a reality set the stage for a battle of the air transport giants.

CHAPTER IV

The First Air Transport Giant

After Edward Hubbard and William E. Boeing of Seattle captured the Chicago–San Francisco air mail contract in 1927 with a bid barely half that of experienced feeder line operators, the disgruntled losers waited to see the rich Seattle sportsman lose his fortune flying the mail. When Boeing began making money from the start, their chagrin turned to amazement. Asked how he did it, Boeing explained that his planes were carrying mail instead of radiators and water over the mountains.

This was right. Aside from his financial backing, Boeing had provided the new airline with one other all-important item, a new, air-cooled engine known as the Wasp to power his planes. The Wasp developed double the horsepower with the same weight, enabling the Boeing planes to carry double the payload at no extra cost for fuel or pilots. Other airlines, unable to get Wasps for over a year, kept on flying radiators and water over the airways to cool their old-style Liberty engines, while Boeing's new fleet packed in more mail and even courted passengers.

Boeing Air Transport had Wasp power when rivals couldn't get it because the shy and solemn Boeing, a man of few intimate cronies, had a close friend in the right place. This friend was youthful Frederick D. Rentschler, head of the recently founded Pratt & Whitney engine works at Hartford, Connecticut. Pratt & Whitney had designed the new engine primarily for Navy fighter planes, some of which Boeing had contracted to build in his Seattle airplane factory.

During the summer of 1926, while in the East, Boeing persuaded Fred Rentschler to talk the Navy into letting him have twenty-five Wasps out of the Navy's priority quota for the new air mail planes then in the design stage at Seattle. The Navy agreed, and Rentschler promised the Wasps by the time the airframes were built. Out in Seattle Clair Egtvedt quickly redesigned the Boeing 40-As for the new Wasp power plants, increasing their payloads from 1000 to 1500 pounds, and thereby adding about $400 potential income for each flight.

Rentschler kept his word. Beginning with February, 1927, he delivered five Wasps a month to Boeing. By June 1 the Boeing factory had the first of the new planes, with a Wasp engine in its nose, ready to fly. After that a plane a day rolled out of the factory, to be trucked to a nearby air strip, tested briefly, then flown to division points along the 1918-mile airway. By June 30 all twenty-five Wasp-powered 40-As were at their stations between Chicago, and Oakland. Boeing Air Transport started operations on July 1 with a $64 question mark hanging over the new-born airline. With an untried, hurriedly designed plane powered by an engine untested in long-haul flying, the wiser men of the industry were sure Boeing was headed for plenty of trouble.

Instead, Boeing Air Transport set a phenomenal record for performance. Where engine trouble and forced landings at the crash-crack-up fields every 25 miles along the route had been accepted as more or less routine by the winged postmen flying Liberty-powered craft, failures in flight with the new Wasp-powered Boeing 40-As were rare events. Operationwise, Boeing Air Transport became almost overnight the country's model airline. The performance of the Wasp-powered 40-As convinced the BAT chiefs that the time had come to fly passengers in numbers. Out in the Boeing airplane factory, Clair Egtvedt and his designers began work on a trimotored flying Pullman, with fourteen seats in its cabin.

The Boeing-Rentschler friendship soon produced an even greater repercussion on the adolescent air transport industry. Fred Rentschler had been an engine man from his boyhood in Hamilton, Ohio, where his father had helped found a machinery plant. After graduating from Princeton while Bill Boeing was struggling through Yale, Rentschler returned to Hamilton and worked as a molder in the foundry of the Hooven-Owen-Rentschler Company. When World War I broke out, he enlisted, was commissioned lieutenant, assigned to the United States Army Signal Corps Aviation Arm, and because he knew metals was assigned to the Wright-Martin Aircraft plant at New Brunswick, New Jersey, to test airplane engines being built for the Allies. When the war ended, Rentschler helped liquidate this war emergency plant.

By this time Rentschler knew airplane engines, both the European type which the Wright-Martin plant had manufactured under license, and American designs not so highly rated at the time. Invited to head the new Wright Aeronautical Corporation, amply backed by New York capital, the intense young Rentschler, just past thirty, pulled together an imposing staff of designers and builders and soon made his company the Number One source of power for military and commercial craft. Outstanding feat of the company was the Whirlwind air-cooled radial engine, top United States power plant at the time, particularly after a Whirlwind-powered Ryan plane carried "Slim" Lindbergh across the Atlantic. More reliable than the old Liberty, the Whirlwind delivered as much power per pound as the Liberty, without the nuisance of flying water up and down the airways to cool the engine.

Rentschler and George Mead, Wright's engine designer, had an idea for a still better engine. The company's directors objected to spending big money developing new engines when the company already had the best in the field. Rentschler resigned, scouted around for new backers, found them in the Niles-Bement-Pond Company, machinery builders who not only owned the idle Pratt & Whitney tool plant in Hartford, but had $1,000,000 of working capital also lying idle. Persuasive Fred Rentschler talked them into letting him have the Pratt & Whitney plant and name, and the capital, too. Then he and Mead and several other engine enthusiasts went to work on the new idea. The first Wasp they built exceeded their own expectations, turning up 410 horsepower from 625 pounds of engine. It was the power plant about which airplane designers had dreamed. The Navy ordered all the Wasps that the new Pratt & Whitney works could build for their rapidly growing carrier force.

Bill Boeing, whose acquaintance with Rentschler dated from World War I days, when the Boeing military planes were powered first with engines from the Wright-Martin plant, then from the Wright Aeronautical Works, followed his friend to Hartford and switched to Wasp power for all Boeing military designs. Whenever Boeing traveled east, he and Rentschler got together to swap ideas. Along in the fall of 1928, after Boeing Air Transport had demonstrated that Wasp-powered Boeing planes could make money carrying cargo and passengers at lower rates, Fred Rentschler tossed Bill Boeing the most startling idea of all. It was: why not pool the Boeing airplane factory and the airline and the Pratt & Whitney engine works to form the nucleus of a well-rounded aviation holding company?

It was an era of consolidations, and the urge to merge was rampant. Other big mergers were beginning to flank Boeing Air Transport with airlines. Particularly aggressive was the so-called Keys Group, whose North American Aviation Corporation had bought into Varney Air Lines and was backing Maddux Air Lines, the western leg of TAT, in an extension from Los Angeles to Seattle which paralleled Boeing's Pacific Air Transport division. Bill Boeing thought the merger of the two money-making noncompetitive companies from the East and West Coasts a great idea. So did Chance M. Vought, former racing driver and successful builder of fast military planes for the Navy, who was sitting in on the conversation. Vought wanted to be counted in on the merger.

The big deal was easy to work out. First Boeing absorbed the Vought plant. Then Rentschler set up a new holding company, United Aircraft & Transport Corporation, swapping ownership of Pratt & Whitney for 800,000 shares in the new concern. Boeing, who owned control of the airplane factory at Seattle as well as Boeing Air Transport and Pacific Air Transport, swapped his shares in these companies for the new United stock. Other owners of shares in the Boeing company followed suit. Rentschler became president of the new company. This was agreeable to Boeing, who shied at being front man for anything. Boeing became chairman of the board. Chance Vought became a vice-president, as did Philip G. Johnson, president of the Boeing company.

To round out the United Aircraft & Transport holdings, fast-moving Fred Rentschler bought the Hamilton Propeller Company, and later added the Standard Steel Propeller Company when the new metal blades became an issue in patent litigation. The "prop" end of plane manufacture was becoming big business. At the time dreamers were predicting that the small private plane soon would be as common as the automobile. To keep a toehold in this field, in case an opportunity developed for a General Motors of the air, United absorbed Stearman Aircraft, which made light biplanes, and Northrop Aircraft, which specialized in military trainers. At the time no one could conceive of airline operation overseas in anything but a flying boat, so Rentschler bought the Sikorsky Airplane works, which was out in front in amphibians. He also added two airport subsidiaries, one in California and the other in Connecticut.

With this varied collection of aviation holdings, each able to supply or patronize the other, ambitious Fred Rentschler, dynamo of the newest aeronautical octopus, had everything he wanted but one all-important unit, namely, a New York connection for the San Francisco–Chicago airline. Boeing Air Transport was recognized as the model airline of the country and the one with the rosiest future. BAT was pioneering passenger service. During 1929, the line carried 6129 passengers in and out of Chicago, where many were dumped because National Air Transport lacked equipment to fly them on to New York.

Also, it was evident by now that plane travelers would not be satisfied with the antiquated railroad precedent of transferring from one system's equipment to another's in Chicago. The main line across country was one logical, unified operation from the Golden Gate to the Statue of Liberty, even if postal authorities had arbitrarily cut the old Columbia Route in two. This consideration, plus the invasion of the Keys Group into Boeing's, now United's, territory in the Far West, by purchase of blocks of Varney Air Lines and Western Air Express stock, convinced Rentschler and his new associates that they had better get to New York before their rivals reached the Pacific Coast. The conviction led to a battle of the giants, reminiscent of the Wall Street battles of the so-called "Empire Builders" for the control of railroad systems.

Rentschler opened United's drive to reach New York in June, 1929, by absorbing Stout Air Services. This gave him a passenger service from Chicago to Cleveland via Detroit, but provided no mail contracts, Stout having voluntarily retired from the air mail business two years before. But Stout had a personnel that knew how to handle passengers efficiently, and it held a permit to extend its line to Buffalo, which was a toe in New York State, at least. Stout also had a fleet of Tri-motor Fords. By the end of the year Boeing Air Transport was flying Tri-motor 14-passenger Boeings, the last word in flying luxury at the time. Air travelers who had flown in these so-called "Flying Pullmans" from San Francisco to Chicago were not going to climb into open cockpit planes for the rest of their journey, and Stout was the only airline flying east out of Chicago that offered a semblance of comfort.

The more logical step, as Rentschler clearly saw, was to pull National Air Transport into the United fold, since Boeing Air Transport and NAT planes fed each other cargo at Chicago. This Rentschler undertook to accomplish early in 1930 by formally inviting the NAT directors to submit a proposal to merge the two airlines to NAT shareholders at their annual meeting on April 10. He soon discovered that the capture of NAT could be achieved only over the prostrate body of a wily adversary, Clement M. Keys, who had raised the first million in New York to found the airline and who regarded it as one of his favorite corporation children. Keys emphatically refused either to consider the merger offer or to submit it to the stockholders.

Rentschler next turned to the so-called Chicago Group, the young financiers who had enthusiastically put up the Chicago quota of the original capital after their elders had cold-shouldered the idea. The Chicagoans were in operational control of NAT, which flew the southwest leg to Dallas for a year before winning the New York–Chicago mail contract. After their city was bypassed by NAT, the Detroit backers took a less active interest in the line. Howard Coffin of Detroit moved upstairs to board chairmanship, and Earle Reynolds of Chicago, largest individual stockholder, became president. John J. Mitchell, Jr., another Chicagoan, was already secretary and treasurer, in control of the purse strings.

Mitchell, Reynolds, Lawrence Armour, and a close little financial group had organized Aviation Securities Corporation, which held 100,000 shares of NAT stock. Mitchell as treasurer of NAT held proxies for 30,000 additional shares held in escrow for employes who were buying stock on time payments. Together, the Chicago group controlled about a third of the 650,000 outstanding NAT shares. And they ran the airline, particularly after Colonel Paul Henderson, NAT's operating vice-president, turned his energies to another of C. M. Keys's corporate offspring, TAT, and Captain Lester D. Seymour, a veteran airman and NAT's chief engineer since its start, took over as the new general manager. Henderson, still a vice-president but in Washington much of the time, announced early in 1930 that by mid-summer NAT would have a fleet of new Curtiss "Condors" capable of handling the Chicago–New York passenger business. This tip-off made it all the more important for United to capture NAT before the Keys Group bagged the passenger traffic on this all-important link of the coast-to-coast main line.

First smoke of battle between the aviation giants occurred on April 4, 1930, when *The New York Times* announced that Rentschler had acquired one-third of NAT's shares through an exchange-of-stock agreement with certain NAT shareholders, without naming them. The story quoted Rentschler as saying that "from an economic point of view, the air between the coasts is not big enough to be divided." The next day, Rentschler went over the heads of the Keys Group, by asking NAT shareholders for proxies for the April 10 meeting. On that day, 70,000 shares of NAT stock changed hands on the New York Stock Exchange. Stocks of both NAT and United Aircraft zoomed on the financial market.

No sooner was the stockholders' meeting called to order in Wilmington, Delaware, on April 10 than a fight for proxies flared. By midnight tellers were still checking and counting proxies. The next day, when the count was completed, the Rentschler representatives attempted to invalidate the meeting by voting only two of the big block of shares they controlled. By holding out, they hoped to prevent a quorum and postpone the meeting until they had

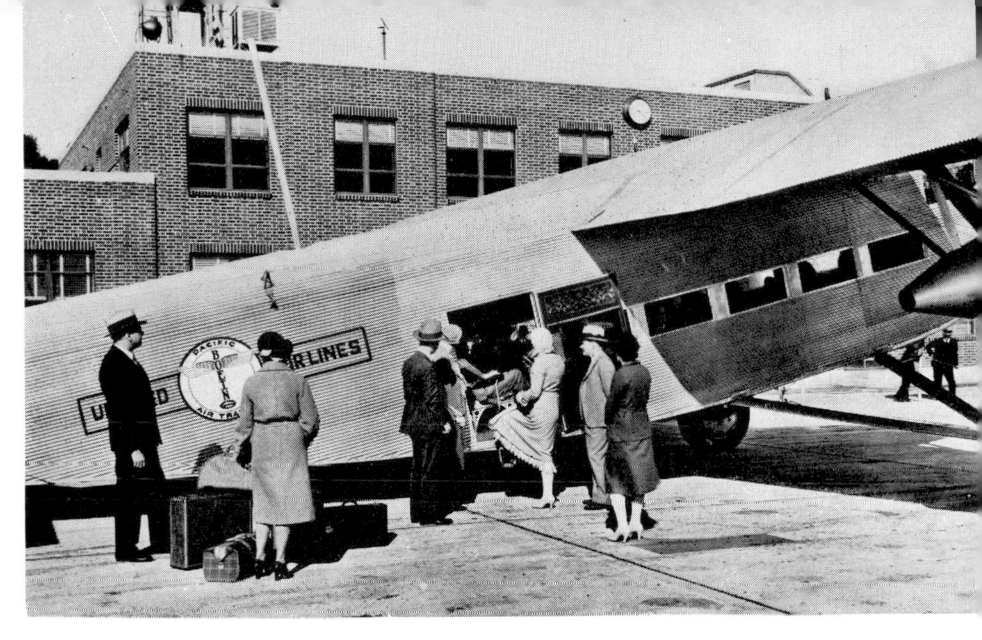

Pacific Coast passengers got a break in comfort when United put a fleet of 10-passenger tri-motored Fords in service on the West Coast in 1931.

This was "spacious air luxury" back in the late twenties. Passengers were squeezed into the four-passenger cabin of Boeing 40-Bs while the pilot rode outside.

The engine that remade the airline industry, Pratt & Whitney's Wasp, being studied by Bill Boeing (left), who first used it in commercial planes, and Frederick B. Rentschler, who dreamed up the engine and organized the staff and company to mass produce it.

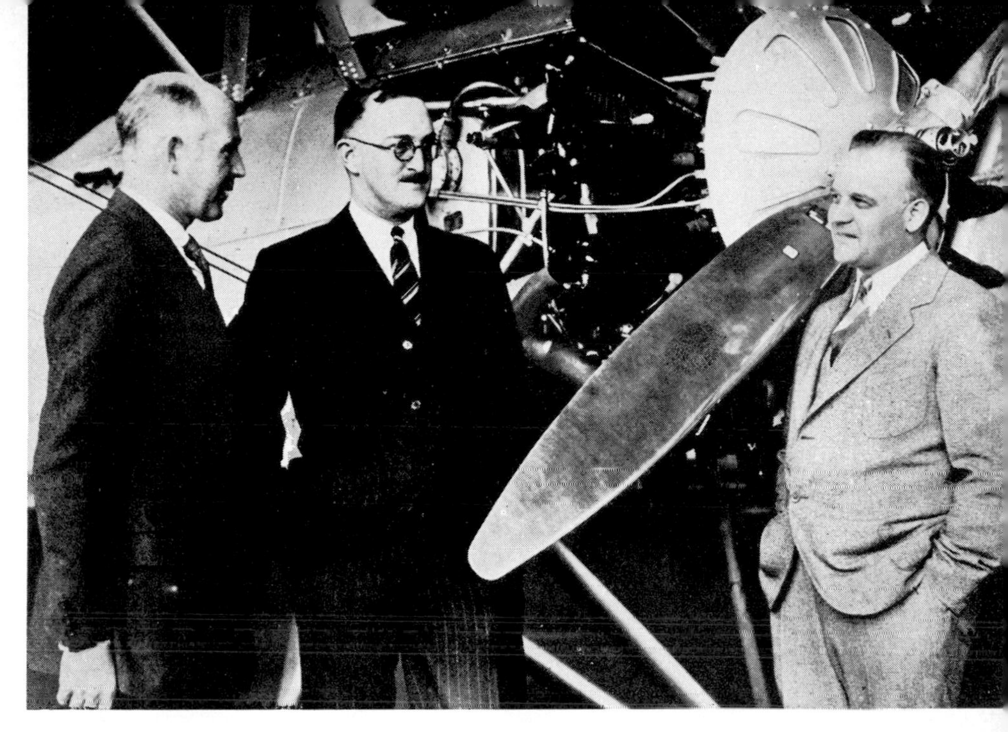

Here were some of the Seattle "brains" responsible for early air transport development. From left: Erik Nelson, who first gained fame as Army round-the-world flier and then became a Boeing executive; W. E. Boeing; and Phil Johnson.

P. G. Johnson, who headed up Boeing Airplane Company and later the United Air Lines network.

Clair Egtvedt, whose genius for design put the Boeing factory out in front both in commercial and military plane production.

Left: Postmaster General Walter F. Brown, whose vision had much to do with air transport's expansion in the late twenties and early thirties. Right: Postmaster General James A. Farley, who had the bitter task of enforcing air mail contract cancellations in 1934.

lined up the majority of the shareholders for their reorganization plan, which included a new board of directors favorable to the merger.

To their dismay, they soon learned that astute Mr. Keys had outsmarted them. Three days before the stockholders' meeting, he had called a directors' meeting, at which the corporation's by-laws had been doctored to meet the emergency. Among other things, they changed the quorum requirements from one-half to one-third of the outstanding shares. They also made a two-thirds vote of the stockholders' meeting necessary to dismiss directors. To make doubly sure that Rentschler would not capture control of the airline, the directors voted to issue 300,000 new shares of NAT stock, and swap them for shares in North American Aviation Corporation, a holding company which the Keys Group controlled beyond challenge. The directors also elected Keys president of the airline, succeeding Earle Reynolds, whom they distrusted.

Shut out from a voice in NAT affairs by these surprise moves, Rentschler turned to the courts. His legal representatives challenged the legality of the Keys changes in the by-laws and secured an injunction in the Delaware Chancery Court restraining the NAT directorate from issuing the 300,000 additional shares to exchange for North American Aviation shares. In and out of Wall Street, Rentschler's financial agent, Joseph Ripley, was busier than a bird dog lining up more NAT shares, by outright purchase or by exchange for United stock. By April 17, Rentschler was able to announce control of 375,000 shares, or 57 per cent of NAT's stock. When the Keys Group still defied him, on the ground that it required two-thirds to change directors, Rentschler sued to have the April 10 stockholders' meeting voided because of the quorum shenanigans.

The battle reached a climax on April 22, when Rentschler called a special meeting of stockholders for May 7, under a joker provision in the NAT corporation by-laws that the Keys Group had overlooked. It stated that any holder of one-fifth of the outstanding shares could call a meeting of stockholders any time. Rentschler announced that at this meeting he would propose rewriting the by-laws to make the shareholders, rather than the directors, the bosses of the corporation. Before the meeting took place, the Keys Group had lost control of the airline. Smooth-talking Joe Ripley, by offering to exchange one share of United stock for three of NAT, instead of one for three and a half, as provided in the original deal, persuaded outgoing president Earle Reynolds to advise all NAT stockholders to take advantage of the offer.

On April 23, a group of United and NAT officers and directors met in C. M. Keys's office at 39 Broadway to draw up a truce, with Keys absent. The United spokesmen agreed to call off their litigation if the majority of the NAT directors would resign. Rentschler was elected to the two NAT top offices, chairman of the board and president, succeeding Howard Coffin and Earle Reynolds and/or C. M. Keys, whoever was legally president. J. F. McCarthy of United Aircraft succeeded John J. Mitchell, Jr., as secretary and treasurer. On May 7 Rentschler called the new stockholders' meeting to order, fixed up the by-laws, formally took over NAT, and announced that the operating personnel would continue to run the airline as a unit of the United system.

An amusing sidelight on the seesaw Keys-Rentschler battle was the April issue of the NAT *Bulletin Board,* house organ of the airline. The issue appeared with the picture of C. M. Keys, as the new president of the company, prominently displayed in a box on the cover. A fortnight later, employes and stockholders received a new April issue, identical in content except that the picture of the new president in the front page box was that of Frederick B. Rentschler and one story had been lifted to make way for another announcing that NAT was now a division of United, the first coast-to-coast airline.

With NAT securely in the United fold, Rentschler reached out for one more airline to complete his airways system. The owners of Colonial Air Lines, serving the major cities of populous New England, were willing to sell or merge. Acquisition of Colonial would enable United to fan out on the Atlantic Coast as it did on the Pacific slope. Unfortunately, Rentschler was unable to contact Boeing before another group snapped up Colonial. Disappointed, Rentschler put his financial agents quietly to work buying up Eastern Air Transport shares, a maneuver that failed to work out. It was a decade and a half before United achieved a hard-won route extension into Boston and Hartford, from whence came the engines that powered the United fleet.

In the Rentschler scheme, United Aircraft & Transport functioned as a family of companies, each operating independently but each helping the other. The merger did two things. It made the Main Line, backbone of the United system, a reality. It also revealed the need of an operating unit to coordinate the four separate airlines in the United fold into one system. To accomplish this end, Rentschler organized a new management company, United Air Lines, Inc., which was to be a business getter and coordinator. United Air Lines owned no planes nor other equipment, signed no contracts, had no earnings. It was a "kept" company, supported jointly by the four member airlines. This unique role was to prove an unforeseen blessing three years later, when innocuous and innocent United became the Cinderella of a wicked industry.

One of the first decisions of the new Rentschler-Boeing management was to merge Stout Air Services into National Air Transport. At the time, Stout's resources consisted of a small fleet of Ford Tri-motors, a personnel with much know-how in the passenger end of the business, an airway from Chicago to Detroit to Cleveland to Buffalo, plus a drawer full of debts. NAT paid Stout $175,000, assumed the debts, and switched the planes and personnel to the Chicago–New York run, abandoning Stout's most valuable asset, the Chicago-Detroit-Cleveland airway. Years later United executives gnashed their teeth in rage at this shortsighted decision which tossed one of the world's heaviest traffic areas into the lap of a major competitor and shut the system out of the flourishing metropolis that had nurtured NAT in the first place in the hope of making Detroit the country's air transport hub.

The place of Stout Air Services in the United Air Lines foursome was taken by Varney Air Lines. When the Keys Group, through TAT, bought into Varney and Northwest Airways, Inc., it was clear that they were threatening the Boeing Air Transport leg of United in its home grounds, the Pacific Northwest. Varney was anything but a money-maker. Its founder and principal owner, Walter T. Varney, an extravagant operator, was always in need of more capital. When United Aircraft & Transport offered to buy the line early in 1930 for $1,000,000, Varney jumped at the chance to get out from under a burdensome load. Luckily for Walter Varney, before he closed the deal he turned negotiations over to Louis Mueller, the San Francisco attorney who became president of the airline when Varney moved up to board chairman.

Mueller drove a hard bargain. When the dickering concluded, United agreed to pay the Varney stockholders two million instead of one, with a six-year $25,000-per-year contract for Mueller himself as chairman of the board, a contract that was bought up for cash in 1933 when Varney Air Lines, Inc., was dissolved and its routes merged into the BAT system. Walter T. Varney, suddenly a millionaire, bought a fleet of ultra-fast Lockheed planes and launched the unsuccessful Varney Speed Lines, a passenger service between San Francisco, Los Angeles, and San Diego. He also started a Rocky Mountain airline. When the money was gone, Varney became a test pilot, and finally a highway truck driver over the same rugged mountains whose horizons his intrepid young pilots had winged with the first western air mail.

The merger of Boeing and National Air Transport in the summer of 1930 reshuffled the entire United States air transport picture. The Main Line became the first coast-to-coast airline under one management since the days of Post Office operation. Over it NAT-Boeing planes carried three-quarters of the country's air mail. With a new interest in passengers, the line was soon transporting a third of the country's air travelers, cutting the San Francisco–New York flight to thirty-three hours. The United system was the first air transport giant. Except for Transcontinental Air Transport, which was still trying to make the unwieldy plane-train scheme work, rivals of the future were still struggling small airlines, eventually to join together into airways systems.

The immediate task was to coordinate operations of Boeing Air Transport, which catered to passengers, with those of National Air Transport, which had discouraged them. To do this, Rentschler and Boeing set up United Air Lines' head office in Chicago. The first United man on the job at Chicago was Harold Crary, who had served in both the western and eastern arms of the swelling air transport system. Crary hailed originally from Seattle, whose glories he had publicized for the Chamber of Commerce. Then he switched to aviation in Chicago in 1927, the year that Boeing and NAT began flying the Main Line.

Crary became secretary of the American Air Transport Association, organized by twenty airline operators to consolidate schedules, expedite the handling of passengers and baggage, and to publicize air travel. That year the airline operators signed with Railway Express to pick up and deliver packages, a relationship that was to endure for decades. The Association also hoped to bring some order to the young industry, and at its 1928 meeting Cliff Ball, one of the more vociferous operators, proposed a system of air traffic cops stationed on tall buildings to direct fliers! No one present foresaw the day of ground control by radio. At this gathering Colonel Paul Henderson predicted the day would never come when passengers would fly over the Alleghenies, because it was too dangerous.

Two years later Crary was setting up shop in Chicago for the very purpose of stimulating passenger travel over those same Alleghenies, and for the very line which Colonel Henderson had helped found. Meantime the energetic Crary covered the country, flying in the rickety planes of nearly every airline in operation. Johnson lured him into the United fold in 1929 because by that time Crary was on first-name terms with every airline head in the country. His first assignment, in his home town, Seattle, was to survey the new business outlook for Boeing Air Transport. While he was at this task, the NAT-Boeing merger occurred and Crary was rushed to Chicago to rustle business for the whole system. At the time, the airlines' revenues were 80 per cent from mail and 20 per cent from passengers and express. One of Crary's objectives was to reverse this percentage, a project he handled so expeditiously that he emerged eventually as United's vice-president in charge of sales. He retired in 1953.

The next executive face to appear in the new United headquarters in Chicago was that of W. A. Patterson. He was still Phil Johnson's man Friday in the Boeing Aircraft plant and in Boeing Air Transport, into which Pacific Air Transport had been absorbed. As a result of the Boeing-Rentschler consolidations, Johnson had been collecting presidencies as most men collect neckties—those of Boeing Aircraft, Boeing Air Transport, Pacific Air Transport, and the new United Air Lines. In addition he was vice-president of United Aircraft & Transport, National Air Transport, Stout Air Services, Varney, and other subsidiaries. A hale and hearty extrovert, Johnson's talent kept him in Washington, selling planes and working on the ever-changing air mail contracts. Johnson liked to build and sell planes rather than operate them. He unloaded the airline operations duties on young Patterson, who thrived on them.

The analytical Patterson brought something new to an industry run largely by men who were fliers and adventurers and dreamers. His first try at aviation was applying business methods to Pacific Air Transport. His next job was systematizing the Boeing airplane factory operations, then those of Boeing Air Transport. Patterson found himself starting at scratch in an industry in which personnel programs, systems of promotion, wage and working condition policies were unknown. With high hopes and sometimes profits, the industry, like Topsy, had just grown. Largely because nobody else topside thought much about it, Patterson became the airline's policy man and planner.

The young ex-banker proved to be the right man for the right job at the right time. When he took over in midsummer of 1931 as general manager of United Air Lines, there was literally everything to be done. But Patterson had a lot to work with. The airline fanned out of Chicago in all directions—1900 miles west to the Pacific Coast, 750 miles east to the Atlantic, 995 miles south to Dallas, and for a time 175 miles northeast to Detroit. The horizons were high and "imagineers" were pushing them still higher. The United system was a loosely hung organization, an octopus in reverse whose tentacles bossed its nerve center, a cooperative of several aviation companies under one corporate ownership. As Rentschler pointed out with pride, the United companies were not "put together" by financial force, but rather were "joined together," each complementing the others. The United transport lines had much know-how, 40,000,000 flight-miles of it, 18,000,000 of them flown by night. It flew the Main Line carrying the bulk of the country's traffic at a profit. In 1931 the system's passenger business tripled to 42,928 air travelers; in 1932 it doubled again to 88,933, and jumped to 127,693 in 1933. These good years were a godsend less than twelve months later when a catastrophe from a source no crystal ball could have foreseen struck the air transport industry like a flash of lightning—a catastrophe made in Washington, D.C.

CHAPTER V

Who's Flying This Plane?

Shortly after W. A. Patterson joined the Boeing organization in Seattle, he picked up the telephone on his desk one day and found the line preoccupied by "The Two Black Crows," a radio team that was currently the rage. Patterson clicked down the receiver, waited a few minutes, tried again. The Two Black Crows were still discussing the fuzz on peaches. The next time he lifted the receiver, the Black Crows were off the line, but a phonograph was playing a popular song, "Why Did Your Dog Die?"

"What's going on here?" demanded the new Boeing executive.

"It's that nut from Yakima, Mr. Hiscock," explained his secretary. "He's playing records over our plant telephone system to create interference for his new radio set."

Patterson made further inquiries, which satisfied him that had she known more about the new man from Yakima, over the mountains, his secretary would have spoken in more respectful terms. Thorp Hiscock was a man to watch.

A former upstate New York banker who learned to fly so well in World War I that he became a "professor of aerial acrobatics" at a Texas Army flying field, Hiscock found the banking business entirely too confining after the excitement of military life and migrated west to Yakima, Washington. There he bought a ranch and established a radio business with William Lawrenz, an electronic Handy Andy whom Hiscock had met during the war. They became the Western Electric company representatives in Yakima. Hiscock, the idea man, and Bill Lawrenz, who worked out the mechanical bugs, were ready to tackle anything in the field of radio with utter disregard for the seemingly impossible.

Hiscock married Bill Boeing's sister-in-law, and thus became one of Boeing's few close friends. One night after he and Phil Johnson had dined at Boeing's house, the trio got word about a plane that had been forced down by a local storm which swept across the pilot's path after he took off. The storm kept the pilot from seeing flares set out at an emergency field to warn him in time to avoid disaster.

"Everybody knew about that storm but the pilot," exclaimed Boeing. "If we only had some way to talk with our pilots when they are in the air."

"What's the matter with radio?" asked Hiscock.

"I have put the problem up to all the big radio companies in the country and they say it just can't be done," answered Boeing.

"It can, too," asserted the irrepressible Hiscock. "It is possible to build two-way radios for planes."

"I wish I knew who could do it," said Boeing.

"I'll do it," declared Hiscock.

Within twenty-four hours he was up to his ears in a project that had baffled communications engineers for many months. Hiscock knew nothing of the technical background of radio, so he resorted to innumerable amateurish experiments around the Boeing plant in Seattle to test his first crude set. When Hiscock seemed hopelessly lost in the electronics maze, Patterson hired an engineer from a major radio laboratory to collaborate with him. He gave the pair a plane with which to experiment. At the end of the first day, the radio engineer quit.

"That fellow is plumb crazy," he declared. "I give up."

Hiscock's approach to a problem was usually the reverse of everybody else's. When other builders of radio sets experimented out in the country far from electrical disturbances, Hiscock located his sets in attics in the crowded cities to be near as much interference as possible. Where others tried to circumvent the airplane motor's troublesome sparkplug interference, he hooked up his set to go through the engine. He rigged up one miniature radio plant on a motor truck and a second on his ranch at Yakima. Day after day he drove up and down the mountain roads of the Cascade

Range talking with the ranch by radio from canyons, peaks, and slopes. When at length he had the sets functioning to his satisfaction, he transferred the one in the truck to a plane, and began talking to his home from the air.

This proved that it could be done. Up to that time the only plane-ground communication on the Boeing system had been that employed by Hebe Miller, an old-time Pacific Air Transport pilot with a voice like a bull. When he wanted to check on the weather ahead, or anything else while he was up in the air, Miller would cut his motor above a town or an airport or a farm and bellow down for information. Miller's system had two weaknesses: not many people on the ground had enough oomph in their vocal cords to bellow back to him, and it wouldn't work in storms. But Miller always insisted that his was the first two-way communication used by any transport flier.

Soon after Hiscock proved that his radio sets would communicate between the ground and planes, he was invited to attend a dinner of the Detroit Aviation Show. At this gathering one of the engineers abruptly turned to him, when the subject of plane-ground communication was being discussed, and said, "We're stumped. Where do we go from here?"

The radio amateur from Yakima pulled some rough diagrams from his pocket and handed them across the table. "You might start building some of these haywire sets of mine. They work."

Boeing established a laboratory at the Oakland terminal of the Main Line to build sets for all of the company's planes. Hiscock and Lawrenz moved there to supervise. Western Electric assigned technicians to work with them. Western Air Express sent Herbert Hoover, Jr., who had been wrestling with the problem with some success, to join them, pooling Western's know-how with that of Boeing for the safety of pilots and air travelers on all airlines. Hiscock's first haywire set was soon refined in so many ways that the resulting battery of electronic aids to pilots quickly became a far cry from the original.

Having demonstrated that it could be done, Hiscock had no more interest in two-way radio communication as such. An odd genius born a quarter of a century ahead of his time, he was intrigued by unsolved problems. Though he seldom flew a plane after getting out of uniform, he had the pilot's viewpoint. He was a pilot groping for precision methods of holding planes on course, of finding airports in fogs and storms, and landing planes safely under any circumstances. Hiscock typified the early airman with the scientific explorer's searching mind.

After the merger of Boeing Air Transport and National Air Transport to form United Air Lines, Hiscock became a sort of free-lance research man, roaming the airway and seeking new ways of reducing the human factor to a minimum in air transport. This became almost a mania with him. When three separate laboratories developed and patented automatic piloting devices, no one of them completely reliable, he appropriated parts from all three and built the first successful robot pilot. It infringed on the patents of all three makers, but Hiscock rode over them rough-shod to build the forerunner of the gyro-pilots used in modern airliners.

When Patterson moved to Chicago to take charge of the newly established United Air Lines headquarters, Hiscock made Chicago the base from which he covered the country, looking for ideas. Hiscock invariably worked on pure inspiration, pulling practical ideas out of the air. One day he was watching the frozen flag hanging stiff from its mast over a Chicago hotel. A wind came up, whipping the bunting, and shook the ice off.

"That's the answer!" he exclaimed.

In the next five days he had worked out the first practical set of de-icers for the wings of planes, a series of long rubber tubes inflated and deflated by changing pressures to accomplish the whipping effect that had de-iced the flag on the pole.

At a machinery exhibit, he became intrigued with the functions of a governor on a piece of equipment designed for Boulder Dam. He immediately bought the governor and carried it to the shop, where technical men had been struggling for months on a device for changing the propeller pitch after a plane gained its altitude.

"Forget electricity," he advised. "Try this method. It does the work by air."

Though the technicians were skeptical, he made life miserable for them until they tried the idea. Before long all commercial air transports were using this idea to change the propeller pitch once a plane had gained altitude, thus flying more efficiently at varying altitudes.

For a time after they located in Chicago, Hiscock and Patterson lived together until their families could move east. It was a period of liberal scientific education for the new operating head of the airline, and one that caused him to lose much sleep. Hiscock's ideas often hit him about three o'clock in the morning, and his voice inevitably came booming through the apartment, "Are you awake, Pat? Got time to listen to an idea?"

While Patterson tried to get to sleep again, Hiscock kept on outlining an idea that had suddenly hit him for a device to control the temperature of fuel while the plane was in flight, thereby increasing the efficiency of the motors and adding to the cruising range.

"It sounds fine. Why don't you go to work on it tomorrow?"

"Tomorrow, hell. I'm going out to the airport and build one now," replied Hiscock, bouncing out of bed.

On this particular occasion, it was three days before he returned to the apartment. During the seventy-two hours he had worked day and night, driving the shop mechanics almost frantic as he hovered impatiently over them directing their work, and munching popcorn, the only form of nourishment he ever ate when he was on an inventive spree. Before he left the shop he had originated a new piece of standard airline equipment.

When this amazing human dynamo with the unquenchable curiosity and the instinct for putting his finger on the fundamental idea in a welter of experiments collapsed and died suddenly in 1934 at the age of forty-one, he was absorbed in an idea for airplane controls so simple that a pilot could push one button to take off and another one to land. It took another decade and the technological impetus of another World War to make this robot control come true. There was never another Thorp Hiscock to take his place, but this erratic airman who launched the electronic era of flying, out of which grew a system of traffic control as dependable as the railroad's block signals or the highway's stop-and-go lights, left his mark on air transport for all time.

Hiscock inspired many young scientific dreamers to the belief that they could overcome any hazard of flying. They could lick the weather; they could see through the fog; they could beat static, the bugaboo of airline communication; they could overcome altitude and pinpoint planes and all other obstructions hidden by darkness or by clouds. "The electronics gang" not only could do this, but before long they did do it.

One of Thorp Hiscock's right-hand men and his successor as a sparkplug of the airline's communications research program was another World War Army pilot named J. R. Cunningham. A native of Spokane, Washington, Russ Cunningham left Washington State College to fly with the Army. When World War I ended, he flew for the Forestry Service spotting fires. Then he joined Pacific Air Transport in the winter of 1926, flying the then hazardous San Francisco–Seattle leg. In five years with Pacific Air Transport, Cunningham survived a major crack-up that contributed to the know-how of ground-plane communication.

Cunningham's obsession was perfecting a technique for "riding the beam" from radio station to station, after Boeing had set up some thirty transmitters between Seattle and Los Angeles and Oakland and Chicago to talk to its pilots in flight. The fliers still held to course by watching for the flashing beacons spotted every 25 miles along the airway. To see the lights they had to fly low under the clouds, a dangerous adventure in the mountainous areas. Russ Cunningham argued that if they could ride the beam by radio, they could fly higher and more safely. Other pilots and the Bureau of Aeronautics authorities were working on the idea, too, but as he flew for Pacific Air Transport, Cunningham carried on his own experiments at the risk of his neck.

One New Year's Eve, for example, while ferrying a Boeing 40-B from Seattle to Medford, Cunningham decided to try out his theory while he had no passengers. A storm moved into his path as he flew over Oregon, and instead of dropping to just above the treetops to wing from beacon to beacon, he climbed up on top, flying by compass but checking his direction by the strength of the radio signals from down below. At 12,000 feet he picked up a load of ice on his wings. The ice was so heavy that his plane lost altitude steadily, about 500 feet per minute. At 6000 feet, nearing Medford but still over the mountains, he knew he would never make it with the ice still on his wings. Pulling his stick back, he pancaked into a mountainside, squashing through the snow into a tree, uninjured and without seriously damaging his plane.

The remarkable feature of the crack-up, though, was the way Cunningham kept coolly talking to the station at Medford over the two-way radio. His last words were, "Keep on talking to me, keep talking to me." The operator at Medford thought that Cunningham was scared silly, or else out of his head. What Cunningham was trying to do was determine the direction to Medford. After his plane plopped into the snow against a pine tree, he sat in the cockpit listening to signals and working on directions. The next morning he started pushing through the snow in the right direction until he came to an empty farmhouse. In the shed was an old auto with the keys in it. Cunningham borrowed the car and reached the Medford Airport a day and a half late, but little the worse for wear.

Before many months had elapsed, "riding the beam" was regular practice for air transport pilots. The airways were soon equipped with directional beams that fanned out in chosen directions. These radio beacons were broken into quadrants, and with special receiving sets which they switched on at will, pilots determined from the nature of the dot-dashes or the dash-dots whether they were on the beam or to the left or right of it. Later, Pilot Cunningham, who had deliberately risked his life proving up the idea of "riding the beam," deserted the cockpit to become Superintendent of Operations on the Pacific Coast run, then assistant to Thorp Hiscock, and finally his successor as director of communications for the entire airline. He retired in 1961.

There were still serious defects in the plane-ground communication system, for all its refinements and the amazing way it guided planes unseen over the airways 95 per cent of the time. The other 5 per cent was a nightmare. Nearly all the crashes of the first few years of the electronics era, beginning in 1929, came in this 5 per cent of the time. The nemesis was static, which crackled into the pilot's earphones, disrupting voices and radio range signals from below, sometimes drowning them out completely. Pilots and electronics technicians knew that before planes could fly safely, they would have to conquer static.

Over on a rival airline, TWA, Jack Franklin, communications

engineer, had an idea that static could be licked by concealing the radio antenna in the nose of the plane. Though this reduced static somewhat, it cut down reception clarity in the 95 per cent of the time when radio communication worked well. Thus it set up an entirely new hazard. Then Franklin devised "the flying doughnut," a ring antenna concealed in a loop about 18 inches in diameter and fastened under the plane's belly. Though this further reduced static, the doughnut still failed at times.

The trouble was, nobody knew exactly what caused static. Up in the Pacific Northwest, Bert Ball, a United pilot with a special interest in weather, tackled static in his spare time between flights. Ball was a former seafaring navigator who had saved up enough money to study aerial navigation and air mass meteorology at the Massachusetts Institute of Technology. In his pilot's reports were often found gratuitous observations about the habits of storms. The reports were so good that the airline's weather men formed a habit of saving them.

Ball made the acquaintance of Professor Marcus O'Day of Reed College in Portland, a life-long student of weather phenomena and a researcher who had spent weeks at a time on the summit of Mount Hood, gathering data on storms up where the elements crackled and thundered. When Ball proposed to take the professor along in a plane to hunt storms, O'Day leaped at the opportunity. Ball asked his superiors if they would let him have a plane. They were dubious that he would find out anything worth the risk of a plane being batted down by the storms. Finally Ball sent some copies of his in-flight weather observations to Patterson.

"This fellow is on the trail of something," said Patterson. "Let's give him a plane for a while."

Ball and a young radio technician named Herbert Hucke assembled a hurry-up crew of five professors from as many different colleges and five radio experts from outstanding laboratories in the country. Day after day for three months they sought storms in their flying laboratory, picking up air mass fronts as they moved in from the Alaska weather cradle and following them over the Oregon and Northern California mountains. They tried out radio sets and antenna of every conceivable design, bristling from the nose of the plane like feelers of a giant beetle.

In the course of these flights Ball and his colleagues discovered that the static was born of the plane itself, hurtling through space. The metal plane picked up lightning-like discharges of high voltage and hurled them back into the clouds. When this electric phenomena burst off the trailing edges of the wings and other flat surfaces, it created pandemonium in the pilot's earphones. When Ball and Hucke dangled trailing wires from these edges, the static discharged itself behind the ship and the radio sets functioned perfectly, even in the worst storm centers. That gave them the clue to the answer—cables which could be unreeled from the plane's wings. Unfortunately these whipped off. Then the experimenters discovered they didn't need a long trailing cable after all; just a 10-inch metal strip would toss off the static. Thus the most serious obstacle to plane-ground communication was overcome.

Not all pilots took kindly to these new electronic gadgets that enabled a dispatcher on the ground to monitor unseen planes in flight miles above him. Many old-time pilots had rolled up safe flying records of a million miles or more, and felt that the reflexes which had made them million-milers were more dependable than the electronic aids. Several serious accidents grew out of this conflict between instincts and mechanics in flying. "Pilot error" became a new term on the airways, the explanation of accident after accident.

"What we need is some way of checking flights," declared R. W. ("Shorty") Schroeder, then manager of operations for the system, "some device that would record weather and altitude at every mile of the flight. Then we would know whether or not our pilots were taking chances."

Safety was a mania with Schroeder. Other executives of the airline agreed that such a magic device on every airliner would be a godsend, but nobody knew how to build one. Then one day Patterson was talking about the idea with an instrument builder in Baltimore.

"Say, we have a new portable recording outfit for testing the temperature and humidity of air conditioning equipment," said the instrument man. "I bet we could adapt it to flight recording for airplanes."

Patterson had two technicians from the airline's communications laboratory at the factory the next week. In a few days they had worked out the necessary changes to transform the humidity tester into a barographic flight analyzer. There were two extra pens on the gadget, and somebody remarked it was too bad they couldn't be put to work. Then somebody else hit on the idea of actuating them electrically to show when the pilot turned the plane over to the automatic robot and when he used the ship's radio transmitter.

When the new recording barographs were installed in the planes, they turned in some astonishing new data on flying. They revealed for the first time the extent to which air transport had been revolutionized since the pilot, sitting in the cockpit, was matching his wits unaided against the elements and the risks of engine failure. The innocuous-looking lines on the charts dramatized, as nothing else could, the answer to the question, "Who's flying this plane?" They revealed that 80 per cent of the time most pilots were relying on their new-found electronic aids to keep them on course and to bring their planes safely into port.

The device that more than any other brought the old-time pilots around to the new techniques in flying—or eliminated them entirely from the cockpit—paradoxically never took off from the ground. It was the Link Trainer, devised by another old Army flier, Ed Link, who came from a family of organ builders of Binghamton, New York. Born with a gift for invention, Ed Link's mind turned naturally to odd uses for the bellows which provide the wind for the organ. He rigged up a machine for taking landlubbers on synthetic airplane rides. It was just a fuselage and cockpit with a pair of stubby wings, mounted on two large bellows that, as the operator wiggled the stick, provided a remarkably realistic imitation of the movements and sensations of flying a plane. Ed Link installed his thriller at carnivals, and set one up just off the boardwalk at Atlantic City, where for 50 cents anyone could treat himself to an imaginary flight without the risk of getting off the ground. One day another pilot tried the on-the-ground airplane ride.

"Listen, this is too good for a stunt," he insisted. "It's the real thing. You ought to fit it up with instruments and use it for a pilot trainer."

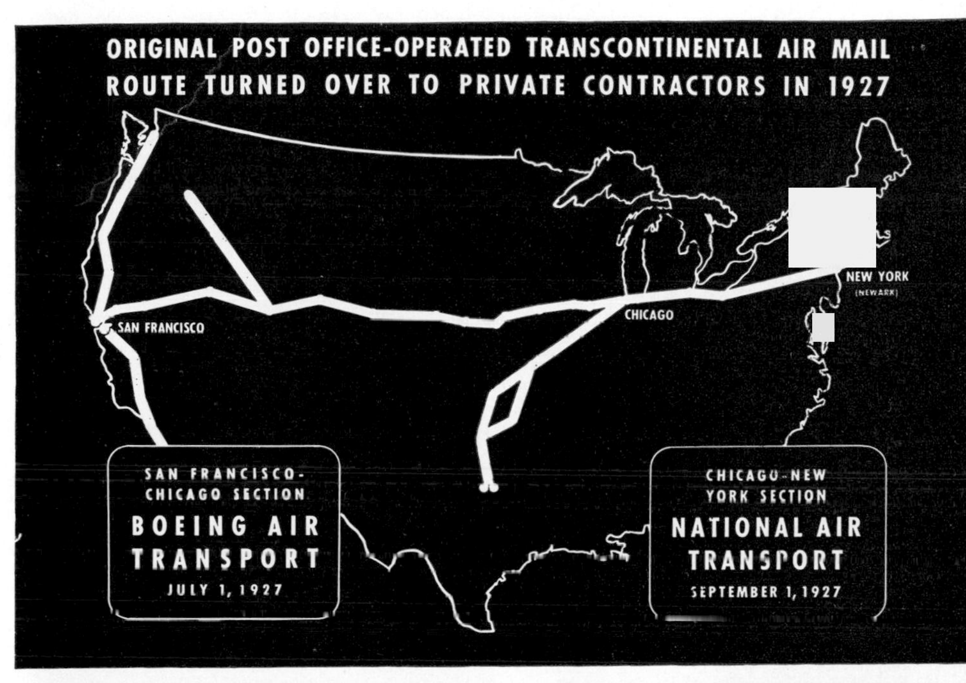

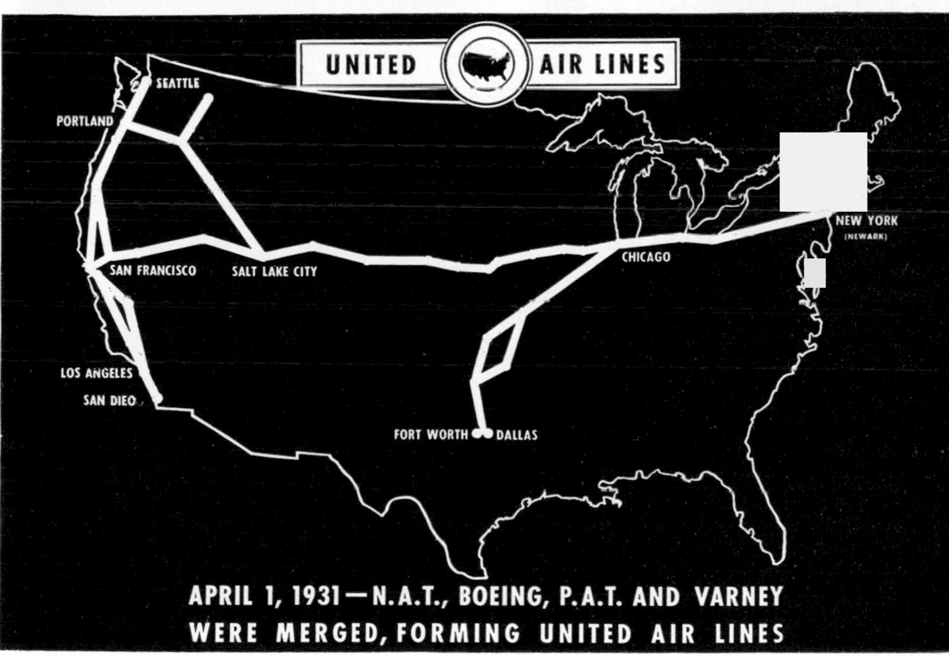

How four key airlines were joined to make the United system, the country's pioneer coast-to-coast airway.

Frederick B. Rentschler, a leader in the formation of United Aircraft & Transport, a well-integrated aviation corporation in which each subsidiary complemented the other. Out of its unscrambling in 1930 emerged an independent United Air Lines.

Joseph P. Ripley, banker and broker, whose persuasive diplomacy won over the Chicago group and other shareholders, making possible the Rentschler victory over the Keys group. Later, it was Ripley's chore to unscramble the aircraft companies he had helped put together.

A new degree of luxury was introduced to the airlines in 1929 when Boeing Air Transport, a United predecessor, placed a fleet of tri-motored Boeing 80s on its San Francisco–Chicago run. Later these and National Air Transport's Ford Tri-motors, operated between Chicago and New York, provided the first coast-to-coast service in multi-engined planes.

Hitherto undreamed-of luxury inside the cabin of the tri-motored Boeing 80-A. It was 1930 or thereabouts. The sandwich-and-apple era was over; the fried chicken era had arrived, and the world's first stewardesses were flying to cater to passengers' needs.

Thus originated the Link Trainer, which in a few hours' operation could simulate the navigation problems confronting a pilot in flying any quadrant of any radio range in the country, and in following the beam safely to the next airport. With the Link Trainer, the pilot no longer had to lose himself aloft in an expensive plane to prove his skill. He could do it without risk in an inexpensive box on a bellows, where every move he made was recorded on a chart under the eagle eye of his chief pilot. If he knew his navigation, he could come down and hit the runway squarely on the nose. If he didn't, he was likely to come down on a mountainside or in the sea, but without damaging himself or his plane or a passenger. The Link Trainer soon separated the seat-of-the-pants fliers from the scientific technicians who were needed as captains and co-pilots in the electronic era of the Mainliners that were soon to emerge from the airplane factories.

During this period the airline pilot changed from a daredevil flier to an engineer. His understanding of electronic communication and navigation became as important as his ability to fly a plane. Also, he had assumed a lot more responsibility. Instead of two to four foolhardy adventurers sandwiched in the cabin in front of him, he had up to a dozen passengers behind him. He no longer sat behind a windshield, out in the open weather, his helmet battered by the wind, snow, and rain. Instead, with the advent of the Tri-motor Fords, Fokkers, and Boeing 80s, he sat in a comfortable cabin, still called the cockpit, in the nose of the plane. To his right sat another, younger flier, known as the co-pilot, at first a general utility pinch-hitter who flew the plane while the pilot worked on his navigation or reports and who passed out lunch boxes to the passengers in flight. Like as not, both the pilot and co-pilot were plenty busy flying and navigating at lunchtime, in which case the passengers helped themselves or went without lunch. In bumpy flying weather, most of the patrons preferred the latter.

The Boeing 80, which took to the air in 1929, was the last word in travel comfort at the time, as the airline's advertising modestly pointed out, but despite the "luxurious appointments" it left something to be desired by the passengers. Returning from a flight to Reno early in 1930, Steve A. Stimpson, Boeing's San Francisco district manager, hit on an idea. The trip was rough, the pilot and co-pilot were fighting the weather, so Stimpson passed out the lunches, poured the coffee from the thermos bottles, and did what he could to cheer the uncomfortable passengers. When he reached his office, Stimpson fired off a wire to his superiors urging that they add a steward, possibly a Filipino boy, to the crew.

Before he got a reply, a diminutive nurse from the French Hospital in San Francisco came into his office with a more intriguing proposition. An Iowa girl who had trained as a nurse in Minnesota, Ellen Church had yearned to fly ever since as a youngster she had seen Ruth Law, the first woman stunt flier, perform at a county fair. Miss Church had taken some flying lessons, but realizing that opportunities for women as fliers were limited, she proposed to Stimpson that Boeing employ young nurses as attendants on the company's planes. She promised to provide the nurses if Stimpson could persuade the Boeing management to employ them. Her visit stretched into a two-hour talk during which, although neither she nor Stimpson realized it at the time, a new profession for women was born. Before she left, Stimpson shot another wire to headquarters saying, "Stand by for important communication following by air mail." In his message, Stimpson practically wrote the ticket for the new calling:

> It strikes me that there would be a great psychological punch to having young women stewardesses or couriers, or whatever you want to call them, and I am certain that there are some mighty good ones available. I have in mind a couple of graduate nurses that would make exceptional stewardesses. Of course, it would be distinctly understood that there would be no reference made to their hospital training or nursing experience, but it would be a mighty fine thing to have this available, sub rosa, if necessary for air sickness.
>
> Imagine the psychology of having young women as regular members of the crew. Imagine the national publicity we could get from it, and the tremendous effect it would have on the traveling public. Also imagine the value they would be to us not only in the neater and nicer method of serving food but looking out for the passengers' welfare.

Although the Boeing management was anything but enthusiastic about Steve Stimpson's brainstorm, and although the pilots grumbled that they didn't have any time to look after a frail female member of the crew in flight, the ebullient Stimpson bombarded his bosses so persistently that they finally told him to employ eight nurses and try out the stewardess idea on the San Francisco–Chicago run for three months. If the nurses made good, they would have permanent jobs; if they didn't, the stewardess idea was out.

Stimpson raced out to the French Hospital to tell Ellen Church and to hire her as chief stewardess, not only Boeing's first but the first on any airline. From the wards of San Francisco and Chicago hospitals, they hired seven more nurses, Ellis Crawford, Harriet Fry, Cornelia Peterman, Jessie Carter, Inez Keller, Margaret Arnott, and Alva Johnson. Miss Church wrote the first specifications for the airline stewardesses: nurses, not over twenty-five years of age, weighing 115 pounds or less, and not over 5 feet, 4 inches tall. The pay was $125 per month for 100 hours of flying. Stimpson and Ellen Church designed the first uniforms, dark green jersey double-breasted jacket and skirt, with a green tam shaped like a shower cap, and a flowing green jersey cape with gray collar and silver buttons for warmth in cold cabins and at colder airports. As Stimpson wrote in one of his memoranda, "I am not suggesting at all the flapper type of girl."

There being no school for the new-born profession, the first eight stewardesses learned as they flew—how to handle thermos jugs of soup and coffee, how to serve meals, check passengers, keep records, and make passengers comfortable when the flying was rough. Boeing's patrons liked the new touch to air travel luxury, and wrote in to tell the management so. Pilots, glad to be relieved of chores for passengers in flight, swung around from critics to boosters. They, too, enjoyed coffee and food served to them in their cockpits. By the end of the three-month trial period, the Boeing management was converted. The first chief stewardess was told to go out and find twenty more nurses for the Pacific Coast flights and to plan a training course for future stewardesses. Other airlines quickly hopped aboard and employed young nurses for stewardesses. The distaff part of the airline crew was on the wing to stay.

So were some other members, down below. At the terminals, other crews were shaping up. The new communications system depended as much upon the technicians in the towers and the weather offices as upon the men in the cockpits. Ground crews became expert in fueling, checking planes, loading and unloading fast, and dispatchers developed new skill in getting planes off the ramp. A new division known as "Reservations" came into being to keep ticket offices and agents from over-selling some flights and under-selling others. The romantic era of the daring and lonely pilot battling through the weather to keep the airline flying had ended, replaced by a new and better age in which airliners were flown by a team, with seven experts on the ground for every three in the air.

CHAPTER VI

Air Transport's Pied Piper

On the morning of March 4, 1929, when Herbert Hoover moved into the White House as thirty-first President of the United States, United Aircraft & Transport moved into a new corporate home at 51 Pine Street, New York City, next door to Wall Street, from whence had come the dollars to finance the Rentschler-Boeing merger. On that same morning, Walter Folger Brown moved down the street from the Department of Commerce to the Post Office Building in Washington, D.C. Brown's move to his new quarters went unheralded at the time, its implications lost in the booming prosperity of the period. Probably not even Postmaster General Brown suspected, on that eventful day, that he was destined to be the Pied Piper of air transport, and likewise the architect of the airways map of the country for decades to come.

An astute Toledo attorney trained in the rough-and-tumble school of Ohio politics through three Republican administrations, Brown, as assistant to Secretary of Commerce Hoover, had handled politics for Hoover, who loathed that aspect of public life. As the new Postmaster General, Brown was expected to do the political chores for the administration while his assistants ran the postal service. This omened well for those airlines making money flying the mail on postal contracts, largely in planes that involved small investments and little overhead. Boeing was one of the few air mail contractors that had invested heavily in new planes with adequate accommodations for passengers. As Secretary of Commerce, Herbert Hoover had prodded the Bureau of Aeronautics into building beacons and emergency air strips, and Brown had shown the same enthusiasm for helping the fledgling air transport industry with Federal funds. Since the Hoover administration was a continuation of the Coolidge regime, the air mail contractors looked forward to four more years of the same.

Their joyful dream endured for the rest of the year, ending in a shocking awakening. By the beginning of 1930 it dawned upon them that Postmaster General Brown was no typical political chief of the Post Office Department. Brown had developed an aviation complex. Instead of letting his aides handle the air mail contracts, he proposed to deal them out himself in a grandiose scheme to parlay them into a vast network of airways, privately owned and operated but kept under the government's thumb until they were nearly self-sufficient without revenues from the Post Office. Knowing nothing about air transport when he became Postmaster General, Brown turned his agile mind on the subject, read everything he could lay his hands on, and by 1930 had a grasp of the industry's problems that few operators themselves could boast. More important, he had a grand plan, one that the air mail carriers did not particularly relish, because it meant they had to absorb the smaller lines into airline systems that flew from somewhere to somewhere.

General Brown became a Pied Piper with intriguing music of new profits as a lure and a bludgeon of "or else" threats to club the doubting airline operators into line. His study of the air transport problem convinced him that he needed new authority to solve it. Calling in Colonel Paul Henderson and Hainer Hinshaw of Aviation Corporation, P. G. Johnson of Boeing, Louis Mueller of Varney, and Harris Hanshue of Western Air Express for advice, General Brown and his assistant, W. Irving Glover, drew up an amendment to the existing Kelly Air Mail Law. The new legislation was known first as the McNary-Watres Act, because it was sponsored in Congress by Senator Charles D. McNary of Oregon and Representative Lawrence H. Watres of Pennsylvania. Later it was known more simply as the Watres Act. The amendment, passed by Congress on April 29, 1930, is still known as "the most scientific job of feed-bagging ever done."

Instead of paying airline operators by the pound-mile for flying mail, the Watres Act empowered the Postmaster General to pay what was called the "base mile rate," with extra pay for night flying, two-way radio, passenger seats, flying over mountains and other so-called "variables." Thus the Post Office paid for cargo space in the plane, whether it was full of mail or not. Extra space could be filled with other cargo or sold to passengers, and any revenue the airline picked up from these sources was so much gravy. Thus operators of modern new planes with plenty of space for cargo and air travelers were paid several times as much as those who still flew converted open-cockpit war surplus planes, or the low-priced planes built for mail carrying exclusively.

The result was a scramble for the bigger planes, Fords, Fokkers, Condors, and the like. Boeing Air Transport, which had pioneered passenger service between San Francisco and Chicago with single engine B-40s, then switched to Tri-motor Boeing 80s carrying twelve passengers, turned the Boeing Aircraft plant at Seattle loose on the design of a new plane that soon would revolutionize air transport. The Boeing builders had already hit on a radical new design in the Boeing Monomail introduced in 1930, a streamlined single-engine all-metal cabin monoplane with retractable landing gear, forerunner of the sleek modern planes to come. Only a few of these were built, because after the Watres Act it was clear that any airline operator using single-engine planes was passing up better pay.

First the Boeing factory assigned Fred Collins, later vice-president, to fly as co-pilot on the San Francisco–Chicago run to find out from Boeing Air Transport pilots what kind of a plane they wanted. While Collins was flying, Clair Egtvedt was designing, and after Collins turned in his report from riding the airways, off the drawing boards came the plan for a low-wing two-engine cabin monoplane, the Boeing 247 that became the prototype of the modern airliner. Collins and Egtvedt wanted to build a 16,000-pound plane around the new Pratt & Whitney Hornet engine, higher powered than the Wasp. Unfortunately the Boeing Air Transport pilots, who had fallen in love with the Wasp engine, didn't want a new engine in their planes. They thought that a 16,000-pound plane was too heavy to land safely, and they demanded Wasp engines for the new Boeing 247s.

Largely because of the pilots' protests, the decision came down from 51 Pine Street, New York City, that the airline would have to get along with a smaller plane. Egtvedt and staff scaled the 247 down to a ten-passenger, 12,000-pound plane with ample room for mail. It was still the most expensive plane on the market, $68,000 as compared to $50,000 for the Ford Tri-motor, but it was so much faster and plushier than anything yet built that United Aircraft & Transport appropriated $4,000,000 to buy sixty of the new airliners to standardize service all the way across the country. The 247s jumped the speed of air travel from 120 miles per hour to 160 miles per hour, an impressive gain that cut the coast-to-coast schedule from 27 to 19½ hours.

The United management, by placing such a huge order, tied up the facilities of the Boeing plant in Seattle, thus making sure that competitors could not share the prestige of flying the first all-metal airliner for considerable time to come. It was a squeeze play with a kickback. Rivals, particularly the newly organized TWA line, turned to a small airplane plant in Santa Monica, built up on a shoestring by an engineering genius named Donald Douglas, which up to this time had concentrated largely on military and mail planes, then pulled a sturdy, all-metal plane off the boards, one that would carry five more passengers than the Boeing 247, and fly them faster in longer hops with fewer stops, particularly when his first DC-2 grew into the 180-mile-per-hour DC-3.

TWA and the newly organized American Airlines bought the faster Douglas planes with higher earning capacity. Other airline operators turned to another small plant in Burbank, California, which came out with the fastest passenger planes in the air, the Lockheed Lodestars. Thus shortly after the 247s were delivered, the airline operators in the United fold found themselves handicapped by an expensive fleet of ultramodern planes that were outmoded not long after they took to air. It was a story often repeated in the airline game, in which today's best is inevitably obsolete by tomorrow.

There was another interesting sidelight to the Boeing 247 deal. About the only customer the Boeing plant could find, after the United order was filled, was the German Lufthansa, which bought two of the new planes. Boeing shipped the 247s and sent a test pilot along to teach the Germans how to fly them. After a few flights, the Lufthansa people said, "Good; you can go home now." Then they began tearing the 247s apart. The Nazis were buying a ten-year leap ahead in design know-how. This may explain why the German bombers of World War II bore a striking resemblance to the Boeing 247.

But regardless of the economic problems the 247s created for United, the performance record they turned in came up to Postmaster General Brown's idea of what an airline should be. The merged United Main Line was what Brown thought all airlines should be, airways that flew "from somewhere to somewhere." When Brown came into office, the country was criss-crossed by a jigsaw puzzle of little airlines, the outgrowth of the earlier Post Office policy of calling for bids on routes established often as a result of political pressures. Many little airlines existed largely on a diet of air mail, making little effort to lure passengers into the air. The first years of air transport had demonstrated that passengers would fly regularly only over the longer routes, where the saving in time compensated for the higher fares, the risk, and the uncertainty of on-time arrival. Though there were three-score or more operators carrying passengers and hoping for air mail contracts, air travel generally was falling into a pattern, typified by the United system. Recognizing this, the big holding companies reached out to swallow little lines, often at fancy prices.

Postmaster General Brown decided to make it his mission to forge a strong network of airlines that flew from somewhere to somewhere with modern streamlined cabin planes in which passengers would ride in comfort. Provisions of the Watres Act gave him power to force his will upon the airlines. In fact, the operators soon learned that they were under the thumb of a tough and determined, but enlightened, dictator. They could do as he said, or else. One clause in the Act, stating that only airlines with 250 miles or more per night of flying experience could bid on the new contracts, automatically eliminated a lot of small fly-by-day operators. Although the Act did not specifically give the Postmaster General authority to award mail contracts by negotiation, he was authorized to make extensions in an earlier law.

Except for the increased subsidy for flying larger planes with cabin space for passengers, these provisions added little to the potential of the United system. Boeing Air Transport flew trimotor B-80s on the San Francisco–Chicago leg, while NAT flew the Ford trimotors it acquired from the discontinued Stout Air Services on the Chicago–New York run, until the new 247s could be delivered. Boeing Air Transport received 95 cents per mile per 125 cubic feet, plus variables adding up to about $1.25 per mile, between San Francisco and Chicago; National Air Transport got $1.15 per mile for flying from Chicago to New York. It was good pay, and the Main Line, which handled nearly all of the transcontinental mail, made money, particularly on the Boeing end.

Before long, however, the cry of "monopoly" spurred General Brown to get some competitive cross-continent lines flying the mail and passengers as soon as possible. Before he could set up some real rivals for United, he had to crack some heads together. Brown's first showdown was with Transcontinental Air Transport and Western Air Express. He had both lines over the proverbial barrel. TAT was eager to abandon its costly plane-train experiment and fly New York to Los Angeles under the lucrative new pay scale. Colonel Henderson, former general manager of the line, had long since eaten his words that "planes will never fly passengers over the Alleghenies." Flying trimotor Fords, the line was sure to make money. There was one catch which Brown used as a club over the heads of the TAT management. Their line had never flown the mail 250 miles or more per night, and therefore did not qualify under the Watres Act for an air mail subsidy.

But the General had an idea for fixing that. Out on the Pacific end of the airway was Western Air Express, which did have enough experience flying at night. Harris Hanshue, Western's president, still had his objections, amounting to a phobia, against flying in the East. Hanshue wanted Western to blanket the Southwest, and with an eye to keeping potential competitors out of his bailiwick had bought Standard Air Lines, flying from Los Angeles to El Paso and Dallas. He had also extended Western's route east to Kansas City and, through subsidiary West Coast Air Transport, was flying north to Seattle. Western had also bid on the San Francisco–Chicago air mail leg and lost to Boeing. But Hanshue drew the line at Chicago. Like the railroaders, he considered Chicago the logical breaking point for transportation across the country.

General Brown's pet idea was a merger of TAT and Western with a small line in Pennsylvania owned by Pittsburgh Aviation Industries Corporation tossed in as flux. An amalgam of some kind was needed, because the TAT-Western merger was a shotgun marriage. Money-making WAE saw no reason for wedding to losing TAT, and Hanshue feared absorption by the Eastern slickers. Neither wanted PAIC, which was whittled down to 10 per cent of the new Transcontinental & Western Air system, but PAIC provided the balance of power and the president of the system, Richard W. Robbins. Neither of the majors in the merger trusted the other with management of the new TWA. Though Hanshue fought bitterly, he was forced to surrender and split off Western's Kansas City line as his contribution to the merger. Transcontinental & Western Air, Inc., became a reality in July, 1930. United no longer had a cross-country monopoly.

TWA was just the beginning of major changes in the airline map. The Postmaster General's grand scheme included a third transcontinental route across the South, from Los Angeles via Dallas to Atlanta. Aviation Corporation, one of the "big three" among the aeronautical holding companies, had already absorbed a string of little airlines in an orgy of mergers so complex that the experts still do not agree exactly what happened when. Out of these swaps of stock emerged the nucleus of the new American Airways system with routes extending as far west as El Paso. American became the third transcontinental airway when it bought Standard Air Lines from luckless Western Air Express. Thus the United system found itself with two competitors, both of whom were eventually granted extensions to San Francisco.

Still busily patching up the airways map of the United States, General Brown had some more fixing to do in the territory United's predecessors had pioneered. At his "suggestion" Boeing Air Transport bought West Coast Air Transport from Western Air Express. West Coast, flying between Los Angeles and Seattle, was a Hanshue experiment in passenger transport only with trimotor Fokkers. It was a losing venture and Brown thought the forced sale would clear up the West Coast picture. About all Boeing got was two Tri-motor Fokkers, shortly grounded as structurally unsound after the crash of a Fokker in the Midwest in which Knute

Rockne, the famous football coach, was killed. But the $100,000 deal got rid of a potential United competitor until some years later when Western launched Seattle flights in its own name.

General Brown next turned his attention to the Pacific Northwest, where the United system, having absorbed the Salt Lake–Seattle Varney Air Lines, still enjoyed a monopoly in the old Boeing home town. But not for long. The Postmaster first decreed that the United system establish a new route from Omaha to Watertown, South Dakota, to appease the clamor of South Dakota politicians. Boeing Air Transport didn't want the route, and the small Mid-Continent feeder line, then known as Rapid Air Transport, did want it. But Boeing got it and flew it daily under orders, and at a loss.

Next, by a series of negotiated extensions, Brown projected Northwest Airlines, which had flown from Chicago to Minneapolis and St. Paul, across the northern states into Seattle. This provided the United system with a third transcontinental competitor, when Northwest connected at Chicago with American Airlines, which bid on and won the Chicago–Detroit–New York route abandoned when Stout Air Services was absorbed by NAT. The good old monopoly days were gone forever for the United system. Where the companies in the United fold had flown without competition on 90 per cent of their airways when General Brown began forging the country's airway system, it now had a monopoly on only a few legs of its system.

Irate over this arbitrary invasion of airline territory it had pioneered, the United management attempted to improve its position without the Postmaster General's blessing. Brokers acting for United Aircraft began quietly buying up shares of Eastern Air Transport, with the idea of fanning out on the East Coast as Pacific Air Transport had blanketed the West Coast. Before anyone but the insiders were aware of it, United's officers had picked up enough shares to pull Eastern out of the Keys-Curtiss fold just as Rentschler had taken over National Air Transport. But someone tipped off the Postmaster General to what was happening, and President Phil Johnson and his right-hand man, W. A. Patterson, found themselves summoned to Washington for a conference. Neither Johnson nor Patterson had engineered the coup, which was handled at top level, but they soon found themselves squirming on the carpet. A "conference" in the Brown scheme meant a meeting with Brown himself, at which the Postmaster General did the talking.

Brown discoursed at length on the evils of monopoly, and how it was becoming increasingly difficult for him and other federal officials to counteract the public's suspicion of and general antipathy toward monopolies. Finally, after his visitors had sweated uncomfortably under two hours of lecturing, the Postmaster General asked abruptly:

"How long do you think it will take for United to unload its holdings in Eastern Air Transport?"

Johnson hustled to New York to report to the other United Aircraft & Transport officials what had transpired. Though the merger of Eastern into the United system was a logical move and exactly what Brown had urged with his "airlines from somewhere to somewhere" philosophy, the United management lost nerve and sold the Eastern Air Transport shares to General Motors, which sponsored the subsequently profitable Eastern Air Lines system.

By the time the Hoover administration, and with it the air transport czar, was swept out of office by the New Deal landslide in 1932, Brown had put the finishing touches on his air transport map. Where the United network had been the only economically sound system when the Postmaster General began his fixing, there were now the makings of four new top-flight domestic airline networks—TWA, American, Eastern, and Northwest—and overseas the colossus of them all, the globe-girdling Pan American system.

The Brown manipulations added little to the United system besides the losing and useless Omaha-Watertown leg. In fact, Brown whittled United down to size by setting up this cross-country competition and refusing to let United expand into the logical east coast population centers. But the Postmaster General's high-handed decisions had brought order out of chaos in a bumptious and burgeoning young industry. His "scientific feed-bagging" had nourished the airways to strength against the days when there would be no more feed-bagging for the major operators.

When Walter Folger Brown stepped out of his office for the last time on March 3, 1933, he left 27,062 miles of airways over which planes were carrying over 500,000 passengers a year. He also left a heritage of hard feelings in the hearts of the small "have not" airlines whose operators did not fit into General Brown's airways scheme. This bitterness soon erupted into a political volcano that all but destroyed the airways system he had labored so single-mindedly to build.

CHAPTER VII

The Air Mail "Purge"

On February 9, 1934, just as United Air Lines was flying handsomely and profitably, its major troubles of adolescence solved and behind it, catastrophe struck with the suddenness of lightning. The bolt came out of the blue in the form of a telegram from Postmaster General James A. Farley which read:

"Pursuant to the authority vested in me by Section 3950, Revised Statutes of the United States, Act of June 8, 1872, and by virtue of the general powers of the Postmaster General, it is ordered that the following air mail contracts be, and they are hereby, annulled effective midnight February 19, 1934."

The telegram landed on the desk of Vice-president W. A. Patterson, who was running the airline. As if to make amply sure of the calamity, four other orders from the Postmaster General were directed to Patterson who, the preceding July, had been named president of National Air Transport, Boeing Air Transport, Pacific Air Transport, and Varney Air Lines. When P. G. Johnson, who formerly headed these companies, resigned to become president of the over-all holding company, United Aircraft & Transport, Johnson's promotion left his thirty-four-year-old man Patterson the boss of all United's air transport operations.

The abrupt air mail contract cancellation confronted Patterson with a momentous decision. Air mail revenues still accounted for 45 per cent of the airline's income. Though the system's fleet of new Boeing 247s was offering speed and comfort never before provided by any flying service anywhere, inside the United States or out of it, and though the passenger and cargo revenues were increasing steadily, they still fell far short of supporting the airline. In fact, the system had achieved almost overnight a reputation as the world's model airline, as was evidenced by testimony of President Johnson in a later suit of Pacific Air Transport against the government for damages arising out of the air mail cancellation. Said Johnson:

"We had developed a system of flying which apparently was well known, because we constantly were being requested by operators from all over the world to permit their men to come over and study our operation, and I believe at some time or other we had representatives come over and spend time over our system from nearly every major European airline. We had them from Sweden, Germany, England, Japan, China, and Russia. I don't recall any major airline in either Europe or Asia that did not, at one time or another, have a group or at least one of their engineers or pilots or executive personnel come over and spend time to look over our line in order to study our methods."

The big question was, should United drastically curtail operations, or quit flying entirely as most of the other air mail carriers proposed to do, and risk losing its organization, or should it keep on flying and lose its cash reserves? Patterson announced immediately that the four operating companies under his presidency would fly all schedules, and that United Air Lines, the business-getting over-all management company, would put on a drive for more passengers, more express, and more freight to replace air mail revenue.

When other executives and some of the directors demurred, Patterson argued, "Our pilots and our ground crews have to eat. If we don't keep them on our payroll, they will get on the government payroll. This is our opportunity to show our people that they are in a stable business."

The United management agreed to go along. It was a million-dollar decision. The United companies slipped into the red more than $1,000,000 during the quarter that followed, flying their schedules with planes half filled. But Patterson still considers this the best buy he ever made, and as events unfolded, many observers concluded that the decision may have saved the United

A brand-new profession for women was opened by United Air Lines in 1930 when it employed the world's first airline stewardesses. Here are the eight pioneers, who were headed by Ellen Church (top left).

Evolution of the airline stewardess. A group of United Air Lines "sky girls" of 1935, when "natty" uniforms and "snappy" hats replaced the conservative suits and capes of 1930.

This was airline meal service in 1933, when United introduced the Boeing 247. The fried-chicken-on-a-plate meals were prepared by caterers, since United had not yet established its own chain of flight kitchens.

How the modern airliner evolved. Above: The Boeing Monomail, a single-engine six-passenger all-metal job with retractable landing gear, which was something of a sensation in 1930. Below: Its successor, the revolutionary Boeing 247, first all-metal low-wing twin-engine transport to take to United States airways.

Another view of the Boeing 247 which, introduced by United Air Lines in 1933, cut coast-to-coast travel time to 19½ hours and set the design pace for both commercial and military planes for some years to come.

States air transport industry for private enterprise. United was the strong airline at the time; if the giant had crumbled under the blow, air transport might have emerged from the hectic next few weeks as a government operation, as it was in nearly every foreign sky.

Other air mail carriers met the emergency as their means permitted. Some reduced their operations to token flights. Some canceled out completely. One of the dramatic episodes was a flight by TWA in the first of the new Douglas DC-2 planes, rushed to completion and test-flown two days before the cancellation order became effective. Jack Frye, president of TWA, was a pilot with a rating. So was Eddie Rickenbacker, new vice-president of Eastern Air Transport. With Rickenbacker as co-pilot, Frye took off from Union Air Terminal, outside Los Angeles, with the last load of mail delivered by the Post Office to the airline. At 10 P.M., Frye lifted the plane off the ground, climbed to 14,000 feet, picked up a tail wind, and pointed for Newark Airport, flying against time to beat a blizzard sweeping down out of Canada. Refueling in a snowstorm at Kansas City, and again at Columbus, Ohio, half an hour before the blizzard closed the airport completely, the intrepid flying executives glided into Newark three hours ahead of schedule, setting a new cross-continent flying record of 13 hours, 4 minutes.

In the public mind, the daring and spectacular flight was the antidote to the diet of propaganda from Washington in which the New Dealers made the airline operators the whipping boys of the preceding administration. It was a welcome relief from the sordid tales of "collusion" and "spoils conferences" spread by the New Deal to justify cancellation.

The cancellations gave the air mail carriers ten days in which to wind up their operations for the Post Office. On February 19, they flew the last sacks of mail. After assuring the 1400 employees of the United companies that the planes would fly and their paychecks would continue, Patterson hurried to Washington to find out what had incited the abrupt and drastic cancellation order and also to answer a summons of the Senate Postal and Post Roads Committee, which had launched an independent investigation of the whole affair. He found the capital overrun with airline impresarios, some of them air mail carriers who had been canceled out, others independents who hoped to bag the contracts the former operators had lost.

To understand what had happened requires some back-tracking to September of the preceding year, 1933, when a special Senate committee, headed by Senator Hugo L. Black of Alabama, began an investigation into steamship and airline postal subsidies. The Black Committee focused its attention on steamship subsidies and apparently had little intention of going in detail into air transport payments, until one day when Senator Black came into contact with an enterprising young Washington newspaper reporter, Fulton Lewis, Jr. In his reportorial rounds, Lewis had become interested in the protests of several small independent airline operators who had been summarily refused contracts by former Postmaster General Brown. Their little lines did not fit into Brown's pattern of a national airways system. The independents got even with Brown by feeding Lewis details of alleged collusion between Brown and the successful air mail bidders. This collusion was supposed to have taken place at a so-called "Spoils Conference" in the Post Office Building at which the airways of the United States were divided up among the big fellows.

The mysterious "Spoils Conference," as subsequent evidence developed, was a meeting of airline executives called by Brown soon after he had worked out his grand plan for building the United States airways system. The conference, which was held in the Post Office Building and duly covered by *The New York Times* reporters and other correspondents, began on May 19, 1930. The meeting was called partly to give each operator an opportunity to state what areas he thought his airline should serve, partly to sell the smaller operators the idea of merging routes so that planes would fly from somewhere to somewhere, thus avoiding delays in transferring mail from one plane to another in transit. Out of the meeting came shotgun mergers that begat the TWA, American, and Northwest Airlines systems. When they found they could not voluntarily agree on spheres, the operators suggested that the Postmaster act as an umpire and make the decisions, a role which Brown accepted with alacrity.

The United quartet invited to the conference—P. G. Johnson, Colonel Paul Henderson, Ray Ireland, and George S. Wheat—

ironically soon found that they were merely spectators. The United companies were already merged into the kind of an airways system the Postmaster General demanded of the others before they could bid for the juicy air mail contracts he was about to grant under the provisions of the Watres Act. The "collusion" with which Phil Johnson and his associates were charged in the cancellation proceedings actually resulted in the creation of three transcontinental rivals whose new cut in the air mail contracts reduced United's share 40 per cent. As Johnson explained in a letter to the United Aircraft stockholders:

"So far as the United Air Lines system is concerned, the action of the Postmaster General in annulling the air mail contracts was wholly without justification. None of the system transport companies has ever entered into any combination to prevent bidding, and the contracts of each of them were originally awarded as the result of public competitive bidding, the award in each case being made to the lowest responsible bidder. Representatives of the system companies were present at the conference above referred to at the specific request of the then Postmaster General. They went into the conference as operators of a fully-integrated transcontinental air transport system, which was the only one then in existence in the country. They came out of it faced by two competing transcontinental lines and the loss of 40 per cent of their air mail poundage."

Justifying the arbitrary enforcement of his ideas on the unhappy and reluctant airline operators, Brown later explained before the Black Committee:

I could think of no other way to make the industry self-sustaining, make it economically independent, than to compel the air mail contractor to get some revenue from the public. Almost all of them were refusing to carry passengers and were depending almost wholly on the Post Office Department, and we were getting nowhere in the development of airplanes. They were just using little, light open-cockpit ships to move the mail with very great dependability, but no progress in a broad sense was being made in the art.

I believed that it was my duty to force them, if I could, under the law to get revenues from nonpostal sources, and the obvious one was passengers; after we could get the people flying themselves, we thought then they would send their freight by plane, and the purpose of it altogether was to develop an industry that could live without a subsidy—that could live on its own.

At any rate, I decided to take the responsibility, and I used the power in the Watres Act, wrote it into the advertisement to compel the carrying of passengers.

That the Postmaster General backed up the courage of his convictions with plenty of physical fortitude is evidenced by his description before the Committee of his early flights to help dramatize air travel to the public.

The time came for starting service on TWA, and I was invited to go out on the first flight. It was a very bitter cold day . . . a terrific wind. In a big Ford we started off on that first trip with passengers over the mountain.

We came into the airport at Camden. I think the wind was blowing around fifty or sixty miles an hour out of the northwest, and the pilot miscalculated his speed as he got ready to set the plane down on the field. He was coming so fast that he was sure he could not stop, so when he was a few hundred yards away from the station, instead of setting the plane down he gave it the gun—I mean he opened his throttles—and started to try to get up again. Of course he did not try to lift the plane at once until he had gathered sufficient speed. We saw the plane going as fast as it could directly for the building on the field, and I wondered whether I had been premature in the passenger operation. Just as he got to the building, he pulled the stick back and lifted the ship over the building, and some of us are just getting over it now. He circled the field and came in easily the next time.

I left the plane at Columbus, because we had gotten over the mountains and over the part that seemed to me hazardous. The plane went on, and the passengers that were in it had their breakfasts in New York and their dinners in Kansas City.

Well, soon after that we had a flight on the line from Atlanta west, and I went down on that, too. We got into some fog near Richmond and the plane was forced down, and we had to go on the train to Atlanta. I wondered again whether I was a little too enterprising. We got to Atlanta, though, and started west for Dallas, and at some point or other one of the planes that was going along with us, a Ford, in taking off had knocked off one of the wheels on the undercarriage. When the plane came in, it had only one wheel in front and the little wheel behind. We watched the boys set that plane down, thinking they would probably kill everybody, but they put the passengers over on the side where the wheel was and put them in belts, and he brought that plane in on two wheels like a bicycle until she lost all of her air, and then she tipped over and took this leg down that had no wheel on it, and the thing spun around like this and nobody was hurt, but it impressed me just the same.

Then we went down on a flight that Eastern Air Transport was making from Washington to Jacksonville, and we got down to Florence. The airport there had very thick sand and a little grass on top of it, and this big Condor plane had eighteen passengers in it. The plane got stuck in the sand, and we had to call on the people who were down there to greet us to help get the plane out of the sand and onto the grass. When the pilot started off and opened his throttles, we were going straight at a high-tension power line. We went over it, but we did not clear it by six inches. That gave us quite a thrill.

I had a speech I had developed with some care, telling how safe it was and how beautiful and how swift and clean it was. We got down at Savannah. We were at the very beautiful club having a luncheon. We had finished our lunch, and I was getting ready to unlimber my safety speech when Mr. Keys was called away from the table. He came back in a minute or two, just as the presiding officer had started to introduce me. He whispered in my ear, "TWA has had a terrible accident. A plane out in Kansas is completely washed out, and Knute Rockne was aboard." I said, "What in the world am I going to say? What happened?" "We don't know a thing about it," he said.

Just then I heard the toastmaster say, "The Postmaster General will now address you." I did not know what to do, so I just made my speech as usual. I did not tell a soul about the accident. The only people who knew about it were Mr. Keys and myself. All the people saw us go out to the airport and we took off to Jacksonville. I speak of these things just to let you know what is the responsibility of a man in ordering service in which you are charged with the lives of your fellow citizens.

There was nothing mysterious or secret about the 1930 meeting of the operators called by Brown. *The New York Times* and other newspapers reported it briefly. But the version developed three years later by Reporter Lewis, with the help of the irate independents, looked like another Teapot Dome scandal. It was so hot that Lewis's superior sent it to William Randolph Hearst for his okay before publishing it. Instead of the "go ahead" signal, Mr. Hearst sat on it for months, refusing to answer queries about it, until Senator Black, getting wind of the suppressed story, wired Hearst and finally subpoenaed Lewis, who sat at the Senator's right at the Committee table, prompting questions for the sweating airline men to answer. Even before they were summoned to Washington, they knew that trouble lay ahead because Interstate Commerce Commission investigators had suddenly swooped into their offices early in October and seized files to tote them off to Washington.

Two of United's executives inadvertently contributed to the free-for-all of scandal that mushroomed from the Black investigation. At the time Colonel Paul Henderson was the United representative in Washington, as he had been during the Brown regime. With his background as former Assistant Postmaster General in charge of air mail, Henderson was invaluable to United in keeping air mail deals straight. Henderson was one of the men called by Brown to help him draft the Watres Act. But Henderson disliked Brown, and resented his dictatorial methods. He thought Brown's deals should be scrutinized for the public records, and told Senator Black so in a private conversation. The Senator asked Henderson to draw up a memorandum on aspects into which the Committee should inquire, which the Colonel did. Phil Johnson happened to be in Washington at the time, and since he agreed with Henderson, he, too, signed the memorandum.

The Black Committee investigation would have resulted only in a revision of contracts, instead of the drastic and calamitous cancellation order, except for the unexpected entry of Franklin D. Roosevelt personally into the picture. Although the cancellation order was issued by Postmaster General Farley and Farley was blamed for the dire consequences, it developed later that he had very little to do with it. What happened was largely the doings of an incoming President, still eagerly throwing the rascals out. Alert for ways of discrediting the Hoover administration anew, the President and his White House advisers picked up the testimony before the Black Committee, spotting a new whipping boy.

When Farley was called to the White House and asked about holdover mail contracts, he agreed that they should be canceled, but advised that the operators be allowed to fly the mail at reduced rates, to be determined after new legislation could be passed.

Overruling his Postmaster General, the President decided upon a dramatic gesture of cleaning the Hoover stables. He called in General Benjamin D. Foulois, chief of the Army Air Corps, and asked if his pilots could take over and fly the air mail. With the Air Corps starved for appropriations, the General recognized an opportunity to make friends and influence Congress. He assured the President his pilots would be ready in a fortnight. It was a well-meant promise that backfired disastrously.

Although the Postmaster General, Assistant Secretary of Commerce for Aeronautics Eugene Vidal, and other advisers counseled otherwise, General Foulois's assurance was all that the headstrong President needed to fan up an artificial emergency, which he did in an executive order issued from the White House on the afternoon of February 9, 1934. It read:

> Whereas by an order of the Postmaster General of the United States all domestic [air] mail contracts for carrying the mail have been annulled; and, whereas the public interest requires that air mail service continue to be afforded and the cancellation of said contracts has created an emergency in this respect;
>
> Now therefore I, Franklin D. Roosevelt, President of the United States, under and by virtue of the authority in me vested do hereby order and direct the Postmaster General, Secretary of War, and Secretary of Commerce together with all other officers of their respective departments to cooperate to the end that necessary air mail service be afforded.
>
> It is further ordered and directed that the Secretary of War place at the disposal of the Postmaster General such airplanes, landing fields, pilots, and other employes and equipment of the Army of the United States needed for the transportation of mail during the present emergency over routes and schedules prescribed by the Postmaster General.

The result was a sanguinary episode in flying history that diverted the public's wrath as nothing else could have done from the so-called "collusionists" to the persecutors of the airline operators themselves. The Army fliers, trained in acrobatics and formation flying but inexperienced in rough-weather flight over strange terrain with heavy loads carried in open cockpit planes designed for other purposes, were lost on commercial air lanes. Though almost two-thirds of the air mail routes were eliminated the day the Army fliers took over, the fleet of 160 observation planes and bombers and the crew of 200 pilots and 324 enlisted men assigned to the air mail detail were no match for the wintry weather that suddenly gripped the nation's airways. By the end of the first week, five pilots had been killed in crashes, six more were critically injured, and $500,000 worth of planes had been smashed.

The tail end of the winter was a terrible time for amateurs to be taking over a highly technical and specialized job. It was terrible flying, even for the experienced pilots, as was proved when a United transport crashed into Utah's Wasatch Mountains in a blizzard, killing the crew and five passengers. The following two weeks were so disastrous and costly in lives that on March 10 the President ordered all air mail flying abandoned. In San Francisco, Chicago, and New York, irate air mail patrons, who had learned to rely on overnight post across the country, made up packages of letters to be air expressed via United planes, then opened and mailed at the other end of the line, a violation of Post Office regulations which the red-faced Post Office authorities ignored.

After a week with no mail planes in the air, the Army pilots resumed service, but flew only by day. Two days across the country was a poor substitute for 19-hour service. Army pilots continued to drop out of the sky. By April, twelve were dead, nine having crashed on the Main Line route alone. Cartoons appeared in the newspapers showing Farley and Roosevelt leading the death march of skeletons of the lost Army pilots. As public anger snowballed, the President recognized that he had a hot potato in his hands. He suddenly decided to accept Jim Farley's advice and let the experienced operators fly the mail on a temporary basis until new legislation authorized new contracts on a more economical and sound system of payment than that provided in the Watres Act.

The disastrous episode was not without its gains. It proved, for example, that air transport flying was a job for specialists and not a sideline for Army pilots. It also showed to Congress that the Army needed more money for better planes and better training of the Air Force. The cost figures were revealing, too. It cost the Army $2.21 per mile to fly the mail, whereas the Post Office had been paying an average of 54 cents per plane mile to the private operators during the year 1933. It ended once and for all the idea that the government could fly the mail or operate the country's air transport cheaper or more efficiently than private operators.

In the public eye, the air mail carriers, who had been pictured as pirates plundering the public treasury, became heroes of free enterprise. But even as he gave them back their air mail cargoes, the vindictive President cut the ground from under them in a White House decree which outlawed for five years from participation in any future air mail contracts all of the airline executives summoned to the former Postmaster General's so-called "Spoils Conference." The decree, naming the individuals arbitrarily blacklisted from their livelihood, was issued in the name of the Postmaster General, but Farley later explained that he personally opposed the purge but was again overruled by the White House. The decree also disqualified any of the former air mail carriers from bidding on the new contracts.

This drastic order forced a reorganization in the air transport industry little short of a revolution. It banished the heads of most of the major airlines, among them Philip G. Johnson, United's president. Paradoxically, Patterson, then president of the four operating companies—NAT, BAT, PAT, and Varney—was untouched, since in 1930 he was a junior officer not invited by the Postmaster General to the meeting in Washington. Thus the United system was less violently shaken than some of the others. Johnson bitterly gave up his presidency of United Air Lines and United Aircraft & Transport to move to Canada, where he organized Trans-Canada Airlines for the Dominion Government and ran it during his five years of exile. Just before World War II broke, he returned to Boeing Aircraft to spark the company's prodigious output of Flying Fortresses and B-29s.

Other airlines quickly changed their hats, under new officers, and resumed operations under new names. Western Air Express became General Airlines for a time, American Airways became American Airlines, Eastern Air Transport revived as Eastern Air Lines under the driving impact of Captain Eddie Rickenbacker. Since the four carriers of the United system were banished from air mail bidding, United Air Lines became an operating as well as a management company, under the direction of Patterson, who became president on April 13, 1934.

The new president was confronted with a crucial decision. The old air mail carriers knew that the independent operators were going to bid low on the new contracts, even if they had to carry the mail at a loss, hoping for an adjustment upward later. So most of the old carriers decided to bid low, too, in order to protect their priority on routes. Patterson argued that the thing to do was figure costs closely and bid on that basis. This is what United did, winning all of its former routes except the Chicago-Dallas run, which it lost to Braniff Air Lines, one of the more disgruntled independents. Braniff bid about half of United's cost. Patterson won the other routes with bids of from 38 cents to 39.5 cents per airplane mile, less than one-fifth the Army's flying cost, as compared to compensation ranging from 42 cents to 45 cents per airplane mile under the previous award.

The New Deal's about-face still left unsettled the question of whether or not there had been any actual collusion to defraud the government in the mail awards and route extensions under the Brown regime. Most of the airline operators, although bitter, were willing to forget the injustice, once they got their routes back. Patterson and the new United directors concluded that their colleagues who had been made to walk the plank were entitled to vindication. They sought it in a suit in the United States Court of Claims for breach of contract and out-of-pocket damages totaling $2,842,-197.90. The case, known as the "long trial," dragged out for seven years, during which United remained in the New Deal doghouse while rivals were awarded extensions. Eventually in 1943, the suit ended in a decision by Commissioner Richard K. Akers exonerating Johnson and his colleagues of wrong-doing and awarding token damages of $368,525.

Thus was written "finis" to a chapter in United States air transport history known among airmen as "The Big Purge."

CHAPTER VIII

United Unshackled

The catastrophic air mail crisis of 1934 left in its wake a bumper crop of problems for a number of characters involved in the historic drama. One such character was suave, soft-voiced Joseph E. Ripley, the Wall Street banker rated by many as the godfather of United Air Lines—and for good reason. Without Joe Ripley's smooth and persuasive dealing on at least two occasions, there might have been no United Air Lines.

The first was in 1929, when blunt Fred Rentschler clashed head-on with C. M. Keys over control of National Air Transport, which United needed to complete the first coast-to-coast airline. When it looked as though the adroit Keys had stymied Rentschler, Ripley moved in behind the scenes and induced the Chicago group to swap their stock for United Aircraft & Transport shares. Then to make the coup complete, Ripley accomplished the impossible by persuading Keys himself to go along with the merger.

It was an era of aviation corporate omelets, and the one that Joe Ripley put together was by far the best of them all, as was revealed by the operations performance and the earnings of United Aircraft & Transport, even after 1929, when the depression years closed in. Each United unit complemented the other—the airlines used the airframes of the aircraft factories, which in turn utilized the products of the engine and propeller plants and the know-how of the engineering group. As Rentschler frequently pointed out, United was unique among holding companies in that its components were "joined together" rather than "put together" in the catch-as-catch-can stock swaps of the day. Rentschler, the head-strong tycoon, took the bows for the organization's success; Ripley, his financial wing man, remained in the background always.

The edicts from the White House, followed by the air mail act of 1934, hit the happy United corporate family hard. Passed by Congress on June 12, 1934, the new air mail act went even further than the F.D.R. decree banishing for five years the men largely responsible for building the major airlines. The legislation made the Interstate Commerce Commission, rather than the Post Office, the dictator of air mail rates. And, more ominous yet, it outlawed any financial or interlocking directorate connections between the airlines and the manufacturing plants that supplied them with planes, engines, propellers, and other parts. The Act forbade salaries over $17,500 for executives of airlines holding mail contracts. It even outlawed Phil Johnson from his job as president of the United unit manufacturing Wasp and Hornet engines, which were bought by the government for military planes.

For the holding companies that controlled the major airlines, these provisions were a body blow. Overnight United Aircraft & Transport had become an illegal corporate monster to be destroyed. The Act gave United's owners five and one-half months to unmerge. Rentschler, Boeing, and the other United chiefs again turned to Joe Ripley, the man who had put the omelet together, and asked him to unscramble it. This was a neat trick, calling for a touch as deft as that which joined the United companies together in the first place.

Astute Joe Ripley was equal to the challenge. He became captain of a reorganization team, which included Philip G. Johnson, purged president of the airlines, and Joseph F. McCarthy, the secretary and comptroller of United Aircraft & Transport. A stockholders' protective association quickly sprang up to safeguard the interests of 23,000 United shareholders. Ripley adroitly pulled it into the operating room to help divide and distribute the $30,000,000 aviation octopus.

Within a month, Ripley had the unscrambling accomplished. In place of the old holding corporation, he set up three new operating companies. Taking over 51 per cent of the assets was a new United Aircraft Corporation, comprising the Pratt & Whitney engine works, the Sikorsky and Vought airplane plants, and the propeller factories, all in the east. The Boeing Airplane Company was turned loose to operate its aircraft factories in Seattle and Wichita. It drew 14½ per cent of the holding company's assets. United Air Lines Transport Corporation, consisting of four airlines, NAT, BAT, PAT, and Varney, the Boeing School of Aeronautics, and the United airport at Burbank, California, inherited 34½ per cent of the holding company's resources. The unscrambling was approved at a stockholders' meeting on July 11, 1934. Each owner of a holding company share received one share of the new United Aircraft stock, one-half share of United Air Lines Transport Corporation, and one-fourth share of Boeing Airplane Company stock.

Everyone was satisfied, except for one little twist which even Joe Ripley could not unravel. Under the new law, the officers and directors of the airline were forbidden to own stock of companies that supplied planes and parts to the airline. The airline operators unhappily unloaded their shares in Boeing and in United Aircraft, the stocks that had turned in the profits. During the five years that United Aircraft had been in the air transport business, only two small dividends had been paid by the rapidly expanding airlines into the holding company's coffers.

Nevertheless, Joe Ripley saw to it that the new United Air Lines system started off free of debt and with $4,000,000 of working capital in the bank. Though the airline represented roughly a third of the assets of the holding company, prior to unmerging, it got more than half of the cash. Ripley's crystal ball must have been working when he made this decision, for the period just ahead was to be known as the "black years" by United Air Lines men.

Another who emerged in the fast-moving drama as a lead character was William Allan Patterson, thirty-five-year-old emergency head of the airline. When the government purge of airline executives who had haplessly attended the misnamed "Spoils Conference" banished Phil Johnson, Joe Ripley urged Rentschler and the other heads of the holding company to name Patterson as Johnson's successor. When they did, Ripley also cast his own lot with United. Under the new law forbidding interlocking directorates, he had to make his choice between being director of the airline or of the manufacturing companies. He chose the airline.

In a sense, the unmerger was an emancipation for Patterson and his airline associates. They no longer had to check with Hartford or with New York before making important decisions about running the airline. No longer was it necessary to keep in mind what was good for the whole family of United companies. They no longer had to fly Boeing planes or buy Wasp engines, if the other aircraft builders offered more alluring equipment. The nerve center of the system had moved from 230 Park Avenue, New York City, to the La Salle–Wacker building in Chicago, where the one small office opened by Harold Crary in 1929 had grown to a beehive covering two floors. Crary himself became the new director of traffic, advertising, and publicity. The vice-president in charge of operations was Duard B. Colyer, veteran of the Post Office air mail days who had been superintendent of operations for Boeing Air Transport. The other officers of the reborn airline were Cyril B. Thompson, secretary, and Charles E. Brink, one of those early-day aviation anomalies, an airline executive who refused to fly, treasurer.

The organizers of the new operating company resorted to a legal device which has confused stockholders and the public ever since. Instead of making United Air Lines, Inc., the business-getting unit of the old holding company, the new operator of the four airlines, they incorporated a new Delaware company, United Air Lines Transport Corporation, to take over outright ownership of NAT, BAT, PAT, and Varney and to operate the Boeing School at Oakland and the United Airport at Burbank, California, as subsidiaries. But to air travelers, United Air Lines Transport Corporation remained simply United Air Lines, and after nine years the transport corporation gave up, eventually adopting United Air Lines once more as the official and corporate name in 1943.

Being reborn was anything but smooth flying for the new airline. Right off the bat, United came near losing the Pacific Coast route. A last-minute clause inserted in the Air Mail Act of 1934 forbade one carrier from holding air mail contracts for more than one primary route and two secondary routes. The four transcontinental airways were defined as primary routes, as were the Pacific Coast and Atlantic seaboard routes. This joker in the Act meant that, though Patterson had won back the old PAT mail contract pioneered by Vern Gorst before either Boeing or NAT flew the Main Line, he could not keep it, except through the device of making Pacific Air Transport completely independent of United.

Fortunately, in response to protests from United and other airlines affected by the joker clause, as well as from West Coast cities and states which requested continuation of United on the Pacific Coast, Congress extended the date of the prohibition until March 1, 1935, to provide time for a Federal Aviation Commission to survey the primary and secondary route designations. By January, 1935, the Commission reported back:

> As the law now stands, it will be necessary before March 1st for United Air Lines to dispose of its route from Seattle to San Diego in order that it may retain its transcontinental route. It will apparently be necessary under the Post Office Department's classification of routes for American Airlines to abandon its Boston–New York route that it and its predecessor company have operated for more than eight years as a condition of being allowed to retain its southern transcontinental. We have laid before us an enormous number of protests against these requirements from civic and commercial organizations and from individual citizens of the areas affected. We have not heard a single word of complaint against the situation now existing, nor any suggestion that the possession of the lines just enumerated actually confers any unfair competitive advantage to their operators. From those transcontinental lines which would seemingly be most seriously affected, and in particular the northern route operated by Northwest Airlines, there has come no protest to us, nor so far as we can discover to the Post Office nor anyone else. Under the circumstances we cannot believe that any serious harm will be done by allowing the present arrangement to continue throughout the present year to permit the perfecting of any permanent changes that may appear desirable in present legislation, and we very urgently recommend that the Air Mail Act of 1934 be amended accordingly at as early a date as may be practicable.

Faced with this unbiased report, Congress granted the airlines a year of grace, and specifically designated the Pacific Coast route as a secondary route, thus removing the threat hanging over the new United management. Later the limitation was removed entirely. Pending the clarification, the airline's stock was held in a voting trust, administered by Martin C. Ansorge, representing the stockholders' protective association, Philip G. Johnson, and Joseph E. Ripley. When the reorganization was finally completed in 1935, United Air Lines Transport Corporation owned BAT, PAT, Varney, the old United Air Lines, Inc., United Airports, and the Boeing School outright, and 99.3 per cent of NAT.

The unmerging of the holding company proved a rebirth for the airline in other ways than corporate ownership. It moved into executive and technical positions men from out on the line. Some, like Jack Herlihy, Bert Lott, Walt Addems, Russ Cunningham, had started as pilots in open cockpit planes. Others had joined the airline on the ramp, or pounded the pavements rustling business, or in shops or offices. They were young in years and in ideas, and one of the youngest of all was the new president. Despite their youth, they were veterans in know-how, most of them veterans of the air transport industry since the Post Office first turned the risk of flying the air mail over to private contractors in 1926–1927. Their advance to key positions made the unshackled United system an airline run by airmen with a passion for dependable operation.

The task confronting the new management was a formidable one. When the directors handed Patterson free rein in deciding what to bid for contracts under the new air mail act, he faced a difficult alternative. He could bid token rates to make sure of getting the contracts back and hope for fairer adjustments later, or he could bid at cost-plus-profit and risk losing the mail entirely. Either way the airline could go broke.

Concluding that the latter plan made more sense, Patterson won most of the air mail back at the highest rates paid any post-cancellation carrier. Only the Chicago-Dallas contract was lost. United planes ceased flying the Kansas City–Dallas route, but continued on the Chicago–Kansas City run for passengers and cargo until May 12, 1934. This left United with 6000 miles of airways, which Crary exuberantly advertised as "air transportation at its best." United flew passengers in "heated, comfortable cabin planes" coast-to-coast in twenty hours for $160, or $288 for the round trip. It boasted 50,000,000 miles of flying experience, and assured passengers their safety and well-being were being watched over by "four experts aground for every pilot aloft."

Though the rebirth freed the United management financially

Thorp Hiscock, eccentric genius and Handy Andy, whose exploring mind penetrated the barrier to ground-plane communication, evolved the first practical de-icers, propeller pitch controls, and other devices that ushered in the era of precision flying.

This was the plane which introduced air transportation to millions, the famed twin-engine 21-passenger DC-3 which first took to the airways in 1936 and which, in the following years, became a familiar sight on airways all over the world. Its carrying capacity, spacious (for those days) cabin, and 180-mile-per-hour speed made it a favorite of travelers and airline operators alike.

Interior of the DC-3, which became the darling of the airways in the prewar and wartime era. The roomy cabin accommodated 21 passengers.

United's flying laboratory of the thirties in which a crew of scientists chased storms until they had the answer to the bugaboo of static, which cut off plane ground communication at critical times.

Inside the weather ship, scientists assembled a battery of instruments for checking static, atmosphere, and other unknowns that once made fighting through storms a nightmare for pilots.

This was the original DC-4, test-flown just in time to become the aerial work horse of World War II. As the Air Force's C-54 and the Navy's R-5-D, it performed herculean tasks of transporting military men and materials on globe-girdling flights.

United crews, flying on contract for the Air Transport Command, island-hopped the Pacific to maintain life lines to the fighting forces in World War II. Above photo was taken at Guadalcanal.

and operationswise, the Air Mail Act of 1934 created new shackles in Washington. The airlines now had three Federal umpires instead of one as in Postmaster General Brown's day. The Interstate Commerce Commission, which knew much about railroads and little about airlines, became arbiter of routes and rates; the Post Office assigned the mail loads and paid the bills; the Department of Commerce maintained the airways beacons, ran the weather service, laid down the safety rules and enforced them. In addition, both the Senate and the House of Representatives had committees almost continuously checking aviation. The life of airline executives became an interminable series of hearings before one or another of these Federal agencies.

By way of cutting its eyeteeth in air mail rate making, the ICC launched a proceeding, at which United and other airlines presented evidence to show that rates should be adjusted upward, based upon a fair and reasonable return upon their investment. Instead of raising the air mail pay, the ICC reduced it for United and most of the major airlines, explaining in its report:

"The costs of service are, of course, important to those who are rendering it, but we are not here fixing the rates for the operators; we are fixing rates for the routes irrespective of the contractors operating them at a particular time."

The Commission rejected a United proposal that air mail carriers be paid on a simple pound-mile, and established a highly complicated structure which cut United's average return on the coast-to-coast route from 38 cents to 31 cents per plane mile, with corresponding reductions on the Pacific Coast and Salt Lake–Seattle runs. Equally involved and serious was another ICC innovation, a 300-pound limit on the amount of mail per plane for which the Post Office could pay. At Main Line airports, stacks of mail sacks weighing more than 300 pounds often piled up, and United had to fly them, pay or no pay. Post Office authorities, recognizing the injustice, tried to compensate the airline by carry-over credits, but the net result of rate cuts and load limits was a hefty net loss which cut deep into United's income. Revenues for 1934 fell below those of 1932, a loss that forced stringent economies, including cancellation of the Chicago–Kansas City passenger-cargo run, the last unit of the route NAT had pioneered eight years before.

Seeking relief, Patterson petitioned the Interstate Commerce Commission for new hearings. It was two years before the deliberate commissioners could get around to an adjustment.

It was tough sledding, but it toughened the industry. As Patterson once remarked, "Looking back, the air mail cancellations, although a terrific jolt to the companies and unfair to individuals, were a blessing in disguise. They stopped the financial manipulations of the earlier era and saved the airlines from the long period of speculation and consequent receivership that the railroads went through. It was a spanking that made us better boys."

In every city served by United, traffic staffs hustled as never before to rustle passengers and cargo. And they got results, in what proved to be the battle of decades for business, particularly on the Chicago–New York run. Figures tell the story. In 1933, United's passenger revenue, $3,955,622 for 68,984,770 passenger-miles flown, constituted 40 per cent of the airline's income. By 1935, it was $4,933,376 for 83,473,000 passenger-miles, and in 1936 the company's planes topped the 100,000,000 passenger-mile mark with an income of $5,844,331 from passenger fares, almost 58 per cent of United's total earnings.

The airline's hustlers pushed the cargo business, too. Though it produced only one-tenth as many dollars as air mail or passengers brought in, this was a virtually untouched field. In August, 1934, Traffic Manager Crary concluded a contract with the Railway Express Agency, whereby the latter agreed to pick up and deliver express handled by United Air Lines, for 12½ per cent of the revenue. The basic rate was set at 4 cents per mile per hundred pounds.

However, United soon found itself at loggerheads with the rest of the airlines on express handling. American, TWA, Eastern, and the other major lines refused to contract with Railway Express on the premise that the Agency would favor the railroads and generate little business for the airlines. Organizing General Air Express, they undertook to maintain their own pick-up and delivery service in the larger cities. It was an expensive experiment. By December, 1935, they were ready to fold General Air Express and join United in negotiating a new blanket contract with the Railway Express Agency, covering the country. Under the new deal, the revenue dollar was split 85 cents for the airlines flying the express, 15 cents for the express company for pick-up and delivery.

Though United's income from express was relatively small, the figures showed an impressive gain, percentagewise at least. In 1933, the planes earned $133,153 flying 184,285 ton-miles of air express. By 1936, boosted by the Railway Express pick-up and delivery service, they garnered $431,653 flying 760,000 ton-miles of air express. That year, express provided 4.27 per cent of United's income. It was only a beginning in the promising cargo business, something to fill vacant space in the planes, but a potential that ultimately called for special cargoliners carrying only mail, express, and freight at passenger speed.

While the United system underwent complete integration, other major airlines were struggling through rebirth likewise. There was one big difference: United's growth was internal, while the transcontinental rivals, notably American, TWA, and Northwest, assimilated new routes and territories. When the Interstate Commerce Commission replaced the Postmaster General as the authority in Washington that issued route certificates, all the airlines scrambled for extensions.

At the time, 1934–1935, United served a score of major population centers, in an area embracing one-fifth of the country's population, and the system still handled more traffic than any other airline in the world; but it was top heavy in the West and needed new outlets in the East. By 1937, United was no longer Airline Number One. American Airlines' new president, C. R. Smith, a dynamic and persuasive young Texan, had doubled the number of population centers reached by his system. American served sixty major traffic centers, and blanketed territory in which one-third of the country's population lived. American was Airline Number One, and United was Number Two.

There were two reasons for this change in positions. One was the decision of the United management to develop intensively the Main Line territory, the historic overland route from coast to coast. The other was that United's petitions for route extensions went unheard or unheeded in Washington, while those of other airlines were acted upon. The company was still in the official doghouse because of "The Long Suit" to clear Phil Johnson's name, a case that Patterson stubbornly continued, even after friendly Post Office executives tipped him off that "we could see United's problems more clearly if smoke didn't get in our eyes."

While United got nowhere in applications to serve larger population centers just off the Main Line, American and TWA were granted certificates to fly United's heaviest traffic route between Chicago and New York. TWA flew between the country's two largest population centers via Pittsburgh, American via Detroit and Buffalo. It was tough competition, because with their new Douglas planes, both TWA and American advertised nonstop five-hour flights between the two cities, while United's slower Boeings were forced to refuel at Cleveland.

Shut off from route extensions by government certificate, Patterson attempted to increase United's potential by buying or building up feeder lines. One proposed deal in 1936 involved the purchase of Pennsylvania Airlines & Transport Company, flying an air mail route between Milwaukee and Detroit and a passenger line from Detroit to Washington via Cleveland and Pittsburgh. This was definitely United territory. Pennsylvania Airlines was in financial difficulty. The merger would salvage a sick airline, and build up United's traffic. The purchase was blocked by the ICC and Pennsylvania merged with Central Air Lines to form what later became Capital Airlines, another competitor for United on the eastern leg of the Main Line.

Another negotiation, for the Cheyenne-Denver leg of the Wyoming Air Services, Inc., ended more successfully. Since the inauguration of air mail service, Denver, the capital of the Rocky Mountain empire, had been off any major airway just as it had been off major transcontinental railways and highways. Proud and ambitious Denverites resented the fact that their city was served only by feeder lines. Early in 1934, United filed for permission to route some of its coast-to-coast flights via Denver, only 99 miles off the Main Line. In spite of pressure from the Denver people, nothing came of the petition until February, 1937, when after two years of dickering United was able to buy the Cheyenne-Denver leg of Wyoming Air Services with its air mail contract for $209,000. For the first time Denver was on a major airway. It was an extension of vast importance in the years to come, when

Denver unexpectedly became the nerve center of the entire United system.

When United switched to Douglas DC-3s at the end of 1936, the airline had a surplus of equipment, the rugged 247s that had flown millions of miles on the coast-to-coast run. They were probably the sturdiest airliners ever built, as was demonstrated in 1933, when the company turned a 247 over to the Army Air Corps Matériel Command at Dayton to be deliberately static-tested to destruction to prove its structural strength. Instead of selling the surplus 247s for much-needed cash, Patterson made them available to feeder lines, such as National Parks Airways and Pennsylvania Airlines, connecting with the United system, on a lease or easy payment purchase agreement. This was in line with the policy of intensively developing the United territory, which rapidly became one of the most air-minded sections of the country.

The battle for passengers rapidly deteriorated into a dog-eat-dog affair. It was a contest that did not pay off immediately. Some of the rapidly expanding airlines almost went broke. Even United, serving the heaviest traffic route in the country, had difficulty staying out of the red. In 1934, the year of reorganization, when United still carried more passengers than any other airline in the world, Patterson had to report to his stockholders at the end of the year that he had dropped over two million of the $3,995,000 that Joe Ripley had lured from the old holding company's surplus to endow the airline. The following year, United managed barely to break even. In 1936 it made $371,000 and stockholders got a small taste of a dividend, 20 cents per share, the last taste they were to have for years.

It was a period of experiment to coax more travelers into the air. United, TWA, and American inaugurated expensive overnight sleeper service from coast-to-coast to lure Pullman passengers aloft. American hit on the idea of air travel scrip books which enabled passengers to save 15 per cent in the purchase of tickets. The other airlines adopted it, too, and Patterson persuaded the rival presidents to make travel scrip interchangeable on all lines. The scheme lured more passengers into the air, but at reduced revenues.

The airlines were fighting not only each other for the passenger business, but a more formidable opponent whom many did not recognize at the time. This was fear. The earth-bound public had not yet accepted the idea that leaving firm ground was safe. Though tens of thousands made barnstorming flights or air trips for the thrill or adventure of it, they returned to the rails and the highways once they were back on terra firma. Out on the Pacific Coast, Steve Stimpson, United's alert district manager, after listening to scores of men explain that they would fly and save time, except that their wives objected, came up with an idea.

"Why not take your wife along free as guest of the company?" he asked.

The United management let Stimpson try out his idea on the San Francisco–Los Angeles route for three weeks, then extended it to the Chicago–New York run for one month. When sixty-eight wives decided to accompany their husbands between these two cities in a single day, the traffic department knew that it had the key to a lot of new business. The plan was extended coast to coast. Other airlines adopted it, too, and before long the distaff side of the passenger list was almost as heavy as that of the men. It remained that way long after the take-your-wife-free inducement was discontinued.

The experiment had its humorous side, too. As a follow-up clincher for the flying wives, Stimpson prepared a cordial letter to the venturesome spouses, telling them how pleased United was to have them in its planes, hoping they had enjoyed the experience and that they would soon fly again. Now and then a letter backfired on Stimpson because some thoughtless male passenger had neglected to tell his wife that he had taken her along.

Though these and other come-on-and-fly inducements got thousands of new passengers into planes, the taste of prosperity was short-lived. Toughened by adversity, United was healthy in every way but financially. Adding to the gloom of the black years was a sanguinary series of eight airline crashes in 1936, followed by five more in 1937, nearly all of them headline-makers. One was a Western Air Express plane which disappeared in Utah's Wasatch Mountains; another was an American plane which crashed in Arkansas. Then, as 1936 drew to a close, a United Boeing 247 en route from San Francisco to Los Angeles flew into a cloud-shrouded peak near Los Angeles, killing all on board. In January another Western Air Express plane piled into a mountainside near the scene of United's crash. Among the dead was the famous explorer Martin Johnson. Early in February one of United's new DC-3s, coming in for a landing at San Francisco Airport, plunged into the bay. All aboard were drowned. Stunned, because the plane was on course and piloted by one of the company's best pilots, United had the plane fished out of the water. Investigators found the answer: the co-pilot had dropped his microphone, which had jammed the controls, preventing the pilot from pulling out of the glide.

The newspaper headlines that announced these crashes panicked passengers right out of the air. Reservations were canceled by thousands. In one day United's passenger revenues dropped from $25,000 to $5000. Many planes flew empty, piling up losses. To cap the series of disasters, the Post Office arbitrarily canceled one of United's daily mail flights between New York and Chicago. In a move to whip the bad fortune, Patterson made Major R. W. Schroeder manager in charge of operations when D. B. Colyer quit in 1937 to join Phil Johnson with Trans-Canada Air Lines. A veteran of World War I Army Signal Corps flying, and of the old Ford line, "Shorty" Schroeder had served with the Bureau of Air Commerce in charge of air safety. Schroeder lived and dreamed airline safety; it was a religion with him. If any man could lick the bugaboo of airliner crashes, Schroeder could do it.

Though Schroeder's safety campaign got results and was a step in the right direction, it was only a step, as President Patterson pointed out to his directors. Patterson argued that though air transport had come a long way since the air mail days, it still had a long way to go before it could offer travelers the safety and comfort of the railroad. He persuaded the directors and the stockholders to increase the company's shares from 1,200,000 to 2,000,000. Despite the run of bad news, the shares were readily bought by stockholders, by employes, and by the public. Patterson had four million new dollars in the kitty to finance the next momentous milestone, not only for United Air Lines but for air transport as a whole.

CHAPTER IX

The Modern Magic Carpet

Among the marvels of science on display at the 1933 World's Fair at Chicago was one of the first Boeing 247 passenger and cargo planes rolled out of the plant at Seattle. The low-wing streamlined aircraft was so new and revolutionary that hundreds of thousands came to marvel at this veritable magic carpet. Bigger planes had been built, but they were strut-and-canvas jobs, whereas the Boeing was a compact, all-metal vehicle that seemed as much a single unit as a giant bird. Gazing admiringly at the graceful monoplane, one of Boeing's engineers exclaimed, "It will be a long time before anyone builds a better or faster plane than this."

The "long time" was less than a year. The better and faster plane made its spectacular debut the following February, when Jack Frye, president of TWA, and Eddie Rickenbacker, vice-president of Eastern Air Transport, flew the last load of mail out of Los Angeles, prior to cancellation, to Newark in 13 hours and 4 minutes in the first DC-2 built by Donald Douglas. That flight was an omen of faster, better, and bigger magic carpets to come during the phenomenal next seven years, during which the United States air transport matured from an experiment into an established industry.

It was a propitious time for a revolution in the business. Before cancellation, an air mail contract was considered reason enough for operating an airline. After the reorganization, it wasn't. The new air mail contracts at reduced rates were no longer manna from Washington; in fact, most airlines lost money flying the mail after

1934. Thereafter the passengers and the shippers had to shore up the budgets, as air mail contracts had done in the past. The passenger, especially, became the prize. In the scramble to lure him into the planes, airline operators lay awake nights thinking up new inducements. The five years following 1934 became the battle of a half decade, particularly between the three major systems, United, American, and TWA. They fought for the transcontinental traveler, and the crucial battleground was the key Chicago–New York run, where all three airlines competed vigorously for the traffic between the nation's two largest metropolitan areas. Out of the bitter competition emerged the finest, fastest, most luxurious and dependable air transportation system yet achieved in any land.

At the start, United seemed to have every advantage. President Patterson had recaptured the old NAT air mail contract for flying the mail over the Chicago-Cleveland-Newark airway, the shortest route between the country's two main cities. The cities on United's Main Line were the most promising sources of bumper loads of passengers. United was the only airline with a fleet of modern planes adequate to handle the traffic. Furthermore, the company had the know-how, not only in flying the route but in handling passengers, on the ground and in the planes. The 247 fleet had already turned in an outstanding record for dependable, on-time flying. There was every reason to expect still better "air transportation at its best." The rejuvenated United management was all set to crack the potential passenger jackpot, not only between Chicago and New York, but all over the 6000-mile system.

This rosy outlook was soon eclipsed. What dimmed it first was the award to TWA of a certificate to fly the Chicago-Pittsburgh-Newark route. Then American Airlines won the Chicago-Detroit-Newark run. Both new routes were slightly longer than United's straight Main Line, via Cleveland, but they brought some hot competition into two markets that had been virtually a United monopoly. TWA launched its route with Douglas DC-2 planes, which were 25 miles per hour faster than United's Boeing 247s. American followed suit. Capitalizing on the advantage this new equipment gave them, both TWA and American adroitly publicized five-hour nonstop flights between the two cities. The best that the 247s could promise was a five-and-a-half-hour, one-stop flight. Actually, the TWA and American planes usually stopped en route for reserve fuel, but even so the new competition held an edge over United in speed.

That was only one of the advantages. The Douglas planes were roomier and more quiet than the Boeing 247s, whose tight-fitting seats lined a narrow aisle broken by a strut over which passengers and stewardesses had to step. Airline passengers changed, too, along with the planes. No longer was the air traveler necessarily an adventurous flying enthusiast or someone flying because of an emergency. The new model passenger was a businessman with a briefcase or a traveler who took to the air because it was the comfortable way to get there. The new passenger was extremely conscious of time. If one airline could save him an hour between New York and Chicago, or four hours cross-country, he switched his patronage to that line. Thus it was with much dismay that United's traffic hustlers watched passengers flocking to the faster TWA and American flights. United's expensive fleet of Boeing 247s was definitely outclassed.

The United management tried every play in the book to meet this unexpected and tough competition. Patterson persuaded the company's directors to earmark $1,000,000 to "beef up" the Boeings with expensive engine changes, three-blade constant speed propellers, and other modifications. This "beefing" stepped up the speed of the 247s from 160 miles per hour to 170, almost that of the DC-2s. Whereupon Donald Douglas, determined to keep his lead, came out with his larger, faster, longer range DC-3, which gave TWA and American a still better travel bargain, namely, a four-and-one-half-hour nonstop flight between Chicago and New York. The Boeings still had to drop down at Cleveland for fuel, and they still required seven hops to cross the country. They still had seats for only ten passengers, while the DC-2 carried fourteen and the DC-3 accommodated twenty-one.

To publicize the dependability of the improved Boeing 247-D, the Boeing Airplane Company decided to enter a stock model plane in the spectacular London-to-Melbourne air race held in October of 1934, and employed two noted racing pilots, Roscoe Turner and Clyde Pangborn, to fly it. Unfortunately, because of a navigating error, the 247-D lost out to a specially built British plane which won the race, and to a Dutch entry which took second. The Dutch entry was a Douglas DC-2 flown by a Dutch crew familiar with the route.

The harried United management undertook to match speed with superior service. Stewardesses served hot meals in specially designed covered trays that kept food warm; they did everything but tuck the passenger's napkin under his chin. Over the highly competitive Chicago–New York route, the United traffic agents touted a sensational new schedule of flights, every hour on the hour all day long. It was a great talking point, but it failed to impress businessmen, who wanted to fly when their work was done, and fast. The experiment established a fundamental rule for the airline business, namely, that passengers don't fly when planes go, but planes fly when passengers want to go.

In spite of United's best efforts to win friends with the 247s, TWA and American continued to skim the cream off the Chicago and New York markets, the testing grounds of air transport. More important, with their greater carrying capacity, the DC-3s made money for their owners as fast as the half-filled Boeings lost it. By the middle of 1935, the United executives could see the handwriting in the sky. The Boeing 247s, despite the sleek lines and sturdy performance, were economically obsolete. They had been from the day that BAT's more conservative pilots persuaded Phil Johnson that a 16,000-pound plane powered by Hornet engines was too heavy and too dangerous to land at airports. When the first Boeing airliner was scaled down instead of up, it was doomed.

This was a costly lesson that Patterson and his associates never forgot. Late in 1935 they appropriated $1,000,000 to buy ten DC-3s from the Douglas factory. For the new fleet of DC-3s, Patterson ordered 14-cylinder Pratt & Whitney Hornet engines. The Hornets cost more than Wright Whirlwinds, they weighed more, and used more fuel. But they gave the United DC-3s more climbing power and either engine could keep a Mainliner aloft with a full load at 11,000 feet, thus adding a margin of safety. And they had speed to spare, if United pilots needed it to keep pace with rivals.

Delivery of United's DC-3s in 1936 touched off anew the battle for passengers on the "blue-ribbon" New York–Chicago run. To offer the customers the last word in luxury, United introduced, in January, 1937, the "Skylounge," a fourteen-passenger deluxe job with swivel chairs, the first extra-fare plane ever flown. This plushy special made the New York–Chicago flight in three hours fifty-five minutes. Passengers paid $2 extra for the leg room and speed; and they grumbled at the extra fare. The Skylounge lost seven full passenger fares for each $28 collected in these fares; it also could not be used on other flights. Eventually the Skylounges were converted into twenty-one-passenger planes, or to DC-3 sleepers, which added a new note of luxury to the overnight flight between San Francisco and Chicago. The sleepers had berths, resembling those in Pullman cars, with soft, light blankets and linen sheets. The harassed "sky girls" became portresses as well as stewardesses. They talked hesitant passengers into going to bed in the air, wakened them before refueling stops to keep their ears from popping, had coffee, rolls, and scrambled eggs ready when they wakened in the morning. Air travel was becoming really luxurious.

Nevertheless, Patterson realized that the DC-3s were merely stop-gap or interim planes. For that matter, all airliners are interim planes, because somebody is always dreaming up a still better sky vehicle. What Patterson wanted was a four-engine skyliner of great carrying capacity with a wide margin of safety, something to overcome the earth-bound traveler's fear of crashes, a series of which had scared thousands of passengers out of the air in 1936–1937.

Back in the happy days before the 1934 air mail cancellation and industry upheaval, the United Aircraft & Transport designers had planned a revolutionary new four-engine plane, which was on the drawing boards when the break-up of the holding company took place. The design was one of the assets turned over to the Boeing Airplane Company when the holding company unmerged. Unfortunately, the Boeing planners were up to their ears in the engineering of a huge four-engine flying boat, known first as the Boeing Clipper and later as the Pan American Clipper. Nobody even considered flying the ocean in land planes at that time, and the Boeing flying boats seemed to be the answer to trans-Atlantic and trans-Pacific air travel. The Boeing staff poured their energies and the company's working capital into the sturdy but slow Clippers, which enabled Pan American to launch dependable overseas service. Unfortunately, not many Clippers were needed, and the decision to concentrate on the flying boats cost the Boeing company its predominant position in the air transport field for a decade to come.

Early in 1936, Patterson revived the four-engine airliner idea as a United project. The first step was to call the company's operations and traffic people together. "What do we want in an airplane?" Patterson asked them. The result was a composite layman's description of his dream plane. Patterson took this to Hartford and laid it before Frederick B. Rentschler, head of United Aircraft & Manufacturing Company. Rentschler, champing to provide Pratt & Whitney power for a four-engine airliner ever since he had launched the design shelved by the Boeing company, called in his chief engineer, George J. Mead, and Commander Jerome C. Hunsaker, aerodynamics expert at Massachusetts Institute of Technology. Mead and Hunsaker soon had the rough design and specifications for a forty-passenger 54,000-pound-gross-load luxury plane, with a speed of 175 miles per hour.

With the specifications in his briefcase, Patterson made the rounds of the aircraft factories. Boeing wasn't interested. Consolidated Aircraft said the airline people didn't know how to design planes. Sikorsky, a unit of United Aircraft, submitted a bid so low that the directors asked Patterson to ignore it. At the Douglas plant, Chief Engineer Raymond said, "Engineering this plane is going to take a lot of time and money; are you just shopping around?" To convince Douglas that he meant business, Patterson offered to underwrite half of the engineering cost, estimated at $300,000, if the factory would foot the rest of the bill.

TWA executives had heard about the dream airliner and asked if they could be counted in. Patterson said sure, come on in. Then Pan American, Eastern, and finally American Airlines joined in underwriting the project, which looked like a million dollars for the first experimental model. Douglas was still willing to pay half the development costs. The other half was divided by agreement signed by the heads of the five airlines, 40 per cent for

United, 24 per cent for TWA, 16 per cent for American, 11 per cent for Pan American, 8 per cent for Eastern.

It was June, 1938, before the big, triple-tailed airliner rolled out of the Douglas factory, ready for its test flight, and May, 1939, before Douglas was ready to turn the job over to United pilots for demonstration flights over the airways. For two months, Benny Howard, veteran flier and flight engineer, soared over the United system, pausing at key airports for more than a million fans to gaze at the silver monster and wonder. The plane more than lived up to its promises. At Cheyenne Airport, 6200 feet high, Pilot Howard cut out one engine as the DC-4 roared down the runway for a take-off. As it lifted into the rarified air on the remaining three engines, Jack Herlihy, vice-president of operations, beamed, "That's the plane for us." When Howard finished his tour, American Airlines pilots took the controls and put the brand new last word in travel luxury through its paces on their airway.

Meantime, defection had split the quintet underwriting the DC-4 project. The dream plane ran into more money than originally contemplated. The experimental model cost $600,000 to build. The price of production models ranged from $450,000 each in orders of five to $182,000 apiece for sixty. The five partners had agreed among themselves not to buy another plane in the 50,000-pound class until the DC-4 was completed, but TWA and Pan American, taking advantage of a new Boeing design, ordered five four-engine, pressurized Stratoliners, 1000 pounds under the 50,000-pound limit. This broke up the cooperative deal. Pan American and Eastern pulled out, leaving United and American holding the sack.

It wasn't as bad as it appeared. During demonstration flights both United and American engineers hit upon modifications that would vastly improve the DC-4 from the passengers' viewpoint. The principal change was a pressurized cabin, which would enable the plane to operate at high altitudes without discomfort to passengers. When the idea was broached to Douglas, he proposed selling the prototype to a Japanese mission which was shopping around for a big plane in which to fly their top brass quickly from place to place in their so-called Co-Prosperity Sphere. This sale let the airlines off the hook. It did the Japanese warlords little good, because the plane plunged into Tokyo Bay as the inept Nipponese took off on a test flight.

Both United and American placed orders for the improved DC-4, but before the Douglas factory could get them into production, Robert A. Lovett, Assistant Secretary of War, sent for Patterson. The Army's air chiefs had concluded that the DC-4 was exactly what the rapidly growing Air Force needed for global warfare air transport. Lovett pointed out that World War II was just around the corner and asked Patterson to cancel United's order so that the Douglas plant could concentrate on a military version. United canceled and American followed suit. The DC-4 became the Douglas Skymaster, and, bearing the Army C-54 or the Navy R-5D designation, it became the aerial workhorse of the war, carrying statesmen, military leaders, troops, munitions, and other cargo to the far corners of the earth during the five years that followed.

No other new plane ever had such a shake-down period in which to work out the mechanical bugs. But by the time the Douglas plant was free to build the commercial version in 1945, the DC-4 was no longer the last word in travel luxury. Three new high-flying pressurized airliners, faster and larger, had emerged from the wartime splurge of aeronautical design. They were the Lockheed Constellation, the Douglas DC-6, and the Boeing Stratocruiser, postwar luxury flying vehicles that fulfilled the air traveler's dream of flying high and wide around or above the weather. It took time to build them, and before they could be delivered to the airlines, the DC-4 had its day on the air lanes as hundreds of reconverted C-54s tided over the interim.

When the DC-4 was in the drafting-board stage, Douglas and United engineers found themselves face to face with a by-problem, which proved that the modern magic carpet was more than engines, wings, speed, cruising range, and seating capacity. This was the designing of a brand new galley from which a stewardess, or pair of stewardesses, could serve meals to fifty or more passengers in the short time it would take to fly from Los Angeles to San Francisco or Chicago to Cleveland if the plane happened to be in the air on these or other short hops at meal time. It was a problem not exactly aeronautical, but important, because air travelers were beginning to have appetites in the air, and the tradition that they were entitled to meals "on the house"—on the airline—had become well established.

On the United system veteran passengers think of meals aloft in terms of periods. These began with the sandwich-and-apple days, with maybe a cup of lukewarm coffee from a thermos bottle, a period in which most travelers' stomachs were so squeamish that they usually waited to refuel when the planes did at the next landing. In those days, landings were not too far apart. Then, taking a cue from the Sante Fe, BAT set up a Harvey House type of quickie restaurant at Cheyenne Airport to serve coast-to-coast flights. It was poorly patronized, because for some inexplicable reason air travelers liked to stand by the gate kibitzing the refueling and the servicing of planes, and poised like sprinters to dash for their seats, as though their magic carpet might soar off without them.

Once inside, their seat belts buckled, they were hungry, and when BAT equipped itself with the first luxury planes, the twelve-seat B-80s with some room to move around in the cabins and stewardesses to look after passengers' comfort, standard equipment on the planes was a thermos jug of creamed chicken and a percolator that could be plugged in to keep the coffee hot. The stewardesses dished out creamed chicken, rolls, and coffee whenever meal time rolled around, and by the time a cross-country passenger reached the other side of the continent, he was well stuffed with creamed chicken, albeit not hungry. The creamed chicken period was followed by the fried chicken era, which synchronized roughly with the Boeing 247 years. To inject a note of class into service aboard these first modern airliners, BAT employed Henry Dreyfuss, the distinguished functional designer, to evolve a combination lunch box and serving tray made of papier-mâché. When the lid was removed, the tray on the traveler's lap held a feast, which was invariably fried chicken, rolls, butter, a sprig of celery, and a pudding or some cake for dessert. Eventually the airline patrons grew a little tired of fried chicken all the way across the country, and contended they had eaten so much of it, hot or cold,

Left: "Boss" of United's far-flung military contract operations in World War II was Seely V. Hall, who had helped pioneer Pacific Air Transport in the twenties. He retired from United in 1958.
Right: Without prior experience in the north, United crews provided a vital airlift to Alaska and the Aleutian chain when the Japanese threat was at its height.

Outbound, the C-54s were transports carrying personnel and cargoes; returning, they were often flying hospital ships, winging the wounded home fast.

Cargo bound for fighting forces in the Pacific is loaded aboard olive-drab transport flown by United for the Air Transport Command.

At its Cheyenne modification base, United updated more than 5000 Flying Fortresses fresh out of aircraft factories, to keep them apace the fast changing techniques of war. Lessons learned in combat were quickly translated into improved fighting equipment aboard these planes.

In the Boeing School of Aeronautics and at the Denver Training Center, hundreds of military fliers learned their navigation and other skills in schools which United operated under contract.

Army Air Transport Command mechanics in the making at United's Denver Training Center.

Weldon E. "Dusty" Rhoades (right), United's manager of flight engineering, became General Douglas MacArthur's personal pilot following a memorable globe-girdling flight. He is shown with Lieut. Gen. R. K. Sutherland, MacArthur's chief of staff.

that they were sprouting wings and would soon be able to fly without the help of planes.

The DC-4 design enlarged the care-and-feeding-of-passengers problem, because whereas a stewardess found it easy to serve ten passengers in a 247 and could handle up to twenty-one in a DC-3, the much larger airliner of the future meant a lot of trotting between the food compartment and the seats of fifty hungry passengers. Patterson was talking about the problem one day, early in 1936, with a hotel man in San Francisco.

"Say, we just had a firm of hotel efficiency experts studying our place and figuring out easier ways to give better service," said the hotel man. "Maybe they could do something for you."

The upshot was that a few days later Patterson asked the R. M. Grinstead Company of New York to assign one of their best men to ride United Air Lines planes and study the procurement and serving of food and advise the engineers at the Douglas Aircraft plant upon the designing of the DC-4 galley. The assignment hit the Grinstead office while one of the younger partners, Don F. Magarrell, a Cornell-trained food and dining service expert, was in charge of the office.

"The job looked interesting, and they wanted a good man, so I assigned myself to the project," Magarrell explained later, with a laugh.

It was one of those fortunate choices of the right man for the right job. Magarrell climbed aboard a Boeing 247 at Newark Airport on Labor Day of 1936 and hit every stop on the United system, winding up finally in Santa Monica, where he found himself the answer to the prayers of a group of Douglas and United engineers, who knew all about aerodynamic flows but very little about the flow of foods. Magarrell impressed them with a suggestion that a motion-flow study be made to determine the easiest way to get the food into the serving galleys and from the galleys to the passengers. They let Magarrell design the galley, and agreed to move it from the front of the plane to a spot near the doorway, where the containers could be hoisted or lowered by high-lift trucks. This seemingly incidental item in the design of the modern planes was both important and revolutionary, because the day was not far off when many air travelers would choose carriers largely on the basis of food, just as rail and steamship passengers pick trains and ocean liners because of their food and service.

This theme crept into the report made to United's executives when he returned to Chicago, by which time Magarrell had concluded that he, too, wanted to work for United Air Lines. He was so eager to do so that he sacrificed a partnership in the Grinstead firm and took a hefty reduction in income to accept a job overseeing the airline's food service, offered him by Dick Pfennig, director of passenger service. It was a sacrifice that paid off before long, because Magarrell soon stepped into Pfennig's shoes, when the latter was promoted in 1937 to manager of operations. By 1945 the assignment of Magarrell to survey the airline's food problems had led to innovations in the care and feeding of air travelers fully as important as the technical gains in flying. That year he was made vice-president—passenger service. In 1951, he assumed even broader duties as vice-president—transportation services. In 1958, he became a senior vice-president.

One of his early recommendations was that United set up its own flight kitchens at major airports to prepare meals just before flight time, instead of contracting with caterers who had to haul the food out to the planes, usually an hour of jolting from downtown. He was given $3000 to try out the idea at Oakland Airport, then the San Francisco Bay area terminal for lines fanning north, east, and south, and the busiest point on the line. The flight kitchen opened during the holiday rush of 1936, and proved a success from the start. In fact, it paid for itself in the next three months, in the saving of food costs. Magarrell was told to set up a chain of flight kitchens, which eventually grew to fifteen extending from coast to coast.

For his first flight kitchen chef, Magarrell employed a Swiss, John Dietschy, who did so well that when the next kitchen at Portland was opened, Oswald Weber, another Swiss produced by Dietschy, was hired. Soon passengers out of the Pacific Northwest were writing appreciative letters about the meals aboard the planes. When the kitchen at Burbank opened, a third Swiss, Max Burkhardt, was installed. After that, one Swiss chef after another joined the airline as new flight kitchens were opened, except for one Austrian and one Frenchman, who added a note of international rivalry to the airline's cuisine.

Between the Swiss chefs and United Air Lines, it was mutual admiration from the first. The Swiss liked their work because it was nice, clean cooking with no cranky patrons sending back dishes for a little more brown on the sunny side. The customers were usually a hundred miles away and two miles aloft by meal time, and happy to have a meal on the house. Magarrell liked the Swiss because they were meticulous perfectionists with a flair for dressing up the plain foods that people could eat at high altitudes with relish, and they could make a little food look like a lot, an important consideration because airline meals had to be served in cramped space, where the traditional "square meal" looked too hearty to be appetizing.

Magarrell added a note of class to the service with printed menus featuring Swiss-French names for the various dishes. For Magarrell the printed menus were more than a bit of swank. They enabled him to keep a check on the meals. Each chef made out his menus for a month in advance and submitted them to the United diet kitchen at headquarters where they were checked to eliminate the chance of regular passengers getting the same meal too often. After the airline's dietitian approved them, they were printed, and there was no substitution. Magarrell knew that his patrons were getting not only food that they enjoyed, but food that was good for them aloft.

The system and the check on meals developed in the DC-3 decade paid dividends in the period of four-engine big passenger loads that followed as the airline served an increasing number of meals a year, turned out in the chain of flight kitchens strategically located along the Main Line and headed by continentally trained chefs.

Meals were only one item, albeit provocative, as the art of serving passengers aloft evolved. When the DC-3s replaced the 247s on the main route, Magarrell was assigned the task of making them more attractive as well as more comfortable. Transcontinental rivals already flew the DC-3s, so the competitive advantage simmered down to giving better service. United's new planes were soon rechristened "Mainliners," a trade name that became a by-word and one that the United heads hoped would mean something to air travelers. It was Magarrell's responsibility to figure out ways to give the Mainliner name a real meaning.

He haunted the Cheyenne shops where the DC-3s were given the Mainliner touch before going into service. He visited the line's special school where novice sky girls were trained in their high-flying duties. As contrasted with the first stewardesses hired in the '30s, something more than a few practice hops now were required to learn the job. What eventually evolved was a five-week course with new classes starting every few weeks to keep pace with fast turnover and expanding need. (At one time the average career of a stewardess was thirteen months; in recent years it has stabilized at twenty-four to twenty-six months. Main reason for "grounding": matrimony—sometimes to pilots or passengers but more often to the boy back home, concerned about his new high-altitude competition.)

The stewardesses had a lot of new duties, and serving meals with the right touch was only one of them. Fewer air travelers were airsick than in the early days, but a passenger who felt fine wanted more magazines and had more questions to ask. Stewardesses had to keep the cabins from getting too hot or too cold, and make sure that no heavy objects were on the overhead racks. They looked after children, knew about the routings, the scenery, and how high the plane was flying. The sky girls became the airline's best contact with the flying public.

On the ground, the running of the modern magic carpet became infinitely more complicated. It was no longer limited to servicing planes or unloading them. Where there had been hundreds of passengers to think about, now there were thousands daily. Where a passenger once considered it his own bad luck if he was grounded or missed a connection because of weather, he now blamed it on the airline. He stayed aloft with his favorite airline as long as it kept him on the wing; after a grounding, he switched to a rival or returned to the rails. It was no longer safe for each office to sell all the tickets it could, because many flights carried a full load. A central reservations system, launched in 1935, became a part of Magarrell's passenger service department in 1936. This was the forerunner of a gradually developed system whereby a traveler could walk into any United office and buy a seat on any flight without waiting for the ticket agent to wire for space.

Eager to make sure he was giving United's passengers everything their hearts desired, Magarrell placed in the literature pocket by every seat on the DC-3s an already addressed letter to the president of the airline, inviting passengers to fill in the blank lines with their ideas. The letters poured in by the thousands. Some of the passengers' brainstorms were brilliant, if unfeasible—windows in the floor so they could look straight down at the scenery over which they were flying, for example. The first-timers wrote ecstatically of their thrills, and some of them even burst into poetry. Now and then a passenger threw a brick, but so many of the replies were bouquets that Magarrell reluctantly concluded it was better to let the customers write their own letters. They have done so ever since. Bouquet or brickbat, all are answered; all are studied carefully. They provide a potent pen-and-ink measurement of the strengths and weaknesses of United's day-to-day service, the company believes.

For United, and for other major airlines as well, 1939 marked a new spell in air transport. Stimulated by better times and World's Fairs at both ends of the line, New York and San Francisco, passenger revenues increased $2,000,000 over the preceding years. The DC-3 Mainliner fleet flew with heavy loads. United pulled out of the red ink, with a modest $777,000 profit for 1939.

More important yet, the outlook on the high horizon was rosy. The Civil Aeronautics Act of 1938 had deposed the Interstate Commerce Commission as dictator of airline routes and rates and set up a new five-member body, the Civil Aeronautics Authority, whose name was later changed to the Civil Aeronautics Board, to avoid confusion with the CAA which administered the government's flying aids and the airways safety regulations. It was the era of alphabet soup in Washington, as Federal agencies were born or reborn almost weekly. Created in August, 1938, the new CAB froze existing rates and routes while it organized for business, but the very existence of a body devoting its energies solely to domestic and foreign airline transport was a promising omen.

The 1938 Act theoretically emancipated the airlines from the

Post Office air mail contracts. Up to that time, an airline was regarded as a route over which mail should be carried on contract, and over which passengers might travel, too. Between 1934, when the New Deal air mail act was passed, and 1938, passenger revenues had outstripped air mail revenues. The Civil Aeronautics Act in effect canceled the Post Office contracts, replacing them with certificates of public convenience over the routes which airlines should operate, carrying mail more or less incidentally to passenger traffic.

An interesting provision known as "the grandfather clause" had a far-reaching significance to the air transport industry. This provided that a permanent certificate of convenience over a route a company had flown satisfactorily became a franchise, which the airline owned, and which could not be taken away from it at the whim of the Post Office or the ICC or any other Federal agency. Similarly, certificates of convenience for new routes became franchises. Airlines no longer had to bid for air mail contracts. The CAB had authority not only to set air mail, passenger, and cargo rates, but it could establish competition over routes and remake the airways map, if it chose to do so.

As might be expected, there was a scramble among the air carriers to cut themselves in on bigger slices of potential business. United, which served only seven of the country's twenty largest population centers, as compared to sixteen tapped by American and a dozen by TWA, launched a drive to crack into Boston, Baltimore, Washington, and Pittsburgh to round out service in the East; to gain entry into St. Louis and Kansas City; to fly directly from Denver to Los Angeles; and to operate certain feeder flights from smaller cities along the system. Rivals were just as eager for extensions, and the CAB, swamped with petitions, took them under advisement so deliberately that years elapsed before many of them were acted upon.

Impatient of the delays, Patterson tried more direct action to strengthen the United system. Though the passenger business had increased in volume, the company's position had deteriorated decidedly. In 1934, United handled 44 per cent of the country's air passenger business; by 1937, it was down to 23 per cent.

In mid-1938, Patterson tried to buy Pennsylvania-Central

Airlines, flying a shortline network connecting Washington, Pittsburgh, Cleveland, Detroit, Chicago, Milwaukee, and intermediate points. The losing Pennsylvania network complemented the United Main Line. Unfortunately, Patterson was unable to reach an agreement on price with Pennsylvania's operators and their bankers, and the deal fell through by the end of the year. Shortly thereafter he had a bigger deal simmering out west. Nine owners of 55 per cent of Western Air Express agreed to swap their shares for United stock. Patterson agreed to buy the other 45 per cent from the other shareholders on the same basis, three shares of Western for one of United. This deal was a natural, too. Over half of Western's passenger revenues came from its connection with the United Main Line at Salt Lake City, but both companies were losing out in the growing Los Angeles–Chicago–New York traffic to TWA and American, which offered through service, whereas the Western-United passengers had to change planes at Salt Lake. The ICC had arbitrarily refused to allow interchange of Western and United equipment to provide similar through service.

With stock of both companies deposited in escrow in a Chicago bank, the merger was all set by the end of June, 1939, except for the CAB's approval. Opposition quickly mounted from three sources, TWA, American, and WAE executives. It was the CAB's first big controversial case, and soon became such a hot potato to handle that the Board stalled until January, 1940, then appointed the distinguished Dean Roscoe Pound of the Harvard Law School as examiner to hear evidence from the airlines involved and the traveling public. After due deliberation, Dean Pound recommended the merger as a convenience to the traveling public.

To the amazement of the United management and Western's majority stockholders, the CAB reversed Dean Pound's findings and denied the merger. United appealed for a rehearing, which failed to change the CAB's decision. As a final gesture, the company's attorneys filed suit in the Federal court, which refused to consider the case. The merger collapsed, but the CAB did grant United and Western the right to exchange equipment and offer through service between Los Angeles and Chicago. Western painted the United "Mainliner" trademark on the nose of its two new DC-3 sleeper planes, and United sleepers were flown by Western crews between Salt Lake and Los Angeles without disturbing the passengers. The interchange, which evened the competition with TWA and American somewhat, lasted until sleeper service was abandoned at the outbreak of war.

In the welter of applications before the CAB, United fared little better than it had in petitions to the ICC. Its planes were denied entry into St. Louis and Kansas City, where the company still owned a hangar that had served the old NAT line. The long-delayed new deal on air mail pay, instead of the hoped-for pound-mile rate on the basis of service rendered, was an even more complicated formula than the ICC's, being based on the CAB's idea of what an airline might need to make both ends meet. In short, air mail was still rated as a Federal subsidy. Some of the feeder applications were granted, but before United could start service into smaller communities over which its Mainliners had flown, the country was at war and the scramble for routes had ended in a CAB freeze. The airline braced for a more stupendous air transport task than airmen had ever dreamed that wings and engines could handle.

CHAPTER X

War Wings

Late in 1941 the airline chiefs of the country were called together in an emergency session in Washington, D.C., by Edgar S. Gorrell, president of the Air Transport Association, who warned that it was only a matter of time until the United States would be involved in World War II. It took no crystal ball to foresee that the airlines, with their long-range-flying know-how, would be one of the nation's useful weapons, because the War Department had already moved in to commandeer the output of DC-4 transports.

"If you don't want your airlines to be taken over completely, you had better get together on a plan for fitting them into the war effort," Gorrell told the apprehensive executives.

They fell to feverishly, and came up with a plan for pooling resources and know-how and for putting planes, shops, pilots, technicians, and experienced operations men at the services of the armed forces overnight. The idea was to offer the government a global war transport system ready-made and ready to fly.

It was fortunate the astute Gorrell warned them when he did, because immediately after the Japanese attack on Pearl Harbor touched off the war, he was called to the White House by the President. General H. H. Arnold, chief of the Air Force, was already there. President Roosevelt showed Gorrell an executive order he had signed, authorizing seizure of the airlines for the duration of the war and turning them over to Arnold's command.

Gorrell argued against the wisdom of the seizure order, and presented the carriers' own plan for fitting into the war picture, pointing out that the airlines were ready to start flying for the Army or Navy or any other war agency that day, whereas under the seizure program it would take weeks to organize a government air transport system. Impressed, the President asked Arnold what he thought about the proposition.

One of "Hap" Arnold's great gifts was persuading people out of uniform to handle difficult and often impossible jobs for the Army, to which the Air Force belonged at the time. Arnold had already talked the aircraft builders into doing millions of dollars worth of designing and experimental plane building long before Congress authorized funds for the work. This gamble by private enterprise had put the Air Force many months ahead in its armament program. To the President's surprise, Arnold pleaded eloquently for leaving the airlines in the hands of the operators who knew how to run them and for contracting with them for war work.

F.D.R. picked up the executive order and tore it up. For the second time in eight years, the United States air transport system had been saved in the nick of time for private enterprise. But it had a job to do. During the next five years, the operations grew until United States military air routes flown jointly by the Army, the Navy, and contract operators girdled the globe with a network of airways. The operation grew so stupendous and functioned so successfully that it revolutionized the thinking about the role of air transport. For one thing, it disposed for good of the bugaboo of government ownership. For another, it fostered grandiose ideas on the part of certain operators, who, after a taste of overseas flying, scrambled for a cut in the fantastic transoceanic flying bonanza. Nearly everybody in the air transport game hoped to hit the jackpot flying millions of air-minded passengers around the earth.

But as of January, 1942, as the nation's war effort swung into high gear, the problem was to carry many people with few planes. The air transport fleets of all the airlines consisted of 363 planes, of which United's share was 69 planes. The Army and Navy needed transport planes for military uses faster than the aircraft plants could deliver them, so the airlines were called upon in the next few weeks to sell all but 200 planes to the government. By May 1, 1942, this left United with 33 DC-3 planes to fly routes that had kept 69 planes busy. Berths were ripped out of sleepers to increase their passenger capacity; everybody sat up day and night. Everybody had to go somewhere in a hurry on some war mission, real or fancied. Thousands of Army and Navy officers and civilians engaged in war work traveled by air for the first time. Two of United's westbound flights were completely sold out night after night to ferry pilots returning to Southern California and Seattle aircraft plants for more fighters and bombers to deliver on the wing at Eastern United States and Canadian bases to plane-hungry Allies.

At first the company sold tickets to regular patrons, subject to cancellation if military travelers needed the seats. Hundreds, then thousands, of luckless passengers were summarily bumped off planes at stops along the line as priority travelers appeared. Planes which formerly had averaged 60 per cent loads now flew at nearly 100 per cent capacity. On the United system, the average daily flying time of planes jumped from 9.3 hours in 1941 to 11.4 in 1943. Half as many planes carried more passengers more miles than the entire fleet had flown the year before.

In fairness to the old patrons, dumped anywhere en route and left to get home any way they could, United reserved big blocks of seats for the military and civilians traveling on government missions. Then the rigid government priority system was established under the Army Air Forces, and United's Traffic Manager Ray W. Ireland was put in charge of it, with the rank of colonel. By the time the five classifications of priority ticket holders were assigned seats, there were few for commercial travelers. United, like most other major airlines, ceased to be a civilian airline for the time being. Travelers without priority ratings were advised to travel by some other means of transportation. Most of them did, though hundreds of "hopers" waited at airports for the seats of "no shows." The flying public changed almost overnight; thousands of confirmed air travelers went back to the rails, while more thousands who had never flown before took to the air on military or war production errands.

The dislocation on the airlines was a sample of the flood of work that hit other departments of the air transport companies. Taking the airlines at their word, General Arnold poured the chores on.

United's overhaul base at Cheyenne, Wyoming, found itself almost overnight a modification center for Air Force bombers, most of them Flying Fortresses bound for Europe. In the fast-moving air war, the bombers were outmoded before they rolled off the assembly lines. The Air Force found it quicker and easier to complete them as designed, then send them to Cheyenne and other centers for overhaul and installation of newer guns, radar, bomb sights, and other improvements for special missions.

The first Flying Fortresses arrived at the Cheyenne base one month after Pearl Harbor. There were two of them. Mechanics began installing extra fuel tanks in every conceivable space. In place of guns and bomb bays, the bombers were loaded with racks for photo equipment. On February 15, 1942, they took off, heading in the direction of Alaska. Months later the mechanics who did the work learned why the B-17s needed so many gas tanks. They had flown the photographic reconnaissance flights over Japan that made possible the sensational bombing of Tokyo by Jimmy Doolittle and his airmen early in the war.

These initial two bombers were followed by 200 more, then a thousand, and eventually by 5680. Bombers spewed out of the two-million-dollar hangars financed by the Air Force much as they rolled out of the factories. At the peak, they came out eleven a day, to be checked and test-flown by United pilots, then turned over to Army fliers. On one day, there were 99 bombers on the field or in the shops at Cheyenne. Though not a factory, the modification center manufactured four million parts in a single year.

United hired all available help in the Cheyenne area, then beat the bushes of the Rocky Mountain region for garagemen, mechanics, or anyone with a skill. Housing bulged to overflowing, including 300 government-owned trailers. Finally a bus service was set up to carry 650 of the 1600 employes of the modification center from Greeley and Fort Collins, 50 miles away over the line in Colorado. Even so, the base was unable to handle the war armada that flowed out of the aircraft plants. Cheyenne became the model for several other modification centers scattered over the land to keep the United States war planes from becoming obsolete before they fired a round or dropped a bomb.

Out at Oakland Airport the Boeing School of Aeronautics, operated by United to train co-pilots, technicians, and mechanics, suddenly found its student body swollen almost a hundredfold. T. Lee, Jr., director of the school, was called back to Washington, along with a dozen other heads of aviation schools, a year before Pearl Harbor. General Arnold wanted the schools to launch a mass training of aviation personnel. The Boeing School started this work in October, 1940, enrolling a new class of future aviation mechanics every ten days. By the end of 1942, it had turned out over 2000 trained mechanics, and had switched to three shifts with 100 instructors, mass-training not only mechanics but radio operators, navigators, and technicians for the Navy as well. The school trained more than 5000 in all. On the side it trained co-pilots for United planes at a special school first in Tracy, California, then at Reno, Nevada, and finally at Denver, Colorado. The Army and Navy sources of co-pilots had dried up, so United had to train them from scratch.

There seemed no limit to the war chores for United's flying crews. The main job was flying transport routes on contract, at home and overseas. When the scaled-down fleets remaining on the airways were unable to cope with the volume of hurry-up air transport, both passengers and cargo, the Air Force assigned back planes it had commandeered, and contracted with the airlines to fly special "milk runs." These changed from week to week, as the flow of military traffic—officers, technicians, emergency cargoes—between bases, plants, and embarkation points fluctuated with the war. United's longest domestic "milk run" was the 2818-mile Route 100 between New York's La Guardia Field and San Francisco Airport. To it was soon added the 1358-mile South Loop out of San Francisco serving bases in Southern California and Arizona, and the 1712-mile North Loop, covering key military points in Oregon, Washington, Idaho, and Utah.

In addition there were hundreds of hurry-up charter flights, from any place to anywhere the Army or the Navy needed somebody or something moved. Random samples of charter flights flown by United pilots were these: 3700 pounds of fleece-lined flying suits from Dayton for Army pilots in Alaska; 800 pounds of serum from San Francisco to San Diego to catch a departing Navy ship, flown in weather when regular flights were canceled; two tons of gun sights flown from Akron to Oakland to catch a Navy transport; daily shipments of 800 pounds of equipment from the Sperry Gyroscope Company in New York flown to the Boeing Aircraft Company in Seattle. A battleship needing 7800 pounds of bearings for speedy repair on Puget Sound got them by air on three flights from Akron. Serums and blood plasma packed in dry ice were routine cargoes. There was almost no limit to the things delivered by air.

The first major contract assigned to United called for the rush airlift of men and materials to Alaska over an emergency route launched early in 1942 when the Japs began moving across the Pacific. It came in the form of a long-distance call from Ed Gorrell in Washington to President Patterson, asking how soon United could start a service to Alaska. Three days later, a survey plane carrying veteran pilots R. T. Freng, Bert Lott, and R. J. Johnson took off from Salt Lake City to chart an airline shortline to Nome. Aboard were Henry T. Harrison, United's veteran weather man; Ted Johnson, Salt Lake station manager assigned to superintend Operation Alaska; and some experienced communications technicians. The proposed route, from Dayton to Calgary, White Horse in Yukon Territory, then Fairbanks and Nome, was entirely new territory to the United fliers.

The survey crew found that pilots had to fly through mountain passes 7000 feet high, flanked by lofty peaks, including Mt. McKinley, more than 20,000 feet. They also discovered that the available maps left much to guesswork, but the radio navigation aids were better than they expected. Air strips were far between and small, but DC-3s could land and take off if the pilots were skillful and daring. To the veteran airmen, the Alaska run was reminiscent of the early days when the daredevil flying postmen and the early Pacific Air Transport and Boeing Air Transport pilots wove their way through Western mountain passes.

United launched the operation between Dayton, Ohio, and Alaska on May 15, 1942. Within two weeks the Japanese hit the outer Aleutian Islands, and the emergency became so acute that crews from six other airlines joined United fliers in rushing military personnel and supplies to the Alaska war theater.

Crews soon found that they were flying not only a supply line but were answering emergency calls from all over the vast Alaskan territory. They flew anything—troops, generals, guns, ammunition, high-octane gas, tools, clothing, medicine. Logs of a few typical flights tell what life on Operation Alaska was like.

Captain J. O. "Jimmy" Johnson, pulled off the New York–Chicago run, was given the Memorial Day job in 1942 of flying an Army officer, two technical sergeants, and a load of ammunition from Anchorage out to Cold Bay in the Aleutians. While he was en route, the Kodiak radio was abruptly turned off. Johnson completed the flight on dead reckoning. Unloading his passengers and cargo, he returned to Anchorage, where he was detailed right back to the Aleutians, this time to Unmak with a 5000-pound load of aircraft bombs. He reached Unmak's metal landing strip in a 60-mile cross wind. No sooner was this cargo unloaded than a sudden gust of wind nosed the plane up and damaged its propellers. While Captain Johnson and the ground crew worked on the plane to get it back into flying shape, the Japanese attacked Unmak by air. Luckily, the visibility was poor, the ceiling was low, and the Jap pilots were poor shots. Their attempt to machine-gun Johnson's transport failed. Unscathed, he and his crew crawled out of the ditch, got their plane into the air, and headed for safer country.

There was the typical hitch of Captain Robert Dawson, another New York–based pilot. Dawson delivered 5000 pounds of ammunition, radio beam apparatus, and two Civil Aeronautics Administration mechanics from Anchorage to Cold Bay, then flew back to the main base at Edmonton, Canada. After a day's rest, he flew a schedule to Anchorage, arriving in the early evening. Before he took off, Dawson checked with the Army Air Transport Command to see if the Army had any special jobs for him. They did. Dutch Harbor had been bombed two days before, and had run out of anti-aircraft ammunition. The Army was unable to get supplies to the Island outpost, so the stuff was loaded in Dawson's plane, while he and First Officer M. W. Ashby planned their flight.

The route from Anchorage to Dutch Harbor had never been flown before at night, there were no lighting or other navigational facilities, and the weather was atrocious. Army planes which had tried to make it in the daytime had been forced back. In addition, there was a Japanese aircraft carrier somewhere in the vicinity of Dutch Harbor. Dawson took off at nine at night and eased down the Aleutian peninsula by dead reckoning. By midnight he was over the airport at Cold Bay. Proximity of the Japanese carrier prevented the use of lights to direct Dawson down to his midnight landing, so he glided down in complete darkness except for the doubtful assistance of masked flashlights held by soldiers on either side of the runway, making a miraculously smooth landing.

"I guess you'd like some rest," said the Dutch Harbor commander to the United crew after the plane had been unloaded.

"Not here," said Dawson. "This is no place for an airplane. Give us some fuel and we'll get back to the mainland."

As Dawson climbed into his cockpit, the Army commander said, "If you happen to spot that Jap carrier out there, we'd like to know where it is."

An hour out of Dutch Harbor, the plane broke abruptly out of the overcast. First Officer Ashby nudged Dawson and pointed downward. "There's the Jap," he said.

Dawson got a brief glimpse of the carrier under his right wing. He lost no time in altering course and dropping down to a few feet above the water. Luckily, no Jap Zeros dived on them and they reached Anchorage at daylight, just in time for another emergency flight with a load of radio equipment and personnel needed at Cordova. That night, when the plane touched wheels again at Anchorage, the log book showed forty-three hours of continuous flight duty for Dawson and Ashby.

Although they were contract fliers for the Army, the United pilots frequently found themselves flying for the Navy, too. One such emergency job was flying a crankshaft to Adak, where a destroyer was laid up for emergency repairs. The crankshaft weighed approximately 3500 pounds and was 20 feet long, extending the full length of the cabin. With the heavy cargo aboard, Captain Hugh Worthington left Anchorage and headed out over the sea late one afternoon, with the warning of the weatherman that the deepest low pressure center ever recorded in the area was located just west of Adak.

Worthington stopped overnight at Unmak, and reviewed the situation the following morning. Adak reported a 600-foot ceiling and two miles visibility, with surface winds of 65 miles per hour

Employe recognition. Above: The 1956 winners of gold DC-7s mounted on walnut desk stands, which are given annually to United employes for such things as sales achievement, community service, and outstanding job performance. Below: Ray Rieder, United employe at New York (right), happily accepts $3,000 suggestion award check from his supervisor. Amount represented 10 per cent of estimated savings to United through adoption of his idea, which concerned a better way of handling laundered uniforms.

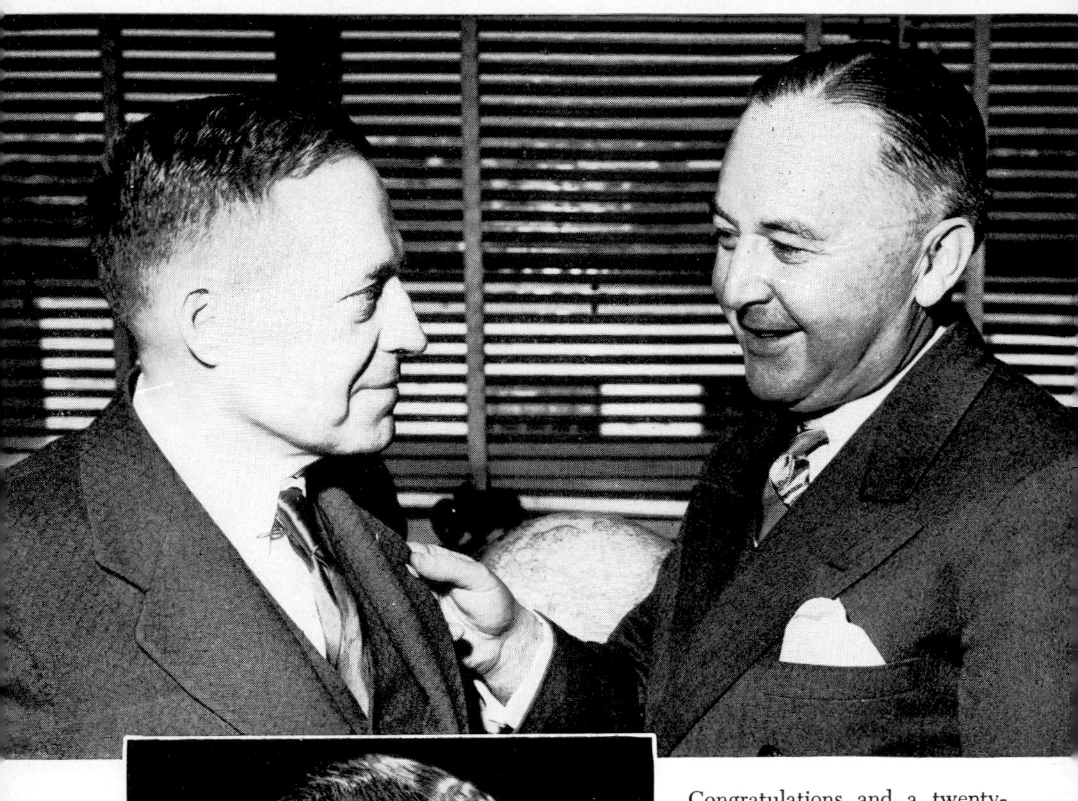

Congratulations and a twenty-year service pin from President W. A. Patterson (right) to Harold Crary, who opened the first United Air Lines office in Chicago in 1929. Crary retired as vice-president—sales in 1953 but continues in consultant capacity as assistant to the president.

Russell F. Ahrens, senior vice-president—personnel, whose first job with Boeing Air Transport was decorating San Francisco mailboxes with "Use Air Mail" signs.

Ellen Church, United's and the world's first airline stewardess, signs autographs for two current-day United sky girls. Miss Church now is administrator of the Union Hospital, Terre Haute, Indiana.

AIRLINE FIRST LADIES

Bernice Johnson Bartholomew, secretary in San Francisco Community Relations office, is United's senior woman employe in years of service. She joined its Pacific Air Transport predecessor in 1926. With her here, on her thirtieth anniversary with United, are two Bay Area co-workers.

The President's Award, highest honor which can be paid to any United employe, went to Capt. R. L. Wagner (right) in 1957. He was completing 30 years as a United pilot—years in which he contributed much to flying techniques and know-how.

PRESIDENT'S AWARDS WINNERS

Recipient of the President's Award in 1958 was W. C. Mentzer, vice president—engineering, who had a major role in United's Jet Age equipment research and planning.

cutting across the runway. This meant that he would have to crab 35 degrees into the crosswind to make a landing. As he approached Adak, the pilot was advised that the ceiling was 200 feet and the visibility was cut down to three-quarters of a mile, with a 90-mile wind blowing 45 degrees across the runway. He had timed his departure to reach Adak at approximately the time the center of the low pressure hit the air strip. Worthington figured he could take advantage of the lull in the center of the storm to make his landing. His analysis and timing proved perfect. He landed safely with his emergency cargo, and ground crews hurriedly tied the plane to tractors to keep it from being blown over while they unloaded the crankshaft.

One stormy March day in 1943 Captain Felix Jones was singled out for an unusual honor, flying General Simon Bolivar Buckner from Anchorage to Seattle. Normally this was an easy ten-hour flight, but strong headwinds and weather turbulent even for Alaska forced Captain Jones to go upstairs and fly between 15,000 and 18,000 feet, where oxygen was necessary to keep the crew and the passengers conscious. As the flight stretched out, all of the oxygen aboard was consumed except for one bottle. Captain Jones had the difficult task of deciding who was more important, General Buckner or himself. Since he was at the controls and responsible for the safety of all on board, Captain Jones decided in favor of Captain Jones. With his co-pilot and radio operator already unconscious, he flew with one hand on the oxygen bottle, the other hand on the wheel. Jones dared not leave the cockpit to investigate the condition of General Buckner. It was only after they made a safe landing at Seattle that he found out. There the General explained that he had stretched himself out on the floor for the greater part of the trip and had not suffered unduly.

When the Alaska operation began, United Air Lines set up a new, nonprofit company, the United Air Lines Victory Corporation, to handle the military contracts. The Victory Corporation consisted of ten shares of capital stock, valued at $100 each, all of them owned by United Air Lines. The purpose of the Victory Corporation was to separate the military activity from its commercial operations and to keep the former on a nonprofit basis. However, the Victory Corporation had to be dissolved later in the year because the government objected to contracting with United on a nonprofit basis and other companies on a profit basis. In place of the Victory Corporation, United Air Lines set up a Military Transport Service on August 7, 1942. At this time, the Dayton-Anchorage flight was turned over to Northwest Airlines, releasing United crews for the still more urgent duty of flying the Pacific.

Five months later, on January 15, 1943, United crews were back in Alaska, flying another route out of Seattle. This emergency airway stretched over Vancouver Island to Ketchikan, Juneau, Yakutat, Cordova, and thence to Anchorage, from which it fanned out to the Aleutian Islands bases. Much of the flying was over open sea, skirting mountainous seacoasts in two-engine planes with few emergency air strips in between. The United pilots were allowed to fly inland behind the mountains by way of Prince George, Fort St. John, and Watson Lake—safer flying but a route that took two hours longer to reach Anchorage.

The Alaskan coastal run was surveyed by Captains John Hodgson and E. L. McMillan on January 15, 1943. After the first month of operation, the pilots reported that if they had a weather man to chart the storms between Seattle and Alaska, they could make the run (at least 90 per cent of the time) in two hops: from Seattle to Juneau or Whitehorse and thence to Anchorage. Whereupon Howard Hoffman, head of United's meteorology department at Portland, was shifted to Seattle to organize an amalgamated weather bureau known as AATMO (Alaska Air Transport Meteorological Office), consisting of government meteorologists and those working for the airlines operating in Alaska. Shortly after this office was set up, United stepped up its Alaska flights to two trips a day. The route was primarily an emergency feeder line for a task force assigned to oust the Japanese invaders from Kiska. When Kiska fell without a fight, the line was shut down and United crews concentrated on Operations Pacific. Despite the rugged terrain and the almost impossible flying weather, United planes completed over two million miles of flying in Alaska without serious mishaps or injury to a crew.

These millions of miles of Alaska flying were a training course for the still bigger military job, "Operations Pacific," first proposed by General H. H. George, head of the Air Transport Command, in

Washington in July, 1942. American forces, after being pushed almost to Australia by the Japanese South Pacific drive, were getting set to push back, hopping from island to island on the long and watery road to Japan. A lot of these dots in the Pacific were little more than coconut-fringed air strips; in fact, some of them, like Johnson Island, had to be lengthened to make adequate runways for the larger planes.

But wherever the fighting forces took a steppingstone, they wanted air transport the day the island was theirs, and sometimes before it was secured. The task outlined by General George was: flying an oceanic airline with one end in San Francisco and the other constantly changing. President Patterson accepted the job and agreed to start within forty days flying an 8269-mile overseas route entirely new to United's pilots, who were to operate strange equipment few of them had ever seen. The pilots got an idea of the scope of the hurry-up new run when they saw a schedule of the route, as long almost as all of the airways flown by the company on the mainland. It read: "San Francisco to Hickam Field, Honolulu, 2446 miles; Hickham to Canton Island, 1908 miles; Canton to Nandi, Fiji Islands, 1250 miles; Nandi to New Caledonia, 865 miles; New Caledonia to Amberly Field, near Brisbane, Australia, 1800 miles." Alternating points in the Pacific were Palmyra Island and Christmas Island.

The planes to be flown were fat-bellied Consolidated C-87s, a transport version of the lumbering bomber known as the Liberator. The more powerful and faster C-54s, which United had helped Douglas engineer, were unavailable except for Army Air Transport and Navy Air Transport operations. Even a spare C-87 on which to learn four-engine flying was out of the question at the moment. The twenty-five pilots and twenty-five co-pilots and other crew members chosen to fly "Ops-Pacific" were checked out at Boeing School in Oakland, where they concentrated on celestial navigation, dead-reckoning flying, radio code work, and meteorology. They also were briefed on use of Mae Wests, life rafts, emergency radio transmitters, just in case they had to ditch in the Pacific. The new crop of ninety-day-wonder navigators came largely from hurriedly trained ticket agents, clerks, accountants, and students from the Boeing School.

Most of the crews learned to fly the C-87s as they flew the new airway. The first C-87 was delivered on September 5. All twenty-five crews were checked out on it. Five more C-87s arrived at San Francisco Airport on September 23, and on that day Captain Jack O'Brien, veteran of the Alaskan operation, as were most of the other Ops-Pacific pilots, took off for Australia. It was an inauspicious start. Three hours out the crew undertook to pump fuel from the emergency tanks to the main tanks. The gauges showed "No Pressure," indicating no fuel. O'Brien decided to turn back while the turning was good. Before he reached San Francisco Airport, the gauges started working again. At the airport a check revealed plenty of fuel in the tanks. Somebody had neglected to warn O'Brien that on the C-87s the gauges worked sometimes, and sometimes they didn't. The captain took off again, and this time, as on subsequent trips, nobody worried about gauges. Then ten days later the plane was back from Australia after flying over 16,000 miles.

Unlike Operation Alaska, Ops-Pacific involved pioneering no new route. Pan American and ATC had already flown the run. So had Consairways, a subsidiary of Consolidated-Vultee Aircraft, set up to help get supplies to the MacArthur forces in the South Pacific in a hurry. The Pacific was smooth, good-weather flying most of the time. The main problem was finding the right dots in the Pacific when the other end of the airway was constantly moving. The enemy held many of the islands until the war ended, as American forces bypassed and isolated Japanese garrisons. The problem of the transport plane crews, after skirting these enemy strongholds, was to land on island airbases often in complete darkness, when lights were blacked out during enemy air-raid alarms.

Though the flying was easier, the work of the Ops-Pacific ground crews was infinitely more difficult. The company had to maintain its own ground crews at most of the destinations. After the long overseas flights, the planes needed careful checking and overhauling. Hangars and shops and living shelters had to be improvised in jungles or on coral atolls. Rain came down in cloudbursts, turning the sod ramps into quagmires. Crews pulled the planes to the edge of air strips and worked under the wings.

When Seely Hall, manager of Ops-Pacific, arrived in Townsville, Australia, with Bill Hoare, superintendent of maintenance, they found the ground crews squatting in a muddy tent city with no lights and no place to hang clothes or keep personal belongings. In the dark, dirty mess hall, meals had to be eaten standing up. The Australian commanding officer had ruled that he didn't want any civilians eating or sleeping in the same building with uniformed men. Hall managed to wangle three wooden barracks to house the ground crews. He billeted the flight crews in Townsville's one hotel. Five tents set up on the hard stand sheltered the shops, the office, the stockroom, the tools, and the clothing of the mechanics, who maintained a guard around the clock to keep equipment from disappearing.

About the time Townsville became livable, Ops-Pacific's destination hopped over to Nadzab Field in the Markham Valley of New Guinea. The field had three landing strips with no lighting facilities. The area was strewn with the wrecks of Japanese and American planes downed in battles preceding the paratroop landing which captured the valley from the Japanese. Here living quarters were three miles up the hillside, where the temperature was cooler but where the rains turned the road into gumbo. Freshets poured down through the tents during the rains. Where meat and vegetables had been plentiful in Australia, they were nonexistent in New Guinea. The crews learned to eat C rations and like them. Between rains, the bright equatorial sun beat down, hot and blinding. Crews, working in shorts, turned as brown as natives.

Seely Hall, checking his crews in Nadzab, found them bathing and washing their clothes in the nearby stream. When he asked what they wanted most from the mainland, they shouted in unison, "A washing machine!" On his return to San Francisco, Hall wangled a hand-powered washer and flew it out, along with two fir trees, in time for Christmas. By this time his men were in Biak on the western tip of New Guinea, a thousand miles nearer Japan. They set up the washing machine and everybody celebrated Christmas in clean clothes. The next day orders came to move to Guam.

Among other United contributions to Ops-Pacific was a clocklike schedule for overseas flying. The 8000-mile haul settled down to a routine with the hazards mainly on the ground. Hall was chief of the Pacific lift as vice-president in charge of United's western division, assisted by Ted Johnson, who had managed the Dayton to Anchorage lift. Hall had a genius for improvising, having helped pioneer Pacific Air Transport in its infant days as manager at Medford, Oregon. The trans-Pacific flight called for so much on-the-spot contriving that in order to spend more time in the Pacific with his men, Hall resigned the western division vice-presidency and devoted full time to scrounging shelters, shops, tools, food, and innumerable other necessities for crews.

He even shared their crashes. Hall and Bill Hoare were in a C-87 taking off from Townsville, Australia, for Port Moresby when the overloaded transport stalled at twenty feet above the ground and plunged and skidded half a mile on its belly, ending up, luckily, in a marsh, with nobody hurt. Other crews in other crashes of the lumbering flying boxcars were not so fortunate. One crashed near Canton Island with the loss of eighteen lives, and another at Auckland, New Zealand, with a loss of fifteen.

The Ops-Pacific pilots never learned to like the C-87 as bomber crews trusted the transport's sister plane, the Liberator. Consequently there were loud cheers on July 15, 1943, when the Army delivered the first C-54 to the United base in San Francisco. It was forerunner of an overseas fleet that established a remarkable record for dependable delivery of personnel, cargo, and materials all over the Pacific. It provided crews with the know-how that later made the San Francisco–Honolulu flight the gravy run for United's veteran pilots. Though most of the 7000 flights were routine, some were outstanding examples of how the war had stepped up the age of flight.

There was the remarkable flight of Captain Jack O'Brien, superintendent of Pacific flight operations, in one of the first C-54s. General George Kenney's Fifth Air Force, stationed at Port Moresby, needed a supply of stabilizers for the bombers operating from that base. Though these stabilizers weighed only 400 pounds, they were so cumbersome that a C-87 couldn't handle a load of them. So a C-54 was called out of the ATC Atlantic service and rushed to San Francisco, where O'Brien and Benny Howard, noted United—and, later, Douglas—test pilot, took over. Taking off at 12:05 A.M. on June 25, 1943, O'Brien and Howard averaged 226 miles per hour to Honolulu. After a fast refueling, they headed for Canton Island, from which they flew nonstop to Amberly Field near Brisbane, completing the 9000-mile trip from San Francisco in 39 hours. Actual flying time was 35 hours. With time out only for refueling, Captain O'Brien flew immediately to Port Moresby to deliver the stabilizers.

Another memorable flight was that of Captain Ralph Johnson with W. E. Rhoades as first officer and Emery Wishon as navigator. Johnson was flying one of two C-87s assigned to bring together an imposing array of top brass planning the big push north. He was located at Perth on the west coast of Australia when orders came to fly to Brisbane, 1960 miles away. The Australians were aghast when Johnson and Rhoades decided to save time by flying straight across the Australian bush country, where there were no emergency landing strips or even settlements. They made it, completing the flight in a little over twelve hours.

That winter "Dusty" Rhoades, by then a captain in his own right, drew one of the historic air transport assignments of the war. Rhoades was in San Francisco when he and his crew were ordered to fly in a C-54 nonstop to Washington, D.C., a trip they made in 10 hours 52 minutes. There Rhoades received secret flight orders from the Air Transport Command and took off with a load of mail and top-secret cargo, plus fourteen officials of the State Department from Washington for Miami, thence to Puerto Rico, Belem in Brazil, Natal, across the Atlantic to Dakar, Marrakech in Morocco, and finally Algiers, where the plane picked up Major General R. K. Sutherland, chief of staff for General Douglas MacArthur. The next day the plane was in Tunis, and on the following morning the party landed in Cairo, where the statesmen and military leaders joined in the top-flight conference held there by President Roosevelt, Winston Churchill, and Generalissimo Chiang Kai-shek.

After short flights out of Cairo to Lydia, Palestine, and Luxor in the Nile Valley, Rhoades continued east with mail, cargo, and passengers bound for India and Australia. When he reached San Francisco via New Caledonia, Fiji Islands, Canton Island, Honolulu, Dusty Rhoades had covered 31,380 miles in his 150 flying hours of globe-girdling. His C-54 had consumed 32,504 gallons of high-octane gasoline. The captain's prosaic report read, "All flights were completed in a routine manner and well within the allotted time without special mechanical or weather delays. The only romance encountered was that within our own imaginations."

Rhoades was wrong about the romance. His flying evidently impressed General MacArthur's Chief of Staff, General Sutherland, himself a pilot. Sutherland frequently relieved Rhoades at the wheel of the C-54. Shortly after his return from the trip, Rhoades was tagged for pilot of General MacArthur's famous plane, *The Bataan*. On leave from United for the rest of the war, Rhoades became a major, then a colonel, and flew the General on the historic hops which finally wound up in Tokyo on V-J Day. Mission 75 (the flight from Okinawa to Japan) found twelve other planes operated by United crews in the spectacular air armada that dropped out of the sky to occupy Nippon. The second plane to take wing was flown by Captain Ralph Johnson.

After V-J Day, the Air Transport Command released United crews rapidly to return to routine commercial operations on the mainland. ATC and NATS flight crews took over in the Pacific. But not for long. The speed with which the Air Force fliers shook their wings for civilian life left the military transport short of flying crews and maintenance men. General MacArthur voiced a vigorous protest because the troops in Japan were not receiving their mail promptly. On short notice, the ATC called the United crews back into a new trans-Pacific service, known as "Ops-Tokyo." Soon United was flying three round trips daily to Tokyo from San Francisco, a service that lasted until January 1, 1947. For a time this operation included eight round trips daily between San Francisco and Honolulu, and tied up seventy-five crews badly needed to fly the increased regular schedules on the mainland. To ease the pressure, United sub-contracted part of the flying to Pacific Overseas Airlines and Trans-Ocean Airlines, organized by veterans of the ATC and NATS. On January 15, 1947, United was able to turn over the Pacific flying entirely to the subcontractors and concentrate on commercial flying. During the five years of Ops-Pacific, United crews logged more than 37,300,000 air miles, transporting 156,000 military passengers, 17,000,000 pounds of cargo, and 18,000,000 pounds of mail. It was an experience that paid off well in the years that followed.

CHAPTER XI

Bedlam on the Airways

By V-J Day, when war ended with the spectacular mass flight of General MacArthur's occupation forces to Tokyo Airport on September 1, 1945, the age of flight had arrived. The momentous drive of the military effort had advanced public acceptance of the airplane as an everyday means of transportation by at least two decades. Prodded by insatiable "Hap" Arnold, aircraft builders had achieved miracles, delivering transport planes that could fly almost anywhere in almost any kind of weather. Both military and airline pilots had settled into the cockpits of these skyway vehicles and girdled the globe in all directions. This wealth of aeronautical know-how was one of the real gains from the devastating war.

Now, with the conflict ended, it was the air-minded public's turn to ride the newly conquered airways. The Air Force and the aircraft builders were not the least bit backward in publicizing their achievements, and air travel loomed most alluring to prospective air travelers. Where before the war it took four hops in a DC-3 to cross the country, the NATS "hotshot," as the Navy Air Transport Service called its cross-country flight for top brass, winged nonstop on regular nightly schedule from Moffet Field south of San Francisco to Washington, D.C. Where prior to the war, airline pilots had flown the beam, a 10-mile-wide dogleg aerial highway, listening in headphones for the dot-dash and dash-dot of the radio range to merge into a hum that indicated on-course flight, military transport pilots now flew around storms, aided by magic electronic eyes that peered through darkness and cloud, and by additional radar eyes on the ground that scanned the skies and guided homing planes back from perilous missions. Pressurized cabins, built into planes for substratospheric military operations, were forerunners of similarly equipped air transports soon to shuttle across continents and over oceans, detouring rough storm-front atmosphere. Speed of planes had doubled, their seating capacity had almost trebled, their range increased fourfold.

To Americans, afflicted as never before by wanderlust, it looked as though the golden age of travel had arrived. The airplane was here to stay. Planes were plentiful; in fact, the War Surplus Administration talked of planes to burn. Priorities were off. Nobody could be bumped off at Omaha or Toledo by a military personality packing a bulging briefcase. Pockets were full of dollars, which had been difficult to spend for anything worthwhile during wartime. The time had come to go places and see things—by air. In 1946, upward of 12,000,000 passengers tossed their dollars on the counter for airline tickets.

To their dismay, what the travel-hungry public found at the airports of the country was not the golden age of flight, but bedlam. Often it required eight to ten telephone calls to reach reservations, where a weary voice explained that the first flight on which seats were available was three weeks hence. The crowded waiting room at the terminal was a madhouse of scrambled passengers, luggage, families meeting arrivals, people seeking information, clerks who didn't know the answers, a confusion made even less appetizing by the blend of tobacco smoke, fumes from the quick lunch counter, smells from the dirty floors and still dirtier washrooms. Chicago Airport, across the street from United's new streamlined and functional executive headquarters, was described by *Fortune* magazine, after a survey of the nation's major air terminals, as follows:

Chicago is the worst; its airport is a slum. Chewing gum, orange peel, paper and cigar butts strew the floor around the stacks of baggage. Porters can't keep the floor clean if people are standing on it day and night. At almost all hours every telephone booth is filled, with people lined up outside; the dingy airport café is filled with standees. To rest the thousands there are exactly twenty-eight broken-down leather seats. One must line up even for the rest rooms. The weary travelers sit or even lie on the floor. The drooping grandmothers, the crying babies, the continuous, raucous, unintelligible squawk of the loudspeaker, the constant push and jostle of new arrivals and new baggage tangling inextricably with their predecessors, make bus terminals look like luxury. In such an atmosphere, the beat-up traveler, interminably waiting for some unexplained reason, has no recourse but to ponder bitterly on the brilliant advertisement that lured him with "Travel with the Easy Swiftness of the Homeward-Winging Birds."

If Chicago with its 1,300,000 passengers in 1946 was "the worst," New York's La Guardia with 2,100,000 passengers to handle was not much better, and conditions were intolerable all the way across the country to Los Angeles's Lockheed Terminal, with 760,000 patrons. Airports built to accommodate hundreds were jammed with thousands. Planes were late departing and still later arriving. Travelers missed connections and sweated it out, impatiently waiting at the gates, hoping for "no shows" whose seats they might inherit on the next flight. There were many "no shows," largely because patrons couldn't get a phone line into reservations to cancel flights. The "go shows," hopers waiting at the gate, became a recognized airline asset. *Fortune*'s diatribe against the airlines in August, 1946, was but one of many. The big question was, what caused the collapse of the air transport technique at the very time when the airlines had a travel bonanza within their grasp?

The answer appeared to be, "Everything at once." The airlines went into the war period as little business; after a phenomenal war record, they came out of it big business. While the industry mushroomed from little to big, many of the key figures who had built the airlines had been drafted into uniform to run ATC, NATS, and other military aviation services. These generals, colonels, and commanders, back at their desks in business suits, had everything to do at once, and they had to do it largely with inexperienced help. During the war, for example, United's payroll tripled to 13,000; worse yet, 1500 of the company's most vigorous young men were in the services. That meant three out of four employes either needed basic training or had to readjust from war thinking before they could become efficient workers. In a drastic move to stem the confusion, Patterson assigned a four-man emergency committee of vice-presidents to visit every United traffic center. "The Atomic Committee," as it was called out along the Main Line, had authority to hire, fire, overhaul schedules or procedures, and spend dollars to get results right now. This drastic treatment helped, but did not solve the problem.

An overdose of grandiose ideas on the part of airline management was one contributing factor to the postwar confusion. These expansive ideas had burst into a lively scramble for overseas routes. To most of the domestic airlines that flew overseas contracts for the Army and the Navy, the postwar transoceanic routes looked like the gravy in the business. Pilots had discovered that overseas flying was no trick at all; in fact, transoceanic service was actually easier than overland operations, with longer flights, not so many landings, smoother flying, fewer ground crews, nothing but long-haul fares. Most of the operators with overseas contract flying experience, and some without it, laid plans to get into the international game as soon as possible after hostilities ceased. At least six of them coveted the trans-Atlantic run, five wanted to fly the Pacific, and several looked enviously toward Latin America, where United had already taken under its wing a struggling Mexican airline, known as LAMSA.

At first blush, the overseas service did look like an airmen's bonanza. But United's statisticians, under Vice-president Hal Nourse, had detected a dark lining in the silvery cloud. Taking an outstanding prewar travel year, 1930, as an index, Nourse projected what the trans-Atlantic traffic would amount to if all the first-class passengers booked on ocean liners could by some hocus-pocus be persuaded to switch to plane travel. The figures revealed that when the ultramodern new airliners projected for postwar oceanic travel were in service, a fleet of fifty planes could handle the entire volume of first-class passenger traffic across the Atlantic. Dividing this improbable potential among the eight nations that proposed to operate airlines meant that fewer than six planes per nation could do the carrying.

On the basis of this crystal gazing, Patterson concluded that United should keep its planes and pilots on the home airways when the war ended.

United's south-of-the-border venture dated from September, 1943, when, at the request of the Mexican government, Patterson made a survey of the struggling Lineas Aereas Mineras, S.A., founded and flown originally by a Yankee adventurer, Gordon S. Berry. The line was launched primarily to fly valuable minerals from remote mines in the rugged interior, and had grown, Topsy-like, into a 1500-mile airline with headquarters at Torreón. It connected a dozen sizable communities, from Nogales on the north to Mexico City on the south, and from Mazatlán on the west coast to Laredo on the Gulf of Mexico. In 1943, LAMSA needed money in a hurry. Its operation was considered important to Mexico's role in the war.

Patterson first loaned the little airline $250,000 out of United's reserves, then helped reorganize the company as Lineas Aereas Mexicanas, S.A. LAMSA's traffic grew, and its prospects were better. From time to time, it needed a shot of capital, and United added to its investment until the quarter million grew eventually to $5,000,000. Somehow the Mexican government never got around to taking over LAMSA, as had been originally planned, nor did the CAB get around to granting a certificate of convenience for a connection with United's domestic routes at San Diego or Los Angeles. Not until 1952 was United able to let go of its south-of-the-border subsidiary. By that time LAMSA operated a fleet of seven DC-3s and had 500 employees. It was eventually purchased by a newly organized Mexican company, Lineas Asociadas Mexicanas, S.A.

The veteran of the intriguing international game, of course, was Pan American Airways, whose astute and wily president, Juan T. Trippe, starting on a small scale in the Caribbean in 1927, had forged a global network, at first flying seaplanes over oceans and landplanes over continents. Pan American, incidentally, was one of the new aviation risks into which Frederick B. Rentschler poured United Aircraft & Transport dollars. Before the war, "Pan Am" had pioneered trans-Pacific flights to Hong Kong and to New Zealand with Sikorsky flying boats, built by a United subsidiary and powered by Pratt & Whitney engines. Pan Am was the first private operator put under contract by the Air Force to fly the 8000-mile South Pacific run with landplanes.

Ubiquitous Juan Trippe, a diplomat of the first water as well as a top-flight airline operator, knew from firsthand experience that if United States airlines were to have landing rights on foreign soil, the planes of foreign nations must have reciprocal rights at United States airports. Trippe foresaw that not only the planes of the British, the French, the Canadians, the Scandinavians, and the

Dutch would be in the international airline business, but the Belgians, the Brazilians, the Colombians, the Chinese, the Filipinos, the Australians, and the Germans, Italians and Japanese as well would want to be in the scramble, too, to mention only some of the potential competitors in a domain that Pan Am had once held largely to itself. More ominous yet, the foreign competitors would be government airlines with state money behind them. Pan American had been generously subsidized by the Post Office, and on some routes foreign governments had helped out with mail payments which would go to their own airlines in the future. If the United States subsidy were spread among the several United States–owned airlines that aspired to compete against a dozen state-owned foreign lines for this overseas business, Trippe could see only ruin for the industry.

To meet the bugaboo before it caught up with him, Trippe came up with a device which he called the "chosen instrument." He proposed a United States air transport cartel in which all airlines with overseas ambitions could join in proportion to the amount of capital they wished to invest in the cooperative. Pan American, the big wheel with the most experience and established contacts abroad, would operate the overseas giant while the rest of the partners would feed it business and share in the profits of the United States flag international air transport.

A howl of "Monopoly!" arose from the industry when Trippe presented his chosen instrument plan to the Civil Aeronautics Board. Under the Civil Aeronautics Act of 1938, it was up to the CAB to recommend what United States airlines should have overseas routes, albeit only the President could authorize operations. Sixteen domestic airlines drew up a counter-proposal for the CAB, urging that they be allowed to compete for overseas business as they battled for passengers in their respective territories. When this declaration of policy was submitted to United Air Lines for W. A. Patterson's signature, he refused to sign it, arguing that the overseas traffic just didn't exist for several competing American companies and for foreign competitors, too. Patterson came out in favor of the "chosen instrument" idea.

For breaking ranks with his domestic rivals, Patterson soon

found himself at odds with the entire industry. Denounced as "a stooge for Juan Trippe," he was soon at loggerheads with Pan American, too. Airlines projected new airways to nearly everywhere. United applied for routes to Alaska and Hawaii, operations that United pilots and ground crews knew first-hand from wartime operations, and which were domestic, even if they did call for overseas flying. The Alaska run was denied, but in due course the CAB granted United the right to fly to Hawaii, first from San Francisco, later from Los Angeles as well.

After the domestic airlines invaded the foreign field, Trippe, as a counter-measure, applied for the right to fly Pan American passengers from points of entry to points of exit, such as San Francisco to New York. Since this would have skimmed the cream off the coast-to-coast operations of domestic airlines, especially United, Patterson soon found himself teamed up with the rival airline presidents who had branded him a "stooge," this time fighting the so-called "Juan Trippe steal."

The Patterson-Trippe relationship was a paradox. As other airlines extended their routes across the Atlantic, into Latin America, to Alaska and the Orient, it was natural that Pan American should feed traffic to United whenever possible and that United should reciprocate. In Hawaii, on the other hand, United's flights soon captured a substantial share of the traffic that had been a Pan American monopoly, and when Los Angeles as well as San Francisco became United bases for Hawaii flights, United passed Pan Am in volume of traffic between the mainland and the Islands.

Shortly after the war ended, the Army and Navy, by Executive Order from the White House, turned over thousands of planes to a new agency, the War Assets Administration, which was authorized to dispose of them in any way it could. Bombers, fighters, trainers, and transports were stacked up at Army air strips, where anyone, but veterans preferred, could buy them for a tenth of their cost, or even less. Hundreds of veterans took advantage of the offer. Some bought planes so cheap they made a profit by merely selling the fuel in the tanks and the instruments off the panels. Others, veterans of the Air Force, set up inexpensive charter flying services. They flew cargoes from anywhere to anywhere, and passengers, too, at cut rates, sometimes barely half those allowed by the CAB for airlines offering transportation over identical routes. Though the CAB had authority to cope with the wildcat airlines flying interstate, it did not exercise its powers. The "non-skeds" were so called because their planes flew at irregular departure times, to avoid being classified as airlines subject to airline regulations. The non-skeds could shift from summer operations in the northern part of the country to winter operations in the south. Where United's fare, requiring approval of the CAB, was $157.85, plus taxes, for the flight from San Francisco to New York, the non-skeds hauled passengers in war surplus planes, operated under different standards, for $88. This new, unregulated competition added to the confusion on the airways.

The new non-sked competition was even more trying in the freight end of air transport. As early as 1940, United had pioneered "flying freight cars," which carried only freight, express, and mail. Toward the end of the war when the Army returned DC-3s that had been in military service, Cargoliner service was launched on regular schedule. At the time, high priority passengers were crowding even the mail bags off the planes, and air mail was piling up at terminals. Postal authorities wanted it moved. So, when the DC-3 transports came home, the seats were left out. Without seats, priority holders could not displace cargo. Daily and nightly all-cargo flights soon had the air mail moving on time. There was extra space in the Cargoliners, and to fill it the company established an air freight department, with special agents in larger centers to hustle business. In cooperation with shippers, the Cargoliners flew fresh fruit and vegetables from California to the eastern markets. They brought clothing, pharmaceutical instruments, and high priority machinery back. The cargo business grew rapidly. Then the non-skeds moved in to skim off the cream. Where United had to fly regular schedules, the non-skeds hopped from city to city, picking up payloads at reduced rates, then switching to another route, wherever the contract flying brought in more dollars. Their hop-skip operations added more to the chaos on the airways.

The non-skeds also put an added burden on the already over-

After a decade in downtown Chicago, United's executive headquarters in 1938 were moved to this functional building across the street from the city's Midway Airport.

Model of new executive offices opened in 1961 near Chicago's O'Hare International Airport. Building contains 373,000 square feet of usable space compared with only 80,000 square feet at Midway; a new wing now under construction will add another 100,000 square feet.

At the Denver Operating Base, opened in 1948, United experts kept 24-hour watch on all the big and little details that go into an airline's daily performance. Representing a new concept in centralized airline control, OPB attracted visitors from all over the world.

"Heart" of the Denver base was this briefing room at which heads of all operating units reported on and reviewed the past 24 hours' record and prospects for the current 24 hours.

The world's largest concentration of electronic flight simulators is found at United's Denver Flight Training Center. Such machines realistically duplicate the flying performance of Mainliners without ever leaving the ground. Above: A DC-6B simulator showing instructors and "trouble panels" in aft section. Below: A DC-8 jet simulator with TV device added to project runway pattern in front of crew on simulated take-offs and landings.

Tempting meals for service aloft are prepared in United's fifteen flight kitchens. Shown here is a casserole (entree) assembly line at the Chicago O'Hare kitchen.

taxed big city airports. During the war few cities had been able to extend their air strips or improve the navigational aids or build new passenger buildings. Air traffic had trebled at many airports, but the authorities were getting along with the same old facilities. While the jam-up of traffic was bad inside the terminals, it was far more serious above them in rough flying weather. The 10-mile wide airways strips converged on major airports like the ribs of a spider web. Airliners still eased down through the overcast on the old prewar system. In low ceilings, maneuvering to make the final approach required from six to twenty minutes. This meant that at best only ten planes an hour could land, and sometimes only three or four an hour reached the runway. The rest were "in stacks," slowly flying figure eights over other fix points established by Federal CAA traffic control men. The planes, cruising in their soupy purgatory, were stacked every 1000 feet up to the 8000-foot elevation. At each swing over the fix point, the pilot dropped his plane 1000 feet. At the bottom of the stack, he was pulled in, unless some plane above developed engine trouble or ran short of fuel and had to be pulled in first, which was of course an added hazard.

Sweating it out in the stacks activated old ulcers in nervous passengers. There were times over La Guardia Airport when planes flew in two to four separate stacks for hours, and other times when they were sent to alternate airports a hundred miles distant. Passengers with appointments in New York found themselves in Boston or Washington or Philadelphia. When they caught trains to their destination, they vowed they would stay on the rails. This dislocation of traffic threw planes off schedule for a thousand miles in all directions. In one day, 400 passengers on a single airline were dumped at alternate airports, at a loss of $6000 for the line.

The irony of it was that electronics equipment and the skill to use it were available to cope with these traffic pile-ups in bad weather. The Army and the Navy had used two systems, known as ILS and GCA, to bring home thousands of pilots returning from military missions. ILS, the Instrument Landing System, utilizing a glide path, a localizer beam, and fan markers, had been approved by the CAA, which proposed to install the necessary equipment at fifty major airports. All a pilot had to do was synchronize two cross markers on an electronic dial before him to follow the ILS beam down to the runway. But the Air Transport Association, which appropriated $300,000 for a study of bad weather landing problems, wanted additional installation of locater stations.

Opposing the ILS method was a "radar eye" known as GCA, or Ground Control Approach, used successfully by the Army and Navy air forces. GCA's revolving eye scanned the skies, picked up approaching planes on the radar scope, through fog or darkness, and "talked the pilot in" without delay until he was in position to drop his wheels on the end of the runway. Military pilots liked the system, but airline pilots distrusted being talked in. While the controversy raged over the relative merits of the two systems, until someone had the happy thought of using both, one to check the other, pilots and passengers sweated their way down through stacks.

Meantime, the war of the airliners raged anew. It was the old 1934 battle for speed all over again, this time on a coast-to-coast scale. The partnership agreement for the development of the DC-4 had fallen apart when the military forces preempted the four-engine transport. During the war TWA had lost its Stratoliners to the Navy, and Howard Hughes, who had gained control of the line, backed the Lockheed Aircraft factory in the development of a larger, faster, high flying pressurized airliner, the Constellation. This, too, became a military project. The first of these flying porpoises were built for the Army, to speed high brass, statesmen, and administrators around the globe. They were the first 300-mile-per-hour transports. The war ended before many of them were delivered to the Army, and TWA, under an agreement with the factory that they were not to be sold to competitive transcontinental lines, took delivery as soon as the military versions could be converted for commercial flight. Later Eastern Air Lines and several foreign lines were allowed to equip themselves with Constellations. Meantime, Douglas was developing for United and other airlines its postwar luxury airliner—the 300-mile-an-hour, pressurized, long-range, high-altitude DC-6.

The 300-mile-per-hour planes gave TWA a great competitive advantage over rivals still flying the 180-mile-per-hour DC-3s. It soon became evident that the DC-6 fleet would be a year, possibly two, in the making. In desperation, United bought surplus military DC-4s, as did American and other airlines. They could be picked up at the bargain price of $90,000. Conversion costs ran an extra $200,000 per plane, and required ninety days in the Douglas plant, more time than it had taken to build them in the first place.

At this point, a coast-to-coast passenger had this choice: he could fly in a 300-mile-per-hour TWA Connie in 11 hours across country; he could take a United or American 230-mile-per-hour DC-4 Mainliner and do it in 14 hours. This happy picture for TWA changed almost overnight. Two crashes of Constellations, for reasons unexplained, led the CAA to ground TWA's fleet while the plane builders, the airline, and the government inspectors hunted for causes of the accidents. United and American, which by this time had delivery of the interim fleet of DC-4s, were flying high once more.

They, too, were riding for a fall. Late in 1946 Douglas delivered the first three DC-6s to United. Patterson, determined to avoid at all costs a grounding such as TWA's, instructed his pilots to fly the new planes for three months without passengers, while they familiarized themselves with the craft and worked out any flaws. The three luxurious new Mainliners rode out storms that forced DC-4s to turn back, and flew more than 600,000 miles in their test flights. On March 28, 1947, one flight of a DC-6, with a helpful tailwind, cut the Los Angeles–New York record to 6 hours 47 minutes 13 seconds. In April and May, 1947, the first eight DC-6s went into service on United's coast-to-coast and Hawaiian runs. American Airlines had them too, and TWA's Constellations were back on the wing. Once more the Big Three were neck and neck in speeding passengers across the continent.

Then in October, catastrophe struck. A United DC-6 caught fire over Bryce Canyon, Utah, and crashed, with the loss of fifty-two lives. The cause of the fire was an unexplained mystery to the airline, the Douglas engineers, and government technicians, who swarmed over the wreckage, scattered for many miles, seeking clues to the disaster. The first reliable tip came a few days later when an American DC-6 was forced down over Gallup, New Mexico, by a similar fire. This time the blaze was extinguished and there were no casualties. The plane was intact. Engineers and inspectors pieced together what had happened on both planes. The fires had broken out while pilots were transferring fuel from alternate tanks to the main tanks. During the transfer gasoline vapors were sucked in through an air-intake in the belly of the fuselage and were ignited by the heating system. Other pilots had made similar fuel changes hundreds of times.

From Chicago Patterson called American Airlines' operating executives. The two airlines voluntarily grounded their DC-6s until they could be modified to prevent such fires in the future. While the $20,000,000 new fleet was on the ground, United made other extensive modifications to bring the luxury liners, fresh out of the factory, up to date. The bad break put TWA once more in the top-dog position. It was an expensive grounding, tying up the DC-6s for months. The loss of revenue to United during this period plus the expense of flying substitute equipment with a higher per ton-mile operating cost resulted in a total dollar loss of about $4,750,000 and plunged the company into the red. It was spring of 1948 before the DC-6 fleet could begin taking to the air again.

The Bryce Canyon catastrophe was the culmination of a series of airline crashes all over the world that frightened travelers by the thousands off the airlines. The nightmare began in 1946, when an American Overseas DC-4 rammed into a Newfoundland mountain. Then an American Airlines DC-3 hit a peak near San Diego. Western Air Lines had two crashes in Southern California. Abroad, the Belgian Sabena, the Dutch KLM, and Air France also experienced fatal crashes. To cap the bad luck, Chinese transport lines cracked up three planes in one day. United had two non-fatal accidents, followed by a DC-3 crash near Laramie in which all aboard were lost, ending a 1,700,000,000 passenger-mile record without a fatality. Intimidated by the frightening crash headlines of the newspapers, passengers turned in their tickets or failed to buy them at all. After turning in a $1,200,000 profit in September and October, United lost $1,000,000 in the next two months. The traffic was slow in coming back. Other airlines faced losses equally serious. American lost $1,000,000; Western Air Lines, flying high earlier in the year, came near cracking up financially. The postwar period of confusion had become so acute that early in 1947 the President appointed an Air Policy Committee to survey the situation and find out, if possible, what had made the lusty wartime industry so sick it could barely stay aloft on its own wings.

An interesting sidelight on the period was that Patterson, who two years before had been warning the industry against an over-expansion when literally millions were fighting for seats on planes, now became the optimist among the airline heads. At a time when traffic was falling off, he set the 1947 sales goal at $93,000,000. While most airlines were curtailing operations and canceling orders for new planes, Patterson was in the midst of a $49,500,000 financing program to pay for a new fleet of twenty DC-6s, seven double-deck Boeing Stratocruisers costing $1,750,000 apiece, and fifty high-speed pressurized Martin 3-0-3s for fast short-haul services; for a new Operations Base at Denver and for enlargement of the maintenance base at San Francisco.

"Why am I so optimistic concerning the ultimate future of air transportation?" asked Patterson, who answered his own question. "It is because now, as a result of wartime development, we are getting the specific facilities which offer for the first time a potential dependability and regularity of service regardless of weather that will compare with surface transportation.

"The big question now is: Are we going to look at our own mistakes and go back and correct them, or are we going to continue to ask the Civil Aeronautics Board to give us something else we think we may want which may possibly remedy earlier mistakes? This might be only a case of piling mistake on mistake, and lead to final chaos in the industry.

"The period we are now passing through is a day of reckoning. False impressions were created by war operations, including the mistaken idea that we could expect unreserved public acceptance before we could complete perfection of our product. We can look at this experience in a way as the most fortunate occurrence. The public can be assured that airline management will be more realistic in considering the immediate problems and in correcting the mistakes of the past. Rather than view this shake-down period with pessimism, I look upon it as an experience that will make air transportation stronger and greater than any of our earlier expectations."

Appearing before the President's Air Policy Committee in September of 1947, Patterson urged that the CAB freeze all applications for route extensions until its program of increasing competition could be re-examined. He also urged the Committee to examine the airways map of the country and see if consolidations, rather than extensions, might not be the answer to many of the airlines' troubles. Very little came of these suggestions or those from other airline heads. Neither the Air Policy Committee nor the CAB could put a finger on the cure for the chaos on the airways.

Before the CAB or any other Federal agency could do much overhauling of the air transport system, the people on the airlines, by a combination of technological wizardry and know-how derived from hard knocks, pulled themselves out of postwar turmoil.

CHAPTER XII

People Make an Airline

In 1933, shortly after W. A. Patterson assumed the vice-presidency of the United Air Lines management company, the directors decided to merge Varney Air Lines, purchased three years before, into Boeing Air Transport, of which Patterson was also president. Merging the properties was simple. Welding the Varney employes into the Boeing organization was something else again, although neither airline had a large payroll. Having an insatiable interest in people, Patterson decided to fly west and oversee the human side of the merger personally. Arriving at the Boeing headquarters in Seattle, he found that the job was almost completed—on paper. The superintendent under whom the Varney line was to be operated handed him a list of Varney employes to be retained and those to be let go. Patterson looked over the list and noted that more Varney people were to be let out than were to be absorbed into Boeing.

"Wait a minute," he said. "We paid two million dollars for Varney Air Lines. The people on an airline are its most valuable assets. These people must be worth something."

"We don't need them," argued the superintendent.

"Well, I'd like to talk with each man before you let him go," insisted Patterson.

Flying the new Boeing Seattle–Salt Lake run, the old Varney route, he talked with all the Varney employes and found jobs for most of them in the United system. Typical of his talks was one with a publicity man, Hal E. Nourse, a former schoolteacher who had given up his teaching to join Varney because he thought there was a great future in the airline business. He was shunted into publicity without previous experience, because that happened to be the only opening at the time.

"What do you know about statistics?" Patterson asked the slight, scholarly Nourse.

"Practically nothing," he replied.

"Neither do I," said Patterson. "Let's learn the game together. I need a statistician in Chicago to dig up facts about this hectic business."

In Chicago, Nourse proved to be a wizard at digging up and organizing facts and figures. Before long, he was head of a staff that could produce sound, factual answers to almost any airline problem. In 1945, Nourse was elected vice-president (in 1958, senior vice-president) of economic controls, a department which Patterson credits with saving United many millions of dollars, particularly in the postwar period when most airlines were diving off the deep end financially to launch new routes and to buy new fleets for mythical traffic that never became a reality. It was Nourse's analysis that persuaded Patterson to count United out of the scramble for overseas traffic, except for the Hawaii run.

Patterson often cites the discovery of Nourse, a misplaced top-flight man on the Varney payroll, as an example of how people make an airline if they can be connected with the right work. Nearly every employe in a position of responsibility in the United scheme of things is someone Patterson or some other executive found out on the line. "Promote from within," adopted early as standard United personnel policy, has continued in effect to the present day. Thus, in 1959, for example, nearly 2,000 United employes—about one out of every ten—earned some sort of job promotion. Ninety per cent of the company's top management people today began their careers "at the bottom" in company offices, maintenance and overhaul shops, or "on the ramp," airline jargon for activities at an airport. The other 10 per cent, generally speaking, are doctors, lawyers, or other professional types employed as highly trained specialists.

"United's most valuable asset doesn't show on the annual statement at all," Patterson has often pointed out. "In the air transport business more than in any other, the human element is everything. That big plane in front of the hangar is only as good as the man who flies it, and he is only as good as the people on the ground who work with him."

Another Patterson axiom is that he has learned the airline business from the people running the airline. Patterson began learning from people long before he was catapulted into the presidency of the United Air Lines Transport Company by the air mail cancellation and the White House purge of the company's older heads. His major task, once the air mail contracts were recaptured, was to merge National Air Transport, Boeing Air Transport, and Pacific Air Transport into one unified system. NAT had already absorbed Stout Air Services, but the big problem was that of the Boeing-Varney merger all over again, on a much larger scale. It was easy for the lawyers and the financiers to join the corporations, and for the operating men to consolidate the fleets. Blending the personnel of five quite different pioneer airlines, three of which had continued to function as independent entities, into one congenial team called for greater understanding.

Full of vim and only thirty-four, the new president decided to cover the entire system, meet everybody on the payroll, and appraise United's human assets for himself. This wasn't as formidable a job as it appears now. Although United was the world's largest airline after the merger, the company employed only 1400 people. Having come up through Boeing via PAT, and knowing the human assets of the western end of the system better, Patterson started out with NAT, whose people he didn't know. It was a good thing he did. He soon uncovered an incipient strike of pilots on NAT. The fliers wanted more money, and above all better working conditions. Though the pilots were the fair-haired employes of the airline, they still worked under rules handed down from the era when the Post Office operated the airline. When pilots failed to fly because of bad weather, for instance, their pay stopped. This, too, was a holdover from the Post Office tradition that the mails had to go through regardless. But there was entirely new emphasis now that the pilots were responsible for the lives of passengers in the cabin behind the cockpit.

In New York one November evening, Patterson received a telephone call from Newark airport. A pilot wanted to know if he would come out and talk things over with three United veterans who had flown since the Post Office air mail days.

"Sure I will," Patterson replied. "I'll be right out."

The session lasted all night. The pilots recounted how they had helped NAT get on the wing, and what was wrong with the airline in general. It was almost sunrise before the meeting broke up. By that time Patterson was sleepy, but his eyes had been opened.

"Well, I think you are 90 per cent right and the company is 90 per cent wrong," he said. "Call off your strike threat and I will cover the whole United system and talk with every pilot and copilot we employ. We will settle every grievance right on the spot."

The pilots agreed and Patterson kept his word. It took two months to cover the route and talk to the fliers. When he returned to Chicago, there was a new spirit on the line and he had a hatful of new ideas. One of them was that he would never again be guided by hard-boiled older heads who counseled against letting employes tell him how to run the business. Instead, he planned four more months out on the line, listening to other groups of employes on the ground.

Patterson spent more than half of his first year as president and over half of the six years that followed talking with people on the system. They included everybody from janitors to superintendents, and they had plenty of ideas. Some were on the beam and some were not. Many of the better suggestions have flowered into standard airline procedures, safety practices such as guaranteed base pay for pilots whether they fly or not, special fares to induce wives to fly with husbands, flying around or over the weather, to mention only a few.

As late as 1945, Patterson made it a practice to try to see every United employe at least once a year. Thereafter, his program overwhelmed him. The United family had grown too numerous, for one thing. Contract flying for the Army and other war assignments which zoomed United's payroll to 13,000 in 1947 made personal contacts with everybody impossible.

Meantime, a lot of good ideas that matured into the airline's unique industrial relations setup had come out of the personal touch with the United family. One was the Personnel Department, started in 1935. Prior to that date, the airlines had been too busy growing up to pay much attention to organized personnel work. More young people wanted to get into the glamorous new game than the operators wanted to employ anyway, and they were willing to work for low wages to get a toehold in the business. In the early thirties, personnel departments were usually for hiring and firing purposes, and the various superintendents could easily handle this duty for the airways. The United Personnel Department was something quite different.

On one of his "meet the people" junkets over the system, Patterson was impressed with a young business hustler in the San Francisco office, Russ F. Ahrens, who seemed to know all about everybody in the Pacific division. Ahrens had joined Boeing Air Transport just before Patterson did. He was one of the bright young men eager to get into the air transport business on any terms. Ahrens and his bride were bursting with pride when he landed a job with Boeing Air Transport. Their pride was short-lived. On the day he reported for duty, Ahrens was handed a bucket of paste, a brush, a roller, and a bundle of "Deposit Air Mail Here" stickers and told to paste them on every mail box in the San Francisco Bay region.

"Better put on some old overalls and save your suit," his superior advised.

Ahrens took quite a joshing when friends spotted him in his overalls, slapping stickers on downtown San Francisco mail boxes. But the thoroughness and zest with which he did the job convinced his bosses he was not only a sticker but a comer. They assigned him to sales—in San Francisco, in Seattle, and, finally, in Chicago. In 1942, Patterson named him director of personnel. He became vice-president of personnel in 1945, senior vice-president in 1958.

United's personnel project was unique in several ways. It not only handled the employment of new people and the upgrading of older employes, few of them as yet out of their thirties, to better jobs, but it undertook to keep up-to-date on a lot of things about United workers that are ordinarily considered none of the employer's business. After his talks with people on the line, Patterson had made it a practice to jot down personal items about them, how many children they had, anniversaries, illnesses, or anything that was of concern to the individual. A gregarious character with a gift for getting on easy first-name terms with anyone in short order, Patterson usually started his visits with groups at hangars, in shops, at traffic offices, with:

"I have some company problems that I want to talk over with you, but let's start on yours first. They are just as important as the company's."

On his return to Chicago, Patterson opened his notebook and dictated memoranda about people he had talked with, their families, and their problems. One of the duties of the Personnel Department was to follow up on this start at knowing the United family and to systematize the information. Personnel soon had a grapevine working over the system that reported in when United people were in trouble or financial difficulty, when babies were born, when there were illnesses or deaths in the family, when an old-timer was celebrating an anniversary, either a wedding anniversary or the tenth anniversary with the company. Over the years this grew into one of the most complete and up-to-date funds of information about employes gathered by any company, either in or out of the airline industry.

This live information was put to use every day. At the start, Personnel put a recap of vital statistics about people on the line on Patterson's desk every morning. To the mother of a new baby, his office then sent flowers; to the baby, a United baby blanket. To the bereaved, he wrote a letter or sent a telegram. An employe reported ill or in an accident received a wire or a phone call asking what United could do to help. Anniversaries were remembered with telegrams, letters, or phone calls.

By the 1950s, United's employe "family" had grown so large that Patterson could not keep up the personal touch by himself. Personnel, through its headquarters office at Chicago and its regional offices at New York, Chicago, Denver, Los Angeles, San

Francisco, and Seattle, had to take over—keeping abreast of and recognizing appropriately new births, illnesses or accidents, marriages, deaths, retirements. Much of the news turned up in this constant "census" still goes to Patterson's desk.

"I keep asking myself, 'What kind of a person is United Air Lines?' " he says. "A man who devotes the best years of his life to United is entitled to the assurance that the company, next to his family, is his best friend in time of need. With most people, it is the human and personal touch that counts."

The policy has paid intangible dividends in ways that Patterson never anticipated. In 1938, for instance, when the management was hard-pressed to make ends meet financially following a series of airliner crashes that frightened passengers out of the air, two pilots came to see Patterson at his office. They said they had canvassed the flying crews up and down the line and found that the pilots were willing to take a 10 per cent cut in wages to help the company over the hump. The proposed wage cut would have saved about $800,000 a year. Instead, Patterson suggested a campaign against waste on the system. The pilots put on a drive that saved $185,000 in the quarter that followed.

Another intangible was that as union labor moved in to organize some 56 per cent of United's people during the war expansion era, the organizers made little headway with the customary "hate the boss" strategy, because nobody could say anything very bad about the company at union meetings without being challenged by someone who had been remembered by the company at some time when it meant a lot.

As a result, United's relationship with the eight unions with which it soon held eleven contracts was unusually amicable. Occasionally, labor leaders objected to the company's personal interest in employes as an infringement on the union's province. Now and then an employe resented it, too, as an invasion of his private life. The vast majority, however, liked to have the company for a friend, particularly when the grapevine reports enabled the management to do something in time of need.

Typical was the old-time pilot who, as flying became more scientific, was unable to pass the periodic pilots' examination. Personnel found a spot for him as dispatcher, as it has found jobs for others who have had to quit the cockpit. The new job involved a decrease in wages. The ex-pilot remarked one day to a fellow worker that he was about to lose an orange grove he had started to buy for his retirement days because he couldn't meet the payments on the mortgage. In a short time the Personnel grapevine reported the pilot's predicament to Patterson's office. Calling the ex-pilot, Patterson said:

"I think it is the company's responsibility to see that you don't lose the investment you made as a pilot. Tell me how much you need, and the company will lend you the money to handle the mortgage."

Another pilot, on leave to fly for the Army, was working with a power saw in his home shop when he cut off two fingers. Realizing that the accident, which might cost the pilot his CAA transport license, would loom as a major nightmare for his family, Patterson called long distance from Chicago to San Francisco. The victim was still in the hospital, so he talked with his wife.

"This is Pat Patterson," he said. "I want to tell you that if the accident should interfere with Jack's flying, we'll have another job for him."

The pilot's wife broke down and cried. A few days later in came a heartfelt letter from Jack Gillespie, telling how the call had lifted a fog of worry for the family. Fortunately, Captain Gillespie was able to resume his flying.

Patterson's idea is that the company is the best friend not only of the employe but of his family as well. On a number of occasions, following the deaths of veteran employes, the company paid the cost of training their widows for positions with the company.

In the fast-changing airline industry, with new techniques evolving overnight, hundreds of people have had to go to school, sometimes periodically, or sometimes, as in the case of pilots, almost continuously to keep from falling behind the procession. During the first decade and a half of its corporate existence, United Air Lines invested over $2,000,000 in training and upgrading its people.

"The best investment we ever made," Patterson has called it, "and one that has given us a staff with not only technical know-how but seasoned by years of experience on the line."

In his early visits to the shops along the line, Patterson was amazed to find that some of the foremen were far more concerned about the efficiency and appearance of machines than of men. It was the common practice to dock employes when they failed to come to work because of illness. When he authorized full-time sick leave pay, Patterson was warned that it would cost the company $10,000 per month.

"It's worth it," he replied. Actually it cost one-fifth that much and paid big dividends in good will.

In 1941, Patterson launched the first pension program set up by any airline. It was a voluntary program underwritten by two big insurance companies, Connecticut General and John Hancock, jointly, and available to flight crews and women employes at age twenty-five or older; to all other employes at thirty or older. Normal retirement age for pilots is sixty; for women, sixty-two; for other employes, sixty-five.

The plan, as originally established, provided for a fixed annuity payable upon retirement. Later (in 1955 and 1957, respectively) two revised plans were adopted for and by pilots and salaried nonunion personnel. The revised plans had two sections—a fixed benefit at retirement providing a guaranteed monthly income and a variable benefit which added a further monthly payment, the amount of which changed with the current value of the common stocks in which contributions to this part of the plan were invested. Together they assured a monthly retirement income with a built-in hedge against the effects of inflation.

Both company and employe contributions finance all three plans. From 1941 to 1961, United had contributed upwards of $43,650,000 while the more than 13,000 employes participating as of the latter date had paid in $38,500,000. More than 85 per cent of all eligible employes were signed up for one of the plans as the program neared its twentieth anniversary (94.2 per cent of all eligible pilots; 85.4 per cent of salaried nonunion personnel and 83.3 per cent of all others). In the first twenty years of the pension plan, 280 employes retired under the plan. In the 1960–1970 decade, 1150 more UALers will join the group.

Returning from one of his early scouting expeditions over the eastern leg of the United system, Patterson fell into conversation with a young co-pilot who was outspoken in his unorthodox ideas. The co-pilot pointed out that the cost of living varied at different communities along the system, and United people who were moved from one station to another frequently found themselves worse off after a promotion involving a move. This struck Patterson as a fair grievance. Before long the co-pilot found himself with a special detail, making periodic cost-of-living surveys in the major United centers, so the company could keep pace, wage-wise.

While Patterson was an apostle of pensions, sick benefit pay, guaranteed income for pilots, "best friend" treatment for employes, he was, paradoxically, dead set against a company-sponsored athletic department, company dances and picnics, Christmas turkeys, and employe welfare activities that he calls "artificial propaganda." His great fear was that the airline would be accused of paternalism. When such activities originated spontaneously with employes, however, Patterson approved them wholeheartedly. Thus numerous employe-organized Mainliner Clubs and Management Clubs soon sprang up on the United system, sponsoring a variety of sports, social, and educational programs.

The company paid a bonus to employes during World War II, but Patterson explained this was only in lieu of increases in wages, frozen by government edict, which lagged behind the cost of living.

Starting in 1937, Patterson began to build up the airline industry's first medical department. Designed primarily to keep flying crews in top physical shape, it also was available for checkups of workers on the ground and provided pre-employment physicals for all new hires.

Patterson spoke of United always as a corporate person. One of the company's executives once objected when he insisted on hiring the widow of a former employe. "What kind of a business are we running?," he asked. Patterson thought a while, then said, "Would you want me to ignore your wife, whom I have known for years, under similar circumstances?" The widow got the job.

Over the years Patterson's curious combination of industrial relations ideas has become ingrained in other executives, superintendents, foremen, and even lesser supervisors. Executives of

This is United's sprawling maintenance base at San Francisco International Airport. Identified are (1) warehouse; (2) jet-engine test cells; (3) jet-engine overhaul plant; (4) piston-engine test cells; (5) jetliner overhaul dock; (6) piston-engine overhaul plant; (7) piston-engine aircraft docks; (8) offices and sheet-metal shop.

DC-8 Jet Mainliner enters maintenance dock at San Francisco Jet Service Center. Specially designed scaffolding encloses plane with catwalks and workstands.

United mechanic at San Francisco base checks reassembly of jet engine after overhaul. Monorail on which it travels can support up to five tons.

Record-breaking dawn-to-dusk flight of 16 hours 51 minutes from New York to Waikiki introduced United's new DC-7 Mainliners to the airways in 1954. Above: Islanders roll out the red carpet with leis, hula dancers, and colorful Aloha Week "king" to welcome press-radio-TV personalities. Below: Territorial Governor Samuel King presents President W. A. Patterson with key to the Islands.

Air freight passed air mail as a source of revenue for the first time in 1956 when United Cargoliners carried nearly every kind of shipment imaginable—medicines, flowers, machinery parts, clothing, pets, and wild animals for zoos. Above: DC-6A Cargoliner being loaded fast at San Francisco Airport. Below: Interior of one of the big "flying freight cars," which can carry more than 15 tons each.

rival airlines view the Patterson personal-touch policy with a mixture of amusement and alarm. Tough, leathery Captain Eddie Rickenbacker, president of Eastern Air Lines, remarked one day that "it's the boy scout in Pat coming out." Patterson has called it "laying a brick a day to build confidence in the company," also "developing the company's human assets as carefully as its physical resources." He apparently has been torn between two fears: that the company will not do all it should for its people; and that the unions might shackle the airlines with featherbedding or pay-for-not-working rules, as they have hamstrung the railroads.

Of the nine unions which have organized 57 per cent of the United people, the largest is the International Association of Machinists, but the toughest is the AFL Air Line Pilots' Association, which for 20 years was headed by David Behncke, an early day Boeing pilot. Though Behncke and Patterson were on "Dave" and "Pat" terms with each other, they frequently clashed in ideas. During Patterson's first sixteen years as president, no strike by the pilots or any other group interrupted United's service, as walk-outs tied up other major airlines periodically. In 1948 it looked as though the enviable record between the company and the pilots was doomed to end. Also, that United might have a new head, when Patterson, his dander up, refused to agree to a "make-work" procedure for settling minor grievances.

Behncke had run a tight union in the higher brackets, probably the highest paid union workers in the world, with members enjoying wages ranging from $900 to $1600 per month for pilots, with co-pilots on their way up drawing from $290 to $570 per month. Pilots were forbidden by CAA regulation to fly more than 85 hours per month, which averaged about 4 hours per working day, in addition to which they spent considerable time on the ground in flight planning and reports. Ever alert to see that pilots enjoyed top working conditions, Behncke bore down hard on grievances. He and Patterson came to an impasse in 1948 over procedure for settlement of minor grievances, which constituted 95 per cent of the issues arising between the pilots and the management. Patterson insisted on settling them on the local level; Behncke was equally determined to work them up the union ladder to the top, which meant that management likewise had to waste time on inconsequential beefs.

To back his position, Behncke called for a strike vote and got it. Patterson said that if the pilots chose to strike, he would be forced to shut down the airline, throwing 9000 other people out of work, too. After a futile ring-around-the-rosy series of discussions, Patterson took off for Denver, the United operating base, to get away from the supercharged Chicago atmosphere.

Mrs. Patterson went along, and they were flying in the Mainliner *O'Connor,* the only plane then in the fleet not named for a state or a city, but instead for jolly and devoted Mary O'Connor, dean of stewardesses, who refused to delegate her chores on the executive plane to any junior stewardess. Just before the *O'Connor* took off, Carl Christenson, a pilot not on the negotiating committee, asked Patterson if he could ride out to Denver to talk things over en route. Christenson explained that the pilots realized Patterson's plan for settling grievances had merit and that they had possibly made a mistake in taking the strike vote. He said the pilots saw the light but could not let the president of their union down. So, if Patterson would give in this one time and save Behncke's face, the United pilots would see to it that the union did not take advantage of the concession.

"Well, how about my face?" demanded Patterson.

Mrs. Patterson, who had been listening, spoke up, "Why not get out of this business and enjoy some peace of mind?"

As Patterson thought about this suggestion, it appealed to him more and more. When the plane reached Denver, he suggested that Christenson tell the union to call off the strike, because he had decided to resign as president so that someone else whose face didn't have to be saved could sign the contract. Thoroughly alarmed, Christenson asked Patterson to hold everything until he could call Chicago and report to the United pilots' Master Executive Council. Early next day he told Patterson the Council had overruled the union and was announcing the strike was off.

Patterson has fought doggedly to keep the airline industry free of the so-called "featherbedding practices" involving make-work or pay-for-no-work that have shackled the railroads. Rather than give in on this principle, United faced up to its first major strike in June, 1951, when the pilots' union arbitrarily demanded acceptance of "mileage limitation," an idea evolved by ALPA to limit a pilot's flying to 17,000 miles or about 70 hours in the air per month.

The over-all objective, as indicated by ALPA's new president, Clarence N. Sayen, youthful former Braniff Air Lines co-pilot who ousted Founder Dave Behncke as spokesman for the pilots, was to force the airlines to employ more crews and thus create more jobs.

When the strike broke, Patterson made another of his spontaneous "million dollar decisions." Refusing to furlough the company's 9000 other employes, thrown out of productive work by the walkout, he ordered full pay for everybody but the striking pilots. Though the decision cost the airline over a million dollars on top of the three to four millions lost in sacrificed revenues, Patterson considers it one of his blue chip investments.

Eleven days after the pilots left their cockpits, the union ordered them back again. Contract negotiations resumed, then bogged anew. The union insisted on "mileage limitation" or a modification which would force the company to hire more pilots by imposing penalty pay for any flying over 70 hours. The company's negotiators adamantly refused to buy the limitation principle. The stubborn contest of wills became a crucial milestone in airline history. Four months later, the union accepted pay increases and other benefits offered by the company before the strike was called—without "mileage limitation."

The next conflict of principles between ALPA and the airlines came in the summer of 1954, when the introduction of the faster DC-7s made nonstop coast-to-coast flights feasible on United and American routes. Though the eastbound flights were flown easily in the traditional eight-hour day, the westbound flights, against head winds, sometimes required half an hour extra. Since pilots on overseas routes flew longer days, the CAB increased the eight-hour flight limit to ten hours for transcontinental nonstops. The pilots' union carried the case to Federal court and lost. Then ALPA struck American Airlines, tying up the system for three weeks. As in 1951, the union eventually ordered its pilots back to work. It appeared that the airline industry had weathered one more ALPA "storm."

The unions have played an important role in Patterson's scheme of things. "When all the ideas are contributed from one side, it is impossible for an employer to know if he is doing everything he can for his people," he has said. "Unions call your attention to things you would never notice." For example, the company once rotated the undesirable night shifts, inevitable in round-the-clock airline operations, so that all employes shared them equally. In 1943 the unions made a big issue of this practice, demanding that seniority determine who worked on the day shifts and who worked at night. The union's plan panned out better than the company's, which apparently upset the home life of a majority of the United families. Similarly, the union spotted other grievances that an executive would never suspect.

When World War II ended, United found itself with a payroll three times as large as when the war broke out. For the first time since Patterson became president, it was a payroll and not a cohesive family of workers. The company had promised every man and woman who left for the armed services that a job would be waiting on his or her return. It might not be the same job, but all a veteran had to do to get back in the United fold was to report to the nearest district manager and ask for a pass to one of the three processing centers at Chicago, Cheyenne, or San Francisco, where personnel experts undertook to fit everybody into the best job possible. This meant that in addition to the 8000 new wartime employes, the company had some 1500 dislocated war veterans trying to readjust themselves to new jobs.

It was a hectic period on the airline, and in an effort to revive the old company family spirit, Patterson and Ahrens, with several other officials, set out in 1945 to talk with as many people as it was possible to meet. To save time, they covered the system in a sleeper plane, which served as their flying office at the thirty-two cities west of Chicago they visited in six weeks. When this man-killing expedition reached San Francisco, Patterson was sent to a hospital, from which he emerged "tired for the next four years," as he put it.

The time to reflect in the hospital convinced him that the days of personal contact with the airline's people were gone for good. Nevertheless, it was more important than ever that workers down the line have an opportunity to ask anything they wanted to know about their company—who was paid what; where the dollars came from; where they went; what about new planes, passes, promotions. Patterson tried to accomplish this through a series of periodic reports to all employes. He had an uneasy feeling that they were too much like the stockholders' reports and not what the United people wanted to know.

This was borne out by the "company dinners" held periodically in major United centers, to which all supervisors and as many of the rank-and-file people as possible were invited. At these gatherings, Patterson kicked off the session with a brief talk, after which the sky was the limit on questions, which he and other executives attempted to answer without pulling punches.

In the summer of 1950, he hit on another idea, a feature in the monthly *UAL News* (later *The Shield*) entitled "Your Visit with the President." In it he answered each month from twenty to forty questions about anything anybody wanted to ask. The questions soon proved that nobody topside could guess what the people on the ramp wanted to know—about passes, jobs, working conditions, routes, services, operations, or a hundred miscellaneous items. The question-answer department proved, as had Patterson's travels out on the line, that it is the little things that count in company relations.

Patterson used the long-distance phone a lot of the time, on the theory that people out on the line like to hear the voice of somebody topside now and then. Frequently, after checking the daily report from the Personnel Department on what was happening in the United family, he reached for the phone instead of dictating a letter or a telegram, sometimes with amazing results.

One day he noticed an item saying that a stewardess, Peggy Johnston, had been bounced around in some bad weather and had injured her back. Inquiring, he found that she had been checked out of the hospital and was at her home, convalescing. Patterson called her on the phone.

"Hello. This is Mr. Patterson," he said. "How are you getting along?"

United stewardesses are coached to be cordial and friendly, but wary of jokers among the passengers, who somehow get their telephone numbers, so Miss Johnston replied, "I don't believe I know you."

"Oh yes, you do," insisted Patterson. "We work for the same airline."

It took a little persuading to convince the stewardess that the president of the airline was calling her long distance to find out how she was recovering. When it finally dawned on her, she was too flabbergasted to talk. She made up for it later, however, by telling about the incident up and down the airline.

"We have grown from an interesting game with a great challenge to a big business with all the problems of a big business," Patterson has pointed out. "We have grown from jacks of all trades to specialists. United has spent literally millions of dollars training employes to keep them up to date on technical developments and management methods. Instead of a few hundred passengers, we have thousands in the air daily. Every time we turn around, we have a new problem in human relations. Our policy is still the same, but now we have to project the human touch through the supervisors who are dealing with the people I used to be able to contact in person, years ago when United was the biggest airline in the world but a relatively small airline at that."

Patterson's industrial relations creed, and the company's as well, is epitomized in a talk he made in 1944 before the Financial Advertisers Association in Chicago, in which he explained:

"In dealing with our employes there is one economic theory we threw to the winds 15 years ago—the theory that labor is a commodity. Employes are human beings and cannot be treated as a commodity. We use the usual methods of selection and training but our basic philosophy, as directors and management, is that capital cannot be put to useful accomplishment unless there are human beings to execute the basic idea for which that capital was provided. We also recognize the fact that employes cannot be gainfully occupied without capital. Therefore, we have an inseparable partnership.

"Our employees are unionized. Our negotiations and discussions for improvement are conducted in a friendly, constructive manner. Although our management is continuously attempting to develop improvements for the best interests of our employes, I contend that it is impossible for any management to think of every little detail without a check and balance such as a union provides. Accordingly, the question of unionization causes no dispute within our company.

"I think it is unfortunate that our government adopted in legislation the term 'collective bargaining.' What is a bargain in the usual sense? It is getting something for less than it is worth, and less than you expected to pay. My conscience would not permit me to complete a bargain with our employes. It is unfortunate that the phraseology of our National Labor Relations Act is such that its very words tend to promote suspicion.

"We accepted many years ago the fact that a human being, responsive to human treatment, deserved an amortization at least equal to that of an inanimate machine which we amortized and protected. A pension plan is not new to United Air Lines. Vacations with pay, which are still being debated in some industries, are over 15 years old with our company. Then there are sick benefits. We never are willing to throw a machine into the scrap heap when it goes temporarily out of service due to a mechanical breakdown—and we don't think human beings should be thrown out under similar circumstances."

Although the question and answer technique, which required two days a week of Patterson's time, plus an attitude survey conducted among employes by the University of Chicago Industrial Relations Center in 1952, brought out into the open many of the doubts and discontents of employes, Patterson still felt there was much to be learned about what the United family was thinking of the company.

Early in 1952, in the Chicago terminal, he noticed that many of the passenger agents and baggage handlers had been there for a long time.

"I'll bet a lot of these people are struggling along day after day with their dreams of doing something different," he remarked.

A vice-president pointed out that almost all of United's people had been carefully screened when they were employed, or later, by trained job counselors to determine their aptitudes. Patterson insisted that this did not tell him much about each man's or woman's secret ambition.

"I'd like to know," he said. "I think we're overlooking something."

A personnel counselor went to work interviewing some 100 employes at Chicago and Des Moines, as sample points. What he learned inspired Patterson to order extension of the survey over the entire system. Of 1800 invited to be interviewed, five out of nine employes were completely happy in their present field of work; many weren't interested in interviews. The other half did have their dreams and more than one-third of these dreamers had not only ambition but aptitude for the work they longed to do. For example, some women ticket agents and stenographers longed to be stewardesses; they were sent to the stewardess school at Cheyenne. Several office workers had ambitions to be sales promoters. They were given the chance. Of 750 employes interviewed, 88 were assigned to new positions. One young engineer in his twenties confessed that his secret ambition was to be president of United. He was studying at night school to round out his training.

"That fellow needs broader experience," said Patterson. "Assign him to job analyzing. Let him find out what is wrong with the company."

Encountering the young engineer some months later, Patterson asked him, "When are you going to be ready to be president? I'm getting pretty old."

In the Patterson scheme of things, employes are infinitely more valuable than machines. "The United family is not only United's greatest asset," he has said repeatedly. "It is our only asset that is irreplaceable."

CHAPTER XIII

The High-flying Mainliners

Air travelers of the thirties who thought they had discovered the modern magic carpet in the Boeing 247 and the DC-3, the first all-metal streamlined airliners, were ahead of their time. The real magic carpet unrolled with the start of DC-6 service in 1947. These luxurious 5-mile-a-minute airliners, pressurized for high-altitude flight, swallowed distance so fast that the Main Line airway between San Francisco and New York shrank to ten hours of flight. The "Sixes," which joined the Mainliner fleet just in time to inaugurate service from New York and Chicago to Los Angeles via Denver, as well as to San Francisco and the Pacific Northwest, soon revolutionized transcontinental flight.

The new flying techniques made possible by the Sixes were dramatized by the experience of passengers aboard Flight 623 flying nonstop Chicago to San Francisco one bright day in 1949. Peering downward four hours out of Chicago, the high-flying travelers were amazed to see the geysers and canyons of Yellowstone National Park instead of the Great Salt Lake gleaming in the sunset. Before anyone could inquire why the airliner was 250 miles off the usual route, the captain's voice sounded over the intercom speaker. He explained that partly to avoid bumpy weather on the Main Line, partly to pick up a 60-mile-per-hour tailwind whipping across the Dakotas, Flight 623 had veered north. Although the dog-leg added 200 miles to the Chicago–San Francisco flight, a tailwind and good flying weather through Idaho and Nevada to California would bring 623 into San Francisco on time.

The skipper more than kept his word. Twenty minutes ahead of schedule, the Mainliner eased its wheels down at San Francisco Airport. Passengers were delighted with the smooth ride and the unanticipated sightseeing. Had they been technically minded, they would have been even more pleased with the log of the flight. Despite the additional mileage, the DC-6, riding the tailwind, had cruised at reduced speed all the way from Fargo, North Dakota, arriving at its destination with hundreds of gallons of gas to spare.

A few days later a Flight 623 passenger was retelling his adventure over Yellowstone when a brand-new arrival on Flight 601 that morning interrupted him.

"Well, listen to this," said 601. "I dozed off right after we left Chicago last night, expecting to wake up over Reno or Lake Tahoe. Instead, the pilot rouses us over the intercom and says, 'If you want a good look at Hoover Dam, it's right below us.' Sure enough, it is. A little later we are looking down on Death Valley. Then we have breakfast over Yosemite, and glide down to San Francisco exactly on time. Can you beat that?"

Neither of these flights was "on the beam," as beams were flown prior to 1948, yet both were on course as airways were flown after 1948, although one plane was 200 miles north of the direct San Francisco–Chicago Main Line, and the other was 350 miles to the south. The two flights were utilizing a technique known as "pressure pattern" flying. Instead of pushing through the storm fronts, pilots flew high and wide, over and around bad weather, thus assuring their passengers not only smoother rides but on-time arrivals.

Pressure pattern flying took advantage of the atmospheric highs and lows moving across the weather map, generally southeast from the polar regions, but occasionally north from the Gulf of Mexico, bringing various combinations of weather—wind, snow, icing conditions, zero ceilings. Like airliners, the pressure patterns were always on the move, but more slowly, so that the fast new planes could easily detour around them. By flying to the side of a pressure pattern, a pilot usually picked up a helpful tailwind and found relatively smooth flying.

Prior to the war it was anybody's guess what kind of weather a pilot and his passengers would find "upstairs"; by war's end meteorologists and pilots had taken much of the guesswork out of the weather. Pan American pilots, for example, pioneering the 8000-mile hop to Australia, discovered that, by angling across the Pacific on dog-legs, thus detouring the moving storm centers, they could save both time and fuel. The Army, Navy, and United Air Lines pilots who joined in the trans-Pacific lift also flew off airways much of the time. United States Air Force bomber pilots headed for Japan often found themselves hopelessly battling a lofty, high-velocity river of wind that swept out of Nippon. Known as the "jet stream," it flowed not only over the Pacific but above the United States. In Denver, United's meteorologists began charting the daily meanderings of this mysterious river of air. Pilots lucky enough to catch a ride in the jet stream clipped hours off their eastbound flights from Honolulu.

The overseas pilots who returned to domestic runs were eager to utilize this improved flying technique across the continent. For the moment, however, they flew head-on into opposition both from the CAA, responsible for airline safety rules, and the airline operators, who pointed out that flying "off the beams," while practical over oceans, might be risky over land where the country's airways had been laid out, like the railroads and highways, to avoid mountain peaks. Furthermore, the unpressurized airliners available immediately after the war were unsuitable for high-altitude flight without discomfort to pilots and passengers. Also, most airliners lacked adequate nonstop cruising range.

Then came delivery of the DC-6 fleet. The pressurized Sixes flew well above the loftiest peaks in either the Rockies or the Sierra Nevadas. They also had long cruising range—3600 miles without refueling. They manufactured their own climate as they winged through the atmosphere three to four miles above sea level. Two marvelous compact gadgets known as "superchargers," whirring at 35,000 revolutions per minute, sucked in the thin outside air and compressed it into atmosphere that passengers could breathe comfortably. The superchargers changed the air in the cabins and cockpits every five minutes, teaming up with a compact little heater capable of warming half a dozen houses, which maintained comfortable temperatures inside the plane even when flying high above the Rockies where subzero temperatures were often colder than over the Arctic. Other superchargers compressed the atmosphere for the engines to keep them functioning smoothly regardless of the altitude.

Also important for pressure pattern flying was a new kind of beacon, a wartime electronic development that helped to emancipate pilots and their passengers from rigid airways flying. This was known as the Omni-Directional Radio Range. During the war, OMNI had proven its value by vectoring thousands of bombers and fighters home from missions over Germany and Italy. Where the old-fashioned beacon sent out beams dividing space into four quadrants, OMNI sent them out like the spokes of a wheel. Where a pilot formerly flew short legs, following beams from station to station, OMNI enabled him, with the help of some ingenious new receiving equipment in his cockpit, to fly a specially charted course for each flight and to pick the most favorable combination of flying conditions. OMNI, using ultra-high frequencies, was unaffected by static. On the other hand, the OMNI-beam traveled like a beam of light instead of following the earth's curvature. Thus its use was limited by the horizon largely to high-flying long-range planes. Since OMNI was made to order for pressure pattern flying, United invested $1,000,000 to equip its new long-range fleet to utilize the ninety OMNI-beacons installed by the CAA along the nation's airways.

Once the new airliners had demonstrated their long-range cruising dependability, the CAA revised its regulations. After January of 1948, pilots were allowed to fly selected pressure pattern tracks above the 14,500-foot level west of the hundredth meridian (roughly North Platte, Nebraska, on the United system) and above the 12,500-foot elevation east of that point.

"We just tacked onto the new OMNI-range every hundred miles or so and flew an approved track all the way to our destination," explained one of United's veteran pilots. "Where in the past we'd been nailed down to the airways, the airplane overnight became the most flexible form of transportation."

United's airmen had an unusual opportunity to prove that their planes were all-weather vehicles during the January, 1949, blizzard, when overland trains and busses were stalled in the Rockies and on the prairies. Winging around or over the weather, the

Mainliners completed 89 per cent of their scheduled flights and even flew special missions to rescue hundreds of stranded surface travelers.

For the overseas service to Honolulu, United added a fleet of seven Boeing Stratocruisers in 1950. These also were high-flying Mainliners, although in the Pacific, over which United pilots had flown 7000 crossings in wartime service, the planes seldom had occasion to climb more than 2 miles aloft, except on eastbound flights to catch a ride on the Jet Stream. From the passengers' viewpoint, the Stratocruisers were air travel at its finest. They were roomy, two-level airliners with a lounge cabin below the main deck. During the ten-hour flight, stewardesses, assisted by Hawaiian stewards, had time to break out champagne and serve meals course by course with cocktails to whet appetites. The Aloha run brought air travel luxury to a new peak. Four years later, when the faster, larger DC-7s became available, United Stratocruisers were sold to British Overseas Airways Corporation.

One catch in pressure pattern flying was that it did not help the short-range flights much. On a 750-mile flight between New York and Chicago, for example, or a 2000-mile hop, such as Chicago to San Francisco, a 30-mile tailwind more than compensated for a dog-leg that added 10 per cent more mileage to the flight. On the shorter runs, off-airways flying was mainly a means of detouring around storm centers which made air travel uncomfortable for passengers—provided a pilot could guess where the storm core was.

What the pilots needed was a seeing-eye to spot these line-squall cores. By 1955 they had it in a new gadget called "C-band airborne radar." This was a relatively lightweight electronic device in the nose of the plane which bounced radar echoes off storm cores 100 miles ahead. If the white fluffy cloud had a vicious, black core inside it, the pilot could detour around it. Airborne radar even revealed storms behind storms, could also detect mountains behind clouds and outline bays or rivers.

This ingenious "radar flashlight" for spotlighting the weather through clouds or night was developed by United's Communications Chief Russ Cunningham, Meteorologist Henry Harrison, and a team of RCA engineers about 1953. By 1954 they had it ready to test. A United crew spent much of the summer aloft deliberately stalking line squalls over the prairies to prove that flying smoothly through them without getting caught in the tempestuous cores was feasible. In 1954 United's directors authorized the expenditure of over $4 million to equip the entire Mainliner fleet with airborne weather radar equipment. It was a $4-million investment in passenger comfort, safety, and on-time operation. Mainliner Convairs, which had the greatest need for weather radar because most of their runs were too short to permit climbing above the storm areas, were equipped with them in 1955; the larger, higher-flying DC-6s and DC-7s were equipped in 1956 and 1957. The installation revealed anew the tremendous increase in the cost of operating a modern airline. The "seeing eyes" for Mainliners eventually cost more than United's entire fleet of sixty Boeing 247s cost back in 1934.

While these flying techniques got the airliners over and around the weather, other electronic eyes based on war-born radar developments were guiding them more quickly and surely down through the ceilings that, two years before, had kept planes circling, when the weather closed in, in "stacks" above the major terminals. At the larger airports, the radar beams of ILS (Instrument Landing System) enabled pilots to glide down through clouds and fog in safety to land under 300-foot ceilings on air strips with a visibility of half a mile, landings that the CAA would have forbidden in 1946–1947. At several major terminals, additional radar eyes on the ground scanned the skies through fog or clouds, double-checking the ILS scopes for the airliners.

Above the country's busiest airports, such as Chicago, Washington, or New York, "stacking" of planes waiting to land became a relatively rare occurrence. At Chicago's Midway Airport, Norman R. ("Huck") Smith, chief of the CAA tower, evolved a precision landing technique that proved the answer at other congested airports as well. Airliners landed at one-minute intervals. Incidentally, Chicago's tower wasn't a tower any more. Smith, like many other tower chiefs, found that the place for a man equipped with electronic eyes to direct an endless flow of incoming and outgoing air traffic was in a nice quiet basement.

By midsummer of 1950, United's pilots found themselves flying war wings again. On July 8, soon after the Communist invasion of South Korea, two DC-6 Mainliners were hurriedly pulled off regular passenger-cargo schedules on the Main Line and rerouted to a dozen airports to pick up 105 high-ranking technicians needed in a hurry by General Douglas MacArthur. Twenty-four hours and forty-three minutes after they left San Francisco Airport, the technicians were in Tokyo. Then the Sixes winged back across the Pacific to Rock Island Arsenal in Illinois, where they were loaded with bazookas fresh off the assembly line. Within two days the weapons were in the hands of hard-pressed American troops.

These trips were forerunners of 1000 others across the Pacific flown by United planes and crews during the following thirty-nine months until the armistice, by which time the Mainliners had logged 13,000,000 miles of military flying over the Pacific. Wrote Lieutenant General Joseph Smith, commander of the Military Air Transport Service, when United's last flight in the lift was completed in October, 1953:

"It is gratifying to realize that the civil aviation companies operating in the Pacific Air Lift, within a relatively short period of the inception of the Lift, were able to so successfully overcome many administrative and operational obstacles and work with such complete harmony as a part of the military team."

At home, United found itself embroiled, in 1950, in another kind of conflict, a rate war brought on by cut-rate coach service of competitors, both scheduled and nonscheduled. While the non-skeds flew as they wished, at any time of day or night or between any points they chose, coach flights of the scheduled airlines were restricted by the CAB to points on their routes and limited to the less popular night hours. Later these restrictions were relaxed, enabling coach flights to operate around the clock.

Before the war United had pioneered coach service between San Francisco and Los Angeles. At that time President Patterson foresaw the possibility of two classes—maybe three classes—of service on airliners. But the United experiment had to be abandoned in 1940 when the war crisis made planes scarce. Before it could be resumed following the war's end, a rash of non-sked operators moved in with cheap war surplus planes to fly bargain flights between the high-density markets. For a time, any war pilot who could wangle a war surplus plane was in the non-sked airline business.

The scheduled airlines met this new competition with reduced-fare coach flights of their own. Capital Air Lines launched coach service on the heavy-traffic Chicago–New York run. TWA and American followed suit, extending the coach service to the trans-continental flights. Western Air Lines flew coach trips between Los Angeles and Seattle. Thus the United system was quickly blanketed by competitors' coach flights on which fares were reduced one-third from first-class levels. No meals were served and passengers were packed like sardines in hurriedly modified airplanes in which smaller seats were jammed closer together.

The original aim of coach service as approved by the CAB was to generate new traffic by making air travel so inexpensive it would lure rail, bus, and automobile travelers into the planes. Also, the scheduled airlines hoped to recover some of the traffic which the non-skeds were happily skimming off their flights between the larger population centers. For a year, conservative United stayed out of the postwar cut-rate war on the theory that the flying coaches might lure more first-class passengers off regular first-class flights than new riders off the ground. In 1950, however, Mainliners went into coach service on the Pacific Coast and trans-continental coach service was soon added.

Always passenger-comfort–conscious, United did not attempt to crowd as many seats into its coach planes as did its competitors. The seats themselves were more roomy, the aisles were wider. This consideration for passengers brought a vigorous protest to the CAB from other airlines, who insisted that United's coach service was unfair competition because the Mainliners did not carry the number of passengers required by the CAB regulations for coach operation. Patterson protested strongly that the high-density seating practiced by other carriers was unsafe. Eventually, by redesigning the interior of its coaches, United met the minimum requirement of the CAB without jamming passengers sardine-style.

Though coach traffic boomed, the idea proved something of a Frankenstein for the airlines. Once launched, it was difficult to discontinue or control. While the scheduled coaches won back some of the traffic lost to the non-skeds, a number of the latter

The DC-7 Mainliner which made its entrance on United's system in 1954 and gave travelers their first nonstop coast-to-coast service. Time, from San Francisco to New York, 7½ hours.

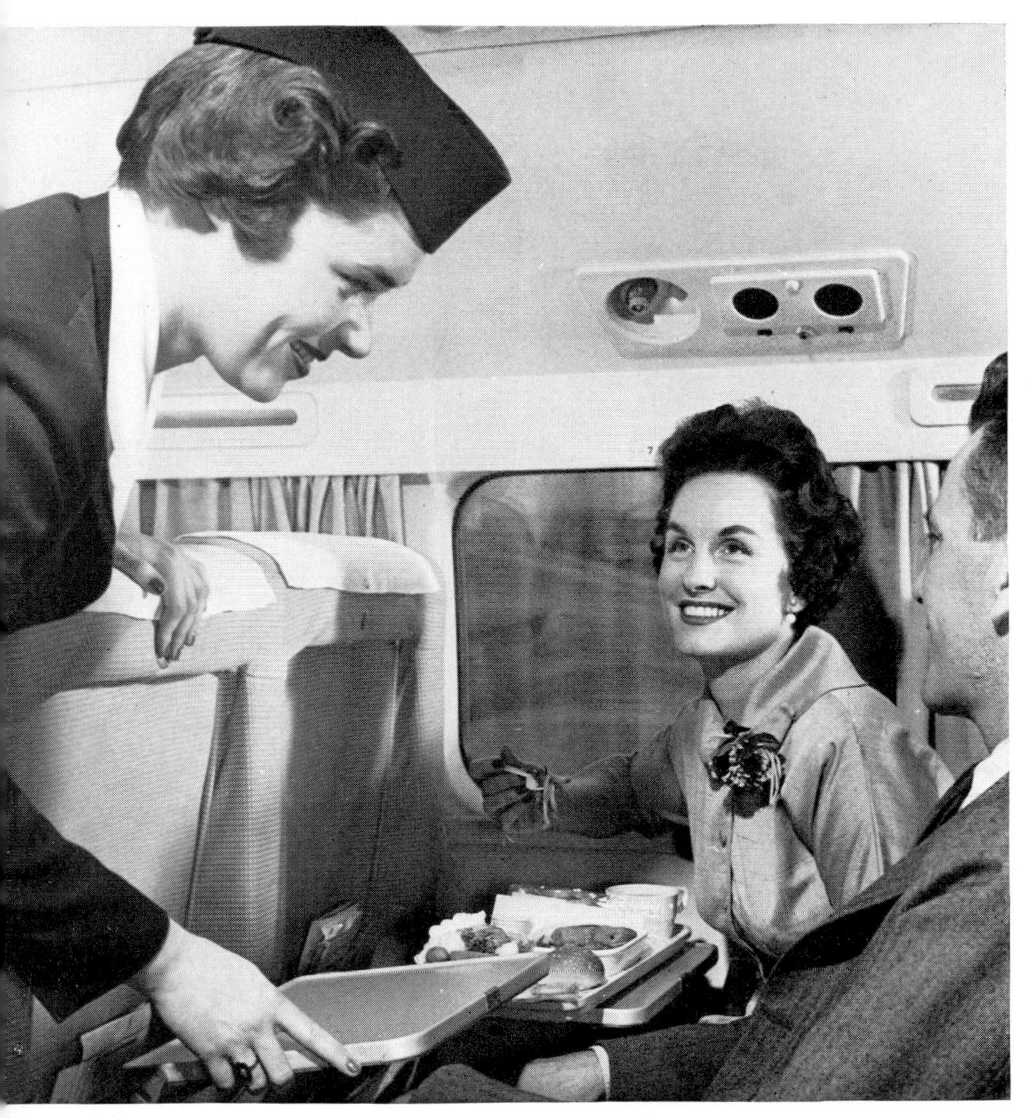

DC-7 Mainliner Custom Coach service, introduced by United in 1957, brought an end to balancing meal trays on pillows. Instead, newly designed seats had table units built into the seat backs ahead.

Popular spot on any DC-7 Mainliner flight was the attractive lounge aft where passengers could chat, play cards, or spread out business papers.

"Rolling out the red carpet," symbol of United's hospitality and service on DC-7 nonstop flights between major traffic centers on the Main Line. This luxury-type service was adopted in 1956, after Kansas City boosters created the "Order of the Red Carpet" to welcome United back to their city after two decades.

lowered their fares still more and continued to operate in violation of CAB regulations. Surveys by the airlines revealed that 35 to 50 per cent of coach traffic was "business you took away from yourself" by diverting traffic from first-class flights. Nevertheless, the coach flights increased. By 1956, 37 per cent of United's mainland traffic and over half of its Honolulu flights were coach. On the latter, a light meal was served. In 1956, Mainliner coach flights carried 1,760,000 passengers who paid $74,304,000 in fares, compared to $161,981,000 earned from first-class ticket sales. Unfortunately, the coach business was highly seasonal, booming traffic in the summer when seats on Mainliners already were in great demand. But whether they liked it or not, the airlines were saddled with an old transportation headache, first-class and second-class travel with too little difference in service to justify the 30 per cent differential in fares.

United's salespeople lay awake nights trying to think up new gimmicks to lure passengers onto the more profitable first-class flights. The best item was the first-class "family plan," under which a passenger could take his wife or children for half-fare on Mondays, Tuesdays, Wednesdays, and later, Thursdays. For a traveling family this meant first-class service at virtually coach price. Tempting food, snacks between meals, on-time service, and Mainliner hospitality also helped keep passengers on the first-class flights.

The question of how to provide more distinction between first-class and coach flights seemed on the way to solution by March 29, 1954 when President Patterson and a group of United executives gathered at the Douglas Aircraft plant at Santa Monica to take delivery of the first of a fleet of twenty-five luxurious DC-7s. The occasion was notable in another way—Patterson and thirty-four other United old-timers, most of them still in their fifties, received twenty-five-year service pins. Two days later, Captain Herb Holloway, UAL's senior test pilot, took the fifty-eight-passenger airliner aloft, came down after three hours with the laconic verdict, "She's a honey."

Two months later, after crews had thoroughly mastered the newest Mainliner, two DC-7s made aviation history in a spectacular dawn-to-dusk flight from New York to Honolulu. A party of press, radio, and TV notables, after breakfasting in New York and lunching in flight, chased the sun across the Pacific to land at Honolulu Airport before sunset, in time for dinner at the Royal Hawaiian Hotel on Honolulu's Waikiki Beach. The sleek new planes dramatized how air transport in three spectacular decades had grown from uncertain infancy into big business. Even the late President Lippman of Wells Fargo Bank would have conceded to his bright young protégé, Patterson, that there was a future in the flying machines, although their cost would have staggered him. Each of the new fifty-eight-passenger DC-7s bore a $1,800,000 price tag.

By the time the "Sevens" went into service, the crews that flew them had changed almost as much as the airliner itself. The pilot was no longer an airplane chauffeur but, as Dick Petty, vice-president–flight operations, put it, "the captain-manager of an operating team." By 1957, United's flying staff consisted of some 2200 pilots, including first officers and flight engineers. Many of the latter were qualified pilots, too, following settlement of a strike called late in 1955 by the flight engineers' union. This settlement established anew the airline's right to determine the qualifications of flying crews. United retained the right to employ pilot-qualified engineers and offered flight training to those engineers who were not pilots. Those who did not desire such training were assured job security as engineers, however.

Most of the captains who directed the DC-7 crews on the top transcontinental and Hawaii flights were veterans who started flying the Main Line in Boeing 40Bs or NAT Curtiss Carrier Pigeons. They won their DC-7 captaincies not only by seniority but by going to school steadily for three decades to keep abreast in the techniques of scientific flying. United pilots knew how they would react in emergencies because all of them had proven their skill, not only in planes aloft, but in amazingly realistic simulators that dramatized just about every flying emergency that might occur on the Main Line. Twice a year each United pilot and co-pilot took a refresher course in Denver or Chicago. Prior to being checked out, pilots graduating from smaller to larger airliners also were trained in the cockpits of the simulators, in which the company had invested $4,500,000 for a battery of seven installed at Denver and Chicago.

There were two emergencies these precocious machines could not simulate and both brought catastrophe to United crews and passengers in the mid-fifties. Shortly after leaving Denver Airport on the evening of November 1, 1955, Flight 629 ceased to report to Air Traffic Control by any of its four communications systems. Then came word that the airliner had exploded near Longmont, Colorado. The wreckage soon was found. Since all passengers and crew members had been killed, no one could report what happened.

The mystery was cleared up weeks later after an extraordinary example of detective work on the part of FBI, CAB, CAA, and UAL investigators. The airliner had been blown up by a bomb planted in the luggage of a woman passenger by her son, who had taken out heavy insurance on her life.

Though the guilty criminal was soon apprehended and eventually executed, the tragedy spotlighted a frustrating problem for the airlines, the epidemic of false bomb warnings. Each one meant planes had to be thoroughly searched, with inconvenience to passengers, interruption of schedules, and added expense for the carriers. Congress, in 1956, made false bomb warnings a Federal offense, subject to a year's imprisonment, a $1000 fine or both. Although FBI agents caught and convicted a number of the hoaxsters, bomb warnings continued to plague the airlines.

The other once-in-a-million catastrophe followed on June 30, 1956 when a United DC-7 and a TWA Constellation ceased contact with ATC simultaneously over the Grand Canyon in northern Arizona. The airliners had taken off from Los Angeles Airport eastbound within ten minutes of each other. Following CAA-approved regulations, both were flying "off airways" to take advantage of favorable tailwinds eastbound to Chicago. The United DC-7 cleared by Air Traffic Control to fly at 21,000 feet took a southerly route, then veered north. The TWA Constellation cleared by ATC to fly at 19,000 feet took a more direct route and, encountering clouds, requested permission to fly above them. The last ATC radio reports from the two pilots gave estimated times of arrival at the Painted Desert "fix" which were within three minutes of each other—United at 21,000 feet and TWA at 21,000 feet "on top VFR" (Visual Flight Rules). This information was discussed by the ATC centers at Salt Lake City, Los Angeles, and Albuquerque; it was relayed to TWA but not to United. That was the last heard from either plane. Subsequently, wreckage of the two airliners and the bodies of passengers and crew members were found on the cliffs of the Grand Canyon. It was the worst crash in commercial aviation history.

Ten months later the CAA issued another painstaking detective report which confirmed what pilots and airline executives surmised. Flight paths of the two airliners had converged in one of the "most spacious sky areas" in the country. Unfortunately, the same accident based on the same airways clearances could have happened anywhere on or off the airways. Up to the time of the Grand Canyon accident there was no really "positive control" exercised in the United States except in the high-density Washington, D.C., area or when all aircraft were flying "on instruments."

It dramatized a hazard that airline managements and the Air Line Pilots Association had warned about for several years. The seemingly limitless sky had become crowded, with 1500 airliners, 18,000 business aircraft, 35,000 military planes, and 42,000 private fliers sharing the space above the country. Though the airliners were only 1.5 per cent of the total flying fleet, they carried the bulk of the passengers. For several years airline pilots had reported up to four near misses a day on a special questionnaire originated and circulated by the Air Transport Association. Most of the reports came from congested areas. However—and very important in respect to this accident—30 per cent occurred en route while cruising.

The demand for new safety measures was immediate, but action was time-consuming. A ten-year lag caused by the nation's failure to build the air traffic control system recommended by the Radio Technical Committees for Aeronautics in 1947 had to be overcome. Even prior to the Grand Canyon accident, because of pressure brought to bear by ATA, two important things had happened, however. The CAA had developed a five-year program for rebuilding its air traffic control system, including a long-range radar network. The Curtis Committee had been directed by President Eisenhower to develop a program for a future control system capable of handling the nation's rapidly growing air traffic.

After Grand Canyon, the only immediate action which could be taken on a national scale was to reduce the CAA's five-year program to three years and provide the funds necessary for accomplishment. It was a year before any real improvement appeared, however, and five years would be needed to do the whole job. The cost—almost one billion dollars.

At the same time federal action was being accelerated, the airlines took voluntary action to relieve the pressure, putting into effect planning developed prior to the accident. Early in 1957, United and the other major airlines agreed to stop all flying above 18,000 feet unless an instrument flight plan had been filed with ATC. Two months later, a dozen HAT routes—high-altitude tracks—which United, American, and TWA had helped develop in order to eliminate off-airways flying, were adopted by the CAA and full traffic control was provided as rapidly as the agency's accelerated facilities program would permit.

This wasn't the end of pressure pattern flying, since United's pilots could choose a north track or a south track or any track in between to find the best weather and winds, but it put all flights on published, designated tracks where air traffic control surveillance and direction could be applied. The benefit of this measure was dubious until the long-range radar system could be completed because it meant greater congestion on the approved routes. But whenever positive control was exercised, with a box of space around each airliner from the time its wheels lifted from one runway until they hit another, the new system meant safer flying.

In 1958, by coordinated action of ATA, ALPA, and CAA, all airline flights in the New York–Chicago–Washington triangle began to operate under IFR rules providing the first real implementation and test of positive control. This plan, coupled with a long-range transition, would place the airlines effectively under positive control over the entire country by 1960.

Early in 1955, a flurry of new route grants by the CAB kicked off a stampede for passengers reminiscent of the battle between United, TWA, and American in the thirties for the New York–Chicago passengers. This time more airlines with more resources were fighting for 35,000,000 passengers who were spending $1,500,000,000 a year to ride the magic carpet. Traffic staffs scratched their skulls to think up attractions to lure new passengers into the air or old passengers from their competitors' planes. The airlines granted new routes promptly ordered all the equipment they could finance, then scrambled to sell seats. This rivalry was keenest on the New York–Chicago run where the new competition jumped the number of seats available 50 per cent, while total traffic only increased 5 per cent annually. Five airlines were battling for passengers over this route.

The hottest contest focused on the coach passengers who had become the bulk of the traffic on several airlines. In 1955, TWA, Pan American, and several other airlines began carrying coach and first-class passengers on the same plane, separated only by a curtain or a thin partition. First-class riders grumbled because sitting on one side of the curtain cost them $30 extra for a drink and a free meal, which coach passengers could buy for $2. American countered TWA's play by putting DC-7s in coach service between Los Angeles and New York. United followed early in 1957 with DC-7 "Custom Coach" flights nonstop from coast to coast and between California and Chicago. Meals en route cost $1.50.

Nobody knew for certain whether the coaches were pulling more passengers off the ground or off the first-class flights. But one thing was sure by 1957; the scheduled airlines with coach service had put the cut-rate non-skeds out of business, except for charter operations, mostly military. And the coach flights, carrying more passengers, were making money.

On first-class flights, the skirmish for passengers continued. Capital Airlines cut in on the eastern end of the Main Line with speedy turboprop Viscount airliners imported from England. One of United's unique come-ons was the men-only "Executives" on which stewardesses served libations and steak dinners, passed cigars on the house, provided slippers for tired feet. The "Execs" were so successful that they were soon introduced to the San Francisco–Los Angeles route as well and a second men-only round trip was added to the Chicago–New York run. On the West Coast, Western Airlines dreamed up "champagne flights" to keep passengers in good cheer.

In 1956 Patterson decided to take another look at the liquor-aloft question. On United planes drinks were on the house, but several airlines sold them with the result that some stewardesses complained they were becoming flying barmaids. A questionnaire to members of the United 100,000 Mile Club indicated that the average passenger enjoyed his drink but preferred good meal service to flowing champagne. United's Dining Department solved the problem, at least partially, by serving a cocktail to those who desired it with the opening course at dinnertime. By the time a passenger had finished his drink and started nibbling on his salad, the stewardess had a hot entree ready to replace the cocktail tray. In July, 1956, United joined five other major airlines in an agreement to limit libations aloft to two drinks, of 1.6-ounce alcoholic content each, per passenger.

When the Mainliners were allowed back into Kansas City by the CAB in 1956, after an enforced absence of twenty-two years, United celebrated by flying a planeload of exuberant Kansas City V.I.P.s to San Francisco, giving them red-carpet treatment all the way. A short time later, R. E. Johnson, vice-president–sales, was in Kansas City for a Chamber of Commerce luncheon. On behalf of the still-glowing travelers, Toastmaster Robert Sweet, president of the chamber, presented Johnson with a charter membership in the newly created Order of the Red Carpet.

Back in Chicago, Johnson reported the incident at a headquarters' staff sales meeting. Out of the ensuing discussion came an idea. Why not order some red carpets and roll them out for passengers boarding United's top-flight DC-7 trips at New York, Washington, Chicago, Denver, San Francisco, and Los Angeles? Thus was sparked one of the most amusing and effective means yet found to impress customers with the quality of an airline's service. The first plush carpets soon were replaced with red rubber rugs, rolled out by ground crews between rows of silvery chains and stanchions to the jocular amusement of passengers waiting to board. On "Red Carpet" flights seats were reserved, eliminating the scramble through the gates for the choice seats.

Once settled into their seats, passengers found themselves surrounded by a new décor dreamed up by a versatile staff of designers called in by Vice-president Magarrell to originate what became known as "the United new look." The traditional gray-blue of the Mainliner interiors was replaced with soft pastels, enlivened by gold, leather, and plastic trim. On the rear wall of the lounge a symbolic navigator's compass was tooled on leather in gold. The window curtains were dusty rose. The new look even included an exterior paint job. Just about everything the design or service experts could conjure up was done to remind the passenger on a "Red Carpet" flight that he or she was king or queen for the flight.

The truth of the matter was, the people who operated the high-flying Mainliners had gone about as far as they could go in providing speed, luxury, and service until the builders of planes had scored a new breakthrough in air transport. That revolutionary step—the jetliner—was not far off.

CHAPTER XIV

Keeping the Mainliners in the Air

The fine record for on-schedule precision operation by the 186-plane United fleet in the late fifties was made feasible largely by people on the ground, as any Mainliner pilot would testify. For every man or woman in the air United had six people on the ground, a total of 20,000 UALers by 1957. The Mainliners that earned their paychecks, which added up to $115,491,000 in 1956, did so only when they were flying. The United fleet represented a $207,000,000 investment, "a lot of money to be sitting on the ground." A DC-7 on the ramp, for example, was $1,800,000 temporarily unemployed. By 1957, the drive to keep the Mainliners flying as much of each day as possible was paying off. The DC-7s and DC-6s averaged better than ten hours of service per day. The Convairs, flying shorter runs, averaged slightly over eight hours per day on the wing.

The people on the ground who kept these Mainliners in the sky belonged to many teams, each expert at its duty. They were the fuelers, who filled the wing tanks with gas; the servicemen, who rolled the ramps up and who hustled the baggage on and off; the airplane cleaners, who kept the Mainliners spick-and-span; the chefs, who whipped up more than 5,000,000 meals per year; the mechanics, who checked the planes before take-off; the agents, who kept the passengers moving.

These were only the people at the terminals. Behind them was an army of 4000 mechanics and technicians at the San Francisco Maintenance Base. There were 2500 ticket agents and traffic hustlers along the Main Line. There were the weather forecasters, the dispatchers, the training staffs at Denver and Cheyenne; the operations experts at Denver, who saw that planes and crews were where they were needed; the management staff in Chicago. In short, the Main Line system had grown in three decades from a simple "seat-of-the-pants" flying operation to one of the most complex and scientific businesses in the country.

As far back as 1940 President Patterson recognized the evolution that was rapidly transforming the airlines. That year the first units of the San Francisco Maintenance Base were begun, to concentrate eventually in one spot the technical know-how and the equipment previously divided between the Cheyenne Maintenance Base and major terminals along the United system. By 1948, 2000 United families had moved to the San Francisco area. It was announced at the dedication ceremonies that the big base was completed. This proved to be the understatement of the day. Scarcely a year elapsed after that without a new addition. By 1954 the base was easily United's largest unit, with 3000 employes. By 1957 it had 4000 employes—engineers, technicians, electronics experts, upholsterers, to mention only a few of the skills needed to keep the fleet in top-flying condition—and it was undergoing a major enlargement to handle the jet airliners on order.

Boss of the huge plant was W. P. "Bill" Hoare, who had been keeping planes in the air since before United Air Lines was organized. Hoare used to scout the war surplus boneyards after World War I, buying up promising-looking Liberty engines for the rickety planes of the flying postmen. As United grew, so did youthful-looking Bill Hoare, until he became the head man of the world's most advanced and scientific maintenance base, which was able to completely renew an airliner and turn it back to operations in five days, better than new.

The San Francisco base was also the headquarters for Vice-president J. A. Herlihy, for W. C. Mentzer, general manager of engineering, and for United's staff of engineers, who worked not only on today's but next year's planes. In 1952, Herlihy headed a group of key United technicians dispatched to Europe to ride in British jetliners and report on the operation and maintenance of jet transports whenever United added them to its ever-growing fleet. While they were in Europe, Herlihy's party visited maintenance headquarters of Scandinavian Airlines System in Stockholm.

"Do you recognize anything here?" he was asked as the group inspected the SAS overhaul base.

"That dock looks familiar," said Herlihy.

"It ought to," replied his host. "We borrowed the idea from you."

Neither foreign nor domestic airlines have had to smuggle from United any idea or technique that has had to do with greater safety in flying. It is available for the asking, as the heads and technicians for scores of airlines have learned while visiting United's San Francisco and Denver bases.

"If it adds to the safety of air transport, it is good for all of us, whether we are competitors or not," explained Herlihy.

After the San Francisco base opened, all Mainliners and Cargoliners were scheduled over the Main Line network in such a way that they flew into SFO—San Francisco Airport—after a specified number of hours in the air. In 1957, DC-6s, 6Bs, and Convairs were overhauled every 2000 hours of flying; DC-7s, every 2200 hours. Regardless of type, each Mainliner covered approximately 1¼ million miles per year and was scheduled into the maintenance base at least twice each year. In addition to these major inspections, it underwent frequent checks along the line at shops maintained in New York, Chicago, Denver, Los Angeles, Seattle, and Honolulu.

Once inside the huge hangars of the base for its periodic checkup, each Mainliner was enveloped by one of the eight huge working docks whose platforms surrounded the fuselage, enabling mechanics to swarm over the plane without the use of ladders. Hydraulic jacks lifted the airframe off its wheels; engines were boosted aloft by overhead cranes that carried them into the enormous shop where each of the 18,000 parts was individually scrubbed in solvent, microscopically checked for wear, renewed or replaced. After being reassembled, they were tested "on the block" in soundproof concrete rooms.

While the engines were undergoing the renewing treatment,

the "brains" of the Mainliner, the electronic equipment and the instruments, moved upstairs to a great dustproof, temperature-controlled shop that suggested a watch factory. In fact, many of the skilled craftsmen in this shop were actually watchmakers. The seats and upholstery from inside the airliner moved to another shop for renewing, leaving only the airframe shell which was checked in the dock. Propeller and de-icing mechanisms were disassembled and double-checked, as were the wiring, the tubing, the landing gear. Five days later, when a glistening Mainliner was released for flight checks with instruments, it was as sound mechanically as the day it rolled out of the airplane factory. The "push-button" base, so named by mechanics because all of the heavy work was done by pushing buttons, delivered up to two dozen rejuvenated airliners per month, including some overhauled on contract for other airlines.

It cost the company $6,000,000 to move equipment and families west and to concentrate maintenance and engineering operations in San Francisco and other operations activities in Denver. By 1957, the investment in the huge base, sprawling over 129 acres adjoining San Francisco Airport, had mushroomed to over $14,000,000. For a short time after it was opened, SFOMB, as the base was known in airline jargon, was referred to by some dollar-minded experts as "United Air Lines' folly."

"I'll tell you how much of a folly it has been," W. A. Patterson once explained to the Investment Bankers Association. "It has reduced manhours on overhaul of engines, aircraft, and instruments by 22½ per cent. With the savings of six years, we paid for the base. I don't think that is a bad investment."

In 1947 Patterson assigned a team of independent appraisers to survey cities along the Main Line and report on the most advantageous site for a similar concentration of Flight Operations and Transportation Services departments. The appraisers came up with some persuasive facts: Denver was within 100 miles of the geographic center of United's mainland network; by DC-6, it was 6½ hours from New York, 6 hours from Seattle, 5 hours from San Francisco, 4 hours from Los Angeles, just 3 hours from Chicago and United's executive headquarters. Denver offered the best living conditions at the lowest price of any major city on the United system and it enjoyed more clear, sunny days than any other large city.

United's Denver Operating Base, something new in air transport, became the nerve center of the 14,000-mile system, which was telescoped by the Mainliners' ever-increasing speed from five operating divisions into a single unit. Denver replaced Chicago as headquarters for two United vice-presidents and their staffs. By 1957, Flight Operations, under D. R. Petty, directed some 3000 employes, including 2200 pilots and flight engineers. Transportation Services, headed by Don F. Magarrell, had 8600 people along the line, including 1100 stewardesses, 950 ticket agents, 750 chefs and dining-service workers in fifteen flight kitchens, and 5500 ground-services workers at eighty United terminals scattered along the system. Housed temporarily in Hangar 5 at Stapleton Air Field, the 1560 Denver members of the United family moved early in 1953 into a handsome two-story Colorado red sandstone unit of the Denver terminal, built by the city of Denver with aid from the Civil Aeronautics Administration and leased to the company for thirty years.

Soon after it opened, the Denver Base became a mecca for executives and technicians from other airlines, foreign as well as domestic. They made pilgrimages there to study the unique "brain center" that stepped up operations to new levels of efficiency. Most spectacular of these was the "Chapel," as it was soon nicknamed, a briefing room in which key executives and technicians gathered every morning at eight-thirty for a quick look and rundown of the previous twenty-four hours' operations from Honolulu to New York and Vancouver to San Diego. Seated before a huge system map covering an entire wall, on which colored lights flashed weather conditions at major terminals and temporary trouble spots along the line, the operating staff listened while experts from various departments reported performances in their respective bailiwicks.

Chapel opened daily with a weather round-up by meteorology chief Henry Harrison or an assistant. In two or three cryptic minutes, the weather man gave the reasons for fog over Los Angeles, thunderstorms over the Midwest, yesterday's northwest cold front that petered out in Idaho, clear weather east of

Chicago, concluding with what could be expected during the next twenty-four hours. Operations reported as to why flights were delayed by weather or mechanical failures; Transportation Services told how the passengers and cargo were moved despite delays, including providing competitors an "assist" when their planes made nonscheduled landings at United terminals. A Maintenance spokesman reported on progress of repairs on planes both along the line and undergoing overhaul at the San Francisco Base. Communications had a few words about the daily torrents of information flowing over United's busy 42,000 miles of telephone and teletype lines, while Space Control revealed that yesterday the airplanes were 79 per cent occupied, but tomorrow, beginning a busy week end, Passenger Service should have seats and meals for an 85 per cent load, including some extra sections. In twenty fast-moving minutes, everything unusual that had happened to any of the 186 Mainliners at all the stations along the Main Line was reviewed with the objective of making the next day's record still better.

This fast look at the system was made possible by the wizardry of Communications, the nerve center of Operations. Actually, Communications operated duplicate nerve networks, one for running the airline, the other for expediting passenger service. Maintaining these networks cost over $4,000,000 a year, more than half as much as the expense of running the entire airline in 1934 when the United system was pieced together. Space Control, a buzzing horseshoe of phone boards, recording machines, and charts, was the nerve center for a 15,000-mile phone network connecting forty-two major traffic-generating centers. Sales offices in thirty-eight other cities used teletype circuits. On the phone circuits, callers used an abbreviated lingo known as "speed talk"—for example, "from LGA post 621 of the 255SFO," which meant "New York is selling five reservations to San Francisco for Flight 621 on March 25." The "speed talk" went automatically onto recording machines, from which it was unscrambled by typists into everyday English.

Up to 2000 reservations messages per hour poured into Space Control during peak periods. A "sell and record" system enabled any United ticket agent in the country to tell a passenger immediately whether or not a seat was available on any flight. Space Control functioned as a wholesaler of seats to regional passenger ticket offices, which sold freely until Denver flashed a "stop sales" warning that a certain flight was sold out. After that seats were sold on that flight only as cancellations came in, right up to flight departure time. Space Control also kept an eye on cargo space, especially after United introduced its unique RAF (reserved air freight) service, which let shippers reserve cargo space on a specific flight just as passengers reserved seats.

Denver likewise was headquarters for United's Dining Service and supervised the far-flung chain of flight kitchens which produced 5,000,000 meals annually. Dining Service kept a careful eye on the appetites of passengers, coordinating menus, testing new recipes, and encouraging the corps of European-trained chefs to ever greater culinary triumphs. Dining Service had to have the right number of meals ready for more than 300 flights a day, even though some of the patrons were "go shows" who waited at the gates in Seattle, Philadelphia or Fresno to slip into seats available at the last minute, often because "no shows" failed to catch airliners at other stations. For coach flights, Dining Service had to guess how many meals passengers would buy as they boarded the planes and have the food ready to put aboard at the last minute. Representative flight kitchen meals cost the company $1.49 apiece, the same meal from caterers $1.74. The easy days when an airline could serve a cold fried-chicken box lunch for every meal were gone. Dining Service not only had to have the meals piping hot, but meals had to be planned so that no passenger got chicken or lamb or filet mignon twice in succession. Dining Service accomplished this feat by having chefs make out menus five weeks in advance, also, by urging them to feature the foods of the area, such as cod out of Boston, salmon out of Seattle, beef out of Chicago.

Among the prides of the Denver Base was the Flight Training Center, which, with a satellite center in Chicago, came to be known as the "airline pilots' postgraduate university." The "university" operated around the year for the men who flew the Mainliners. Denver Flight Training provided co-pilot courses for new members of United crews and upgrading courses for co-pilots graduating to captain status. It also offered graduate training for captains advancing up the line from Convairs to DC-6s to DC-7s and, eventually, to jetliners.

Both the Denver and Chicago Training Centers were equipped with flight simulators, amazing electronic mechanisms that duplicated Convair and DC-6B cockpits and reproduced any flying condition or emergency that might occur. The simulators even simulated realistically such flying problems as engine or propeller failure, hydraulic troubles, icing on wings, etc. They reproduced signals and messages heard on airliners in flight, the sounds of motors revving up, of wheels screeching on landing strips. Pilots emerged from these simulated runs and emergencies in cold sweats, but better pilots for having experienced the emergency and solved the problem without risking anybody's life. A Convair simulator, incidentally, cost $750,000, as much as a new Convair-liner. But in it the flight crew could, as a team, solve emergencies which could not be simulated in actual training flights. Also, each simulator released a training plane for passenger or cargo service.

At nearby Cheyenne a stewardess training school turned out fifty new stewardesses each month to replace those who had resigned, usually to get married. The original eight nurses persuaded by Ellen Church and Steve Stimpson in 1930 to participate in the test of Miss Church's idea of stewardesses aboard airplanes had become a United sky girl staff numbering 1100 by 1957. Stewardesses, too, looked to the Denver Base as their headquarters, although their intensive 4½-week training course at company expense was at the school in Cheyenne. Stewardess requirements had changed over the years. Nursing experience was no longer a requisite. Instead, United sought personable young women, age 20 through 26, with college training or business experience, who had the knack for handling people. Although a few, like jolly Senior Stewardess Mary O'Connor, made a career of flying, the average United stewardess flew 24 months, then embarked on the wings of matrimony. Ellen Church's big idea had grown into a new career for more than 7000 young women employed by the airlines of the world.

Denver was also headquarters for Ground Services, the 5500

men who got the passengers, the baggage and cargo, and the meals on more than 300 daily flights and who fueled and cleaned the airliners in all kinds of weather. Peripatetic Seely Hall, assistant vice-president–facilities, who joined the airline in Medford when Vern Gorst first launched Pacific Air Transport back in 1925, made an important discovery in 1952. Watching the crowds who kibitzed as ground crews swarmed over airliners at terminals, Hall realized that United was running one of the greatest shows on earth. A survey revealed that 40,000,000 people stood on the sidelines each year, enjoying the "ramp show." As a result of this revelation, United put Ground Services workers into smart new uniforms, with colored caps to designate their duties. This and Ground Services training courses stepped up the efficiency on the ground to a new high.

Among the wonders of the Denver Base was the "weather center," organized by soft-spoken Henry T. Harrison, long-time head of United's Meteorological Department. Harrison, now a little grayer and more scholarly-looking, was the same Cleveland weather man whom Jack Herlihy and other early National Air Transport pilots used to call in the flying-postman era when uncertain about risking their necks by taking off into "soupy" weather. Since then Harrison had studied a lot of weather all over the globe. At twenty-four, he was meteorologist with the Byrd Antarctic expedition, discovering to his amazement that some of the best flying weather was over the frigid and cloudless polar regions.

When World War II broke, Harrison was head meteorologist for United's eastern division. A few weeks later he was the AAF hurricane expert at Miami, gateway for the flying caravan of bombers winging to the European war theater. Just prior to the historic Yalta conference, Lieutenant Colonel Harrison was handed one of his most ticklish wartime assignments—getting sixteen planeloads of top brass, including Franklin D. Roosevelt, Winston Churchill, General George Marshall, Secretary of State Stettinius and their staffs, weatherbound at Malta, to Yalta in Southern Russia. Although eager to reach Yalta to meet Stalin on time, Roosevelt and Churchill balked at flying in bad weather. It was Harrison's responsibility, in collaboration with RAF me-

Introduction of the twin-engine Mainliner Convair to United's system in 1952 meant new speed, comfort, and operating efficiency for intermediate cities, long served by the trusty but outmoded DC-3.

Ticket offices in downtown city locations are United's "supermarkets." Typical in its smart appearance is this one on Chicago's famed Michigan Avenue.

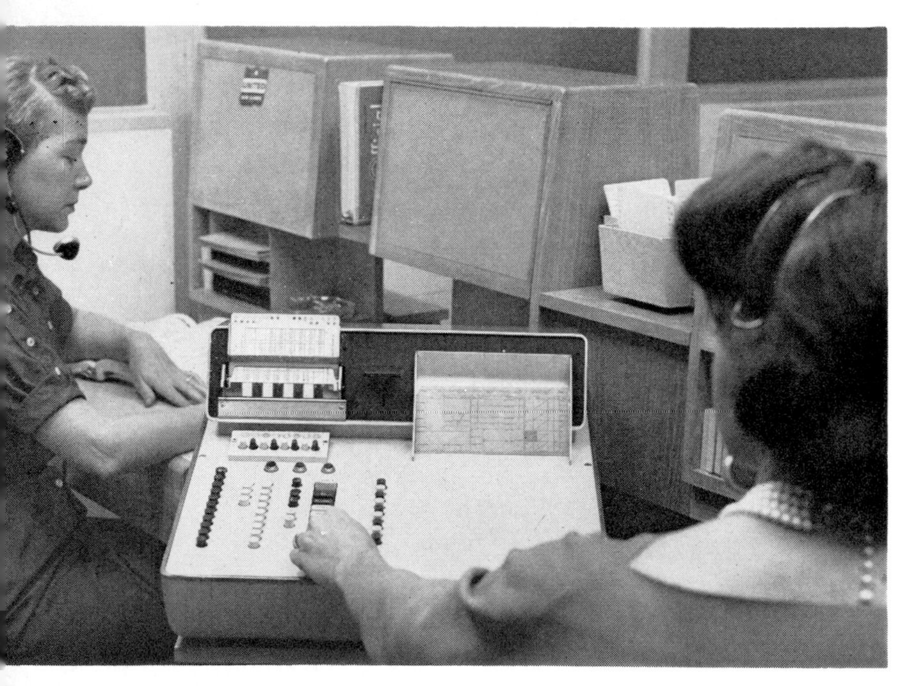

Agent sets like this enable United reservations personnel to determine space availability on any flight in less than a second. Thus does the company keep pace on the ground with the Jet Age in the air.

The Mainliner's weather eye: Mechanic adjusts C-Band radar unit in the nose of airliner, which enables pilots to see through storms and plot courses where flying is smoothest. United's entire fleet was equipped with these weather radar sets by 1957 at a cost of $5,000,000.

Three decades separate the United Air Lines stewardess uniforms shown here. Joyce Strang (left) models the original 1930 outfit—a greenish ensemble which included a matching tam and cape. The Jet Age uniform of Sheri Moore is done in a UAL shade of pink and beige known as "peige."

teorologists, to map a chain of fair-weather dog-legs from Malta to Yalta, over which route the pilots delivered their distinguished passengers on time.

By V-J Day, Harrison was in Manila analyzing pressure patterns for the bomber armadas softening Japan for the invasion. When the war ended, he returned to Chicago to apply new knowledge of upstairs-weather forecasting to the entire United system. By 1948, Harrison and his staff, having set up shop in Denver, were able to tell pilots what weather to expect anywhere, at any time, at any level, along the entire United system. By that time, Harrison had evolved a system that made choosing a track to capitalize on pressure patterns as easy as charting a course via airway beams. When a pilot reported for duty at any major terminal, the meteorologist had already completed last-minute weather mapping. By placing a transparent plastic, on which all the approved tracks were sketched, over a routine weather map, it was evident at a glance where the airliner would encounter the most favorable winds and atmosphere.

In 1955, Harrison and his chief, ex-pilot Dick Petty, vice-president–flight operations, concluded that they were not extracting the full potential from U.S. Weather Bureau facilities. United's meteorological experts were scattered along the Main Line in key centers where the majority of flights originated. After a new look at the weather-forecasting problem, Harrison advised concentrating all of United's meteorologists in one system-wide weather center at Denver. Unbelievable as it may seem, Harrison insisted that the weather in Fresno or Akron or any of United's terminals could be sized up better in one well-staffed weather center in Denver than in a dozen understaffed regional offices. In 1956, except for a small staff in San Francisco specializing in Pacific Ocean weather for Honolulu flights, all of United's weather experts were pulled into Denver. Their concentrated forces, twenty-five meteorologists plus ten weather clerks, made the largest weather staff outside of the U.S. Weather Bureau in Washington, D.C. From Denver they sent out fifty-five to seventy forecasts each twenty-four hours by leased wire to dispatchers along the system. Every three hours pilots in flight received revised up-to-the-minute forecasts by radio.

United's Weather Center pointed up a revolution in airline meteorology to meet the demands of the higher-flying, faster-moving airliners. Pilots had long complained that "You give us wonderful weather service on the ground, but when we're in the air, we're forgotten." The Weather Center utilized reports from high-altitude atmospheric flashes by miniature radio sets known as RAWINSONDE, which were borne aloft by weather balloons all over the country and over weather ships in the Pacific. RAWINSONDE reported temperatures, barometric pressures, and humidity at various elevations up to 40,000 feet. It also told which way the wind was blowing and how fast. As these and other reports poured into the Weather Center, they were processed by teams of meteorologists whose aggregate experience in weather forecasting totaled 503 years. The new facilities plus the new techniques took most of the guesswork out of weather aloft.

As the United fleet grew, one of the more important teams was Sales, directed by Vice-president Robert E. Johnson. Every day Johnson and his staff of traffic hustlers had up to 24,000,000 seat miles to sell to keep United in good health financially. Every year they dealt with over 6,000,000 passengers, many of whom changed their plans after they made their original reservations. Sales had to develop means of keeping track of all these passengers embarking on 1600 departures daily and making 3000 connections. One terminal, San Francisco, handled over 6000 passengers per day.

Bob Johnson, who became an assistant to the president as well as vice-president–sales in 1955, had begun booking passengers onto flying machines even before United became a company. Born in Yakima, Washington, trained in journalism at the University of Washington, he joined Boeing Air Transport in 1929 after being talked by Harold Crary into entering the Boeing publicity department. At first, Johnson split his energies between publicizing Boeing airplanes and Boeing Air Transport service. When United Air Lines was organized in 1931, Johnson joined Crary in the Chicago headquarters, handling the new company's publicity and, later, advertising. In 1935, he married United's chief stewardess, Rosalie Gimple. In 1946, after three years in the

Pacific as a Navy air-combat intelligence officer, Johnson became director of public relations and advertising, then took over sales upon Crary's retirement. In 1959, he became senior vice-president, Sales-Advertising.

By the mid-fifties the task of keeping track of seats sold on 1600 daily flights had outgrown human transmitting and recording capacities. A survey of "no shows" revealed that United was more often at fault than the passenger who failed to board his plane and occupy his seat. In 1955, United helped solve the problem by going electronic. A wizard device in each sales office no larger than a portable radio and known as "Unisel" reported back in a matter of seconds if the requested space was available on any flight scheduled during the next three months. The prospective passenger got his "yes" or "no" immediately. An automatic ticket maker called a "Ticketeer" printed the customer's ticket immediately. The new technique, covering the 14,000-mile system, was rated as "fastest and most efficient ticket sales and reservations set-up in transportation history."

By 1956, United's 200 ticket offices in eighty cities were undergoing transformation, too. On the premise that these offices were United's personality in their areas, Vice-president Johnson assigned a staff of designers and decorators to give Sales the "United new look," keeping pace with the refurbished Mainliners. Starting with the Beverly Hills, Chicago, and Waikiki offices, the designers covered the eighty United cities, creating travel atmosphere with ingenious use of murals, lights, vinyl floors and counters, and travel plaques in United's red, white, and blue color tones.

Air cargo furnished one of the surprises of 1956 when it passed air mail as a source of revenue on the United system. Five new DC-6As placed in all-cargo service that year handled cargoes of great variety coast to coast on schedules as fast as those of passenger airliners. The large liners had pressurized cockpits and areas for live cargoes, notably dogs, which traveled in lightweight deodorized kennels, an idea of the late Colonel A. D. Tuttle, United's former medical director. The Cargoliners carried cut flowers, machinery, medicines, wearing apparel, films, to mention only a few items. Among the year's cargoes were 700,000 pounds of beasts, birds, and insects, the latter largely bees and ladybugs —and five tons of fishing worms. In addition to cats and dogs, chicks, and tropical fish, the Cargoliners transported monkeys, lions, tigers, gorillas, frogs, ponies, and a racehorse. Altogether cargo brought in $10,656,000 in revenues in 1956, thus making United's team of cargo hustlers among the important people who helped keep the Mainliners on the wing.

CHAPTER XV

What Makes United Run?

Shortly before United Air Lines reached its thirtieth anniversary, W. A. Patterson, who had just arranged with three insurance companies and thirty-eight banks to mobilize $150 million to pay for a fleet of jetliners, talked to the Associated Traffic Clubs in Cleveland. Contrasting the company's humble first flight from Elko, Nevada, to Pasco, Washington, in 1926 with the fabulous growth of the Main Line system in three decades, he said:

"It is true that our little company was subsidized when it became the first airline to operate under a private contract with the Post Office. We owned five airplanes which cost $16,000 apiece. We had twenty-three employes. Our passenger business that first year was $1,324; our air mail revenue was $230,000. The (air mail) law at that time read that we were to find some commercial use of the airplane; we were also to develop the art of flying; and we were supposed, eventually, to become self-sufficient. Well, that was not too long ago. Let's see how we have turned out, particularly in assuming those three obligations."

Patterson's 1956 report to the 23,777 stockholders who owned United Air Lines at that time contained some of the answers, but not all. The four little airlines that started flying in 1926 and later merged to form the United system had grown into a 14,000-mile airway network connecting eighty terminals and serving a third of the population of the country. Revenues had zoomed to $262,791,000 in 1956, and only 3½ per cent of this was from air mail. Air mail pay had been cut from $10.80 per ton-mile in 1926 to $.36 per ton-mile in 1956, when for each ton-mile the Post Office garnered $1.50 from the sale of stamps. In addition to this profit United paid to or collected for Federal, state, and local governments more than $59 million in taxes. United had not only become self-sustaining, but Uncle Sam's flier in an air mail subsidy, long since discontinued for the trunk airlines, was paying off well.

In three decades the United system, after growing fabulously, had come to mean a lot of things to a lot of people. It was a fleet of 186 modern, pressurized, and speedy twin-engine and four-engine airliners with more than 10,000 seats that moved on an average of 2000 miles each day. In 1956 more than 6,200,000 passengers paid a whopping $236,285,000 to ride on Mainliners while freight and express shipments earned $15,000,000—50 per cent more than air mail, which, in the '20s and '30s, had provided the biggest part of the airline's revenues.

The United family was over 20,000 strong; its paychecks and benefits totaled $115,491,000 in 1956, 43 per cent of the Main Line's revenues. United's people were scattered from Hartford, with 50 UALers, to Honolulu with 200, San Francisco with 6300, and North Platte with 4. Wherever they were, by their enthusiasm, sincerity, manner of living, and participation in civic affairs they had given United Air Lines a corporate character that made the company a welcomed neighbor in hundreds of communities.

This enviable company personality was more than a lucky heritage. It was planned that way. Ever since he became head of the struggling company in 1934, Patterson had asked himself and other officers, "What kind of a personality is United Air Lines anyway?" A lot of Patterson's zeal and public spirit had rubbed off onto his associates, and from them onto supervisors, and from supervisors to men and women on the ramp, in ticket offices, in Mainliner cabins.

Back in 1948, United had originated an annual meeting known as "Flight Plan"—a one or two-day affair attended by supervisory personnel from all across the Main Line system. Its purpose was a yearly appraisal of just where the company then stood and what plans were in the making for the future.

In 1955, a new, more personal touch was added which quickly became the climax of each year's "Flight Plan" event—the annual awards dinner. Taking part were employes whose performance "has been of such significance and value as to warrant special recognition by the company." The awards were gold-finished Mainliner models mounted on walnut desk stands, each carrying a small gold plaque engraved with the employe's name, reason for award, Patterson's signature, date, and place. The United people who received them were a cross-section of job classifications and locations—their common ground an outstanding job of sales achievement, community service, or special contribution to their individual administration. It was tangible recognition of Patterson's long-time insistence that "people make an airline."

Top honor of them all was "The President's Award," of which not more than one could be given in any one year. In 1955, it went to Ernie M. Weiss of the Denver Ground Services staff for leading rescue teams, at the risk of his life, after the Medicine Bow accident; in 1956, it went to veteran Captain Rube Wagner, soon to retire after 30 years of flying. Wagner, whose logbook told the story of 32,000 hours in the air, was described by Patterson in making the award as "the outstanding technician-scientist-professional man in flying today."

Another award that emphasized how everybody in the clan helped make United run was one in 1955 to Ray N. Rieder, supervisor of plant maintenance at New York's International Airport. This was $3000 for the best suggestion of the year. Rieder's idea was simple: individual lockers near the work areas of Ground Services personnel where soiled work uniforms could be left and fresh uniforms picked up, the lockers being serviced by a laundry. The idea saved the company $30,000 annually. In 1954, A. S. Kingman, a Los Angeles ramp serviceman, won $2640 for suggesting use of recording machines to handle the 2000-per-hour torrent of phone calls to Space Control at the Denver Operating Base. In the first decade and a half after the Suggestion Board was set up in 1941 by Patterson, United people tossed in 98,717 ideas for improving operations or services in some manner. Of these, 19,678 were adopted, bringing cash awards of $337,810 to originators. The ideas saved the company an estimated $3,375,000 in that period.

By 1956, a fourth to a third of United's people found themselves going to school somewhere along the Main Line. The $5,000,000 earmarked annually for training was about evenly divided between Flight Operations training and Personnel's more general Education and Training department.

In two flight-training centers maintained at Denver and Chicago, every pilot, co-pilot, and flight engineer took a refresher course twice a year. In 1955–1956 the Denver center turned out 300 new co-pilots, many of them former flight engineers who elected to become fliers following the 1955 flight engineers' strike.

The comprehensive training program for people on the ground was the brainchild of T. Lee, Jr., who has been United's Number 1 "professor" since the company was founded. About half of this program was technical, too, concentrated at the San Francisco Maintenance Base, where classrooms and home-study courses directed by eighteen instructors taught mechanics, physics, mathematics, and other subjects important in keeping pace in a fast-moving industry. The nontechnical department, based at Cheyenne, featured courses and seminars for training fifty new stewardesses each month, as well as on indoctrination for new supervisors and new techniques for more senior management employes. In New York, Chicago, San Francisco, Los Angeles, and Seattle, local training staffs conducted indoctrination sessions for new United people as well as on-the-job training to make employes more skilled in their daily tasks. Thanks to the opportunities offered by the "world's largest airline university," nobody on the United payroll was standing still, tied to his job, except by choice.

Through the years, United, the country's largest airline system when the company was put together, grew the hard way. Because of "the long suit" to vindicate former President Phil Johnson of conspiracy, United was "in the doghouse" in Washington, D.C., from 1934 to 1943. Competitors were granted new routes for the asking; United got them by paying hard cash whenever the CAB permitted purchases of smaller airlines. That is how United got into Denver, which became the nerve center of the entire Main Line system, headquarters of D. R. Petty, vice-president—flight operations, and staff and of D. F. Magarrell, vice-president–transportation services, and his staff. Denver's rise to a position second only to the executive headquarters at Chicago in the United scheme of things is an unusual chapter in the company's history and calls for a quick flash back to the late thirties.

The early overland air mail route laid out by the Post Office had completely bypassed Denver in favor of Cheyenne, just as had the Pony Express, the overland railroads, and the transcontinental highways. United got into Denver in 1937 by buying a feeder line from Cheyenne to Denver from Wyoming Air Service, Inc.

After the CAB denied a United–Western Air Express merger in 1940, United petitioned for the right to fly from Denver to Los Angeles, to speed up service to Southern California. At the same time Western Air Express, reorganized and rejuvenated as Western Airlines, also applied for the Denver–Los Angeles route. The applications, shelved at the outbreak of war, were heard in 1944 and the examiner recommended in favor of United. Again the CAB reversed the examiner's findings and granted Western a certificate to fly Denver–Los Angeles. Under an ambitious new management headed by William A. Coulter, the line's largest shareholder, Western was on the make, ambitious to expand into a new transcontinental line. Western contracted for a fleet of DC-6s, but until the new planes could be delivered, it handled the Denver service in DC-4s.

The Denver gateway decision had an unexpected denouement. Shut out of the Southern California area via Salt Lake or Denver, the United management tried a new approach. The company petitioned to merge Route 1, its transcontinental airway, with Route 11, the San Diego to Seattle route. There was precedent for this, the CAB having already approved the merger of the Salt Lake–Seattle route into Route 1. The Board favored merging Routes 1 and 11, but if that were done, United Mainliners might fly nonstop from Chicago to any city on the Pacific Coast, including Los Angeles. Without the traffic delivered by United at the Denver gateway, which was 40 per cent of its passenger business, Western, having overexpanded, might be in precarious financial straits. So the CAB stalled on United's petition.

Early in 1947, a CAB member called United's Patterson from Washington to say that Western was in such financial difficulties that the airline would probably go into the hands of a receiver within thirty days unless bailed out. He suggested that Terrell C. Drinkwater, newly chosen president of the company, might be willing to sell Western's Denver–Los Angeles route to United. This was a more significant suggestion than appeared on the surface. Though the Civil Aeronautics Act of 1938 implied that airline certificates amounted to franchises with proprietary value, the CAB had not yet established a precedent by approving the sale of a major route by one airline to another. Patterson called Drinkwater and arranged to meet him at Santa Barbara to see if a deal that would save Western could be worked out. Drinkwater needed fast action to meet his next payroll. Patterson wanted it, too, in order to get the route without having to bid against rivals.

The agreement quickly worked out by the two airline presidents was an unusual one. Drinkwater needed $3,750,000 to save his airline. He and Patterson listed the assets Western could sell in connection with the Denver–Los Angeles route—four DC-4s specially equipped for high-altitude flying at $450,000 each; spare engines, parts, and equipment worth $325,000; ground facilities valued at $125,000; development costs and promotion, $128,000; training pilots, stewardesses, and dispatchers, $245,000. The total still fell short by $1,128,000 of what Drinkwater needed to rehabilitate Western, so Patterson put down that sum as the intangible value of the route, which ironically three years before had been a grant free to Western when the CAB denied United's petition. There was still one catch. The CAB had to approve the transaction and this took time. Drinkwater needed cash immediately to meet his payroll. To keep Western solvent until CAB could approve the sale, Patterson loaned Drinkwater $1,000,000 out of United's reserve funds with equipment as security. He also agreed to assume a Western commitment to Douglas Aircraft for the purchase of five DC-6s about to be delivered, thus letting Western off a financial hook. In the end it turned out to be a million-dollar bargain, because in Western's contract the planes were priced at $600,000 apiece, whereas Douglas was asking $825,000 per plane in new quotations.

Conclusion of the negotiations touched off a flurry of actions by the CAB. Now that it was no longer necessary to bolster up Western's volume by transcontinental United traffic from Denver west, the Board approved on May 19, 1947, the merger of United's Routes 1 and 11, permitting United to fly nonstop between Chicago and Los Angeles, as well as via Denver. On the same day, the CAB granted TWA a nonstop route between Chicago and Los Angeles and certificated American to fly into San Francisco via Phoenix. Western was permitted to extend its Los Angeles–San Francisco route to Seattle, in competition with United. In September, the CAB formally approved the United purchase of Western's Los Angeles–Denver route in what was hailed by the industry as a milestone decision.

Elsewhere, other decisions affected United's Main Line. The CAB also agreed to consolidation of the routes to Washington and Boston into Route 1, giving United entry into New England and the nation's capital. It also granted United's San Francisco–Honolulu application, but postponed decision on the Los Angeles–Honolulu run until 1950. This reshuffling extended far beyond the United routes and became precedent for a general remaking of the airways map to take advantage of the new speed and longer cruising range of modern air transports.

The major airlines—United, American, TWA, Eastern—which carry the bulk of the country's domestic air traffic, have been peculiarly vulnerable to the whims of the ever-changing CAB administrations. At the time of the 1947 reshuffle, the CAB's idea was to make the majors completely self-supporting and use the Federal subsidy funds to shore up the feeder lines that served smaller communities. This policy of force-feeding the feeders was carried to ludicrous ends. An example was Southwest Airways, which competed with United up and down the Pacific Coast from Los Angeles to Medford, Oregon, where it connected with another feeder, West Coast Airways, serving Oregon and Washington communities. In 1948, the CAB authorized the Post Office to pay Southwest $30 a ton-mile for carrying mail over the same route for which United was paid $.63 per ton-mile. To reduce Southwest's competition, the CAB several years later temporarily suspended United's certificate to serve some cities, such as Santa Barbara and Monterey, where Southwest thus inherited a monopoly on service. That suspension lasted until 1955.

The major airlines had not only grown independent of subsidy; they were making money for the Post Office. In fact, they were carrying mail so economically that in 1953 postal officials decided to experiment on certain routes with the idea of flying all first-class mail, whether the letters bore air mail stamps or not.

By 1955, when Ross Rizley became chairman of the CAB, such a stack of applications for new routes had been filed by airlines, United included, that Rizley decided to clear the log jam with drastic action. The board members, who were convinced by the spectacular growth of air traffic that the sky was unlimited, raced through the dockets, making expedited decisions and granting a rash of new routes that changed United's competitive position almost overnight. In fact, it amounted to a reversal of the old concept that a CAB route certification was a franchise to operate between centers of population, with just enough competition to protect the public interest. Under the new CAB decrees, some routes were packed with competitive airlines scrambling for passengers to keep their planes even partly filled.

The Denver service case decision brought TWA into Denver from Los Angeles and Chicago; gave Continental Airlines a Los Angeles–Denver, San Francisco, Chicago route; put Western Airlines into Denver from San Francisco via Salt Lake; gave American a San Francisco–Chicago nonstop route; and put United back into Kansas City, an old Main Line traffic center lost in 1934 following the air mail purge.

The Chicago–New York case granted Northwest and Capital Airlines nonstop schedules between these centers, bringing the number of competitors on this route up to five; it also granted United a New York–Pittsburgh–Chicago route. The East Coast case increased the competition between New York and Washington to nine airlines. United gained the right in this latter decision to fly between the Atlantic seaboard terminals of Washington, Baltimore, Philadelphia, New York, and Boston, a service long sought, but with the restriction that flights had to originate or terminate west of Toledo. The Southwest–Northeast case put Braniff and Delta into New York from the South. United also won back Santa Barbara and Monterey, which had been suspended previously in the effort to bolster Southwest Airways. Though the decisions meant new competition, they also rounded out the United system, adding important population centers and increasing Main Line mileage to a new peak, 14,000 miles.

Having remade the airways map of the country, the CAB turned to a long-range study of the fare structure. Though the airline industry was booming, judged by increases each year in passenger traffic, it was zooming into a decline, earningswise, for a number of reasons. One was the increased cost of everything—wages, fuel, planes, parts, leased wires, equipment. A DC-6, which was a $600,000 investment in 1948, cost $1,000,000 plus in 1956, while a DC-7, which carried virtually the same number of passengers, but faster, cost $1,800,000.

In the scramble for passengers, one airline after another put its costliest and fastest planes into coach service, at fares one-third less than first-class fares. To meet the competition of American Airlines and TWA, United put DC-7s in nonstop transcontinental coach service early in 1957. It was reminiscent of the costly battle for traffic between Chicago and New York in the mid-thirties, except that this time the struggle was on a continental scope, with the prospect of going broke on a still more colossal scale. In 1957, United and six other airlines unsuccessfully petitioned for a temporary 6 per cent fare increase until the CAB's fare investigation could be completed, pointing out that while airline fares remained at the 1940 level, railroad and bus fares had climbed over 40 per cent.

The crisis involved more than keeping the airlines financially healthy, which the CAB was charged with doing by the Civil Aeronautics Act. The airlines' fleets were a key arm of national defense under a program known as CRAF (Civil Reserve Air Fleet) set up following the Korean War. Under this plan, roughly one-fourth of United's larger airliners were modified for long-range overseas flying at any time they might be needed by the

Department of Defense. The planes and their crews were kept on the alert to fly on short notice to designated mobilization points. Along with the planes, some 1500 United technicians and mechanics were in the reserve.

The CRAF program made available to the Defense Department within forty-eight hours some 360 fast, 4-engine airliners for which twenty-four airlines had paid over $400,000,000 CRAF, which saved the Federal government an investment of $400,000,000, plus an annual $300,000,000 maintenance cost, was labeled in Washington as "Uncle Sam's Best Buy." By way of contrast, the Federal Maritime Administration had agreed to pour $1,500,000,000 in eight years into subsidies to modernize the United States Merchant Marine. Thus "Uncle Sam's Best Buy," a defense air arm for free, was a crucial responsibility of the CAB members.

The rising cost of providing air transport was illustrated by the price tags on United Mainliners, as of early 1957. The average cost of each type of plane was: a DC-6, $841,000; a Convair 340, $637,000; a DC-6B, $1,114,000; a DC-7, $1,794,000. As of March, 1957, United's fleet consisted of 7 DC-4s, 42 DC-6s, 5 DC-6As, 25 DC-6Bs, 55 Convair 340s, and 32 DC-7s. In the remaining months of 1957, 7 DC-6Bs and 11 DC-7s were to be delivered, followed by 4 DC-6Bs and 9 DC-7s in 1958. United's propeller-driven fleet, 200 planes with the addition of 1958 deliveries, represented a $207 million investment—soon to be nearly doubled by the addition of a 30-plane jet fleet.

This was only part of the investment, albeit the larger part. Every gate at a major airport called for $30,000 worth of mobile ramp equipment. The arrival of a Mainliner "Red Carpet" flight was, as Patterson put it, like the arrival of a Queen Mary, except that it took place several times daily. Behind the ramp, and unseen by the kibitzing public, were still more costly servicing facilities, kitchens, baggage-handling vehicles. The airport itself had become a major investment, not for the airlines, but for the communities themselves. A number of terminals had grown from civic headaches into money-making facilities, notably Los Angeles, San Francisco, Denver, Detroit, and Chicago's Midway Airport.

In the years since Jack Knight barnstormed the Main Line, talking chambers of commerce into transforming cow pastures into landing strips for the intrepid flying postmen, airports had grown, like the airliners that used them, into vast, complex, multimillion-dollar investments. United was one of the few airlines that ever invested its own dollars in demonstration terminals—at Burbank, California, and Reno, Nevada. It turned out to be expensive demonstrating.

"All we got out of spending our own money was a greater appreciation of the airport problem," recalled Patterson, after the Burbank Airport had been sold to Lockheed Aircraft Corporation for its cost, $3,000,000. The Reno venture demonstrated why airlines could not afford to operate airports. After pouring $500,000 into a model small-city terminal, the runways and other facilities suddenly required enlargement at a cost of an additional $700,000, mainly to accommodate the Nevada National Guard and private-plane operators. When the city asked for an option to buy the airport, United's management jumped at the opportunity to get out of the airport business for good.

After the war, many cities inherited military landing strips or emergency wartime airports built by the CAA. A boom in airport building began, with designers split into two schools. One school favored the centralized terminal, such as Seattle's imposing building, completed in 1951. The other school advocated the sprawling Chicago-type terminal, in which each airline had its individual passenger station. The $14,000,000 San Francisco International Airport, opened in 1954, represented a compromise in the thinking of the two schools.

Although owned and operated by the city, the San Francisco Airport was a major United interest, since United's flights, north, south, east, and west, accounted for more than half the traffic. United's veteran airport managers contributed much to the planning of facilities for passenger, baggage, and freight handling.

The four-story, highly functional terminal represented at the time the latest in airport engineering, with loading wings and levels designed to completely separate incoming and outgoing streams of traffic. But spectacular as it appeared on opening day, September 1, 1954, the terminal did not completely solve the problem of moving passengers and luggage on and off planes as expeditiously as the Mainliners could airlift them from city to city. Each modern new terminal introduced new ideas as architects and ground service experts strove to anticipate the rush of traffic when jetliners would load or unload a hundred or more passengers and their luggage in a cascade at the gates.

United's engineers came up with a brainstorm for passenger and baggage handling in 1954, an "air-dock" into which an airliner could be pulled sidewise for boarding and deplaning. After building one at Denver experimentally, they were $175,000 wiser; the air-dock wasn't the answer. From that early experimentation, however, came the eventual answer—a telescoping corridor called a "Jetway" that could be extended from the second-floor level of a terminal building to a plane's passenger loading doors. Where such units were installed—San Francisco, New York, Seattle, for example—United's passengers were fully protected from the weather as they boarded or deplaned. Equally important, such pedestrian traffic was removed from the ramp area where ground servicing activities were taking place.

At the Los Angeles International Terminal, another inspiration of United's engineers went far toward the baggage delivery dilemma. It was a belt conveyor with a slowly moving ejector that spread the bags over a wide area, thus eliminating passenger pile-ups around baggage counters. The conveyor worked so well that before long others were delivering rivers of luggage at terminals along the Main Line. Each new device helped break the airport bottlenecks.

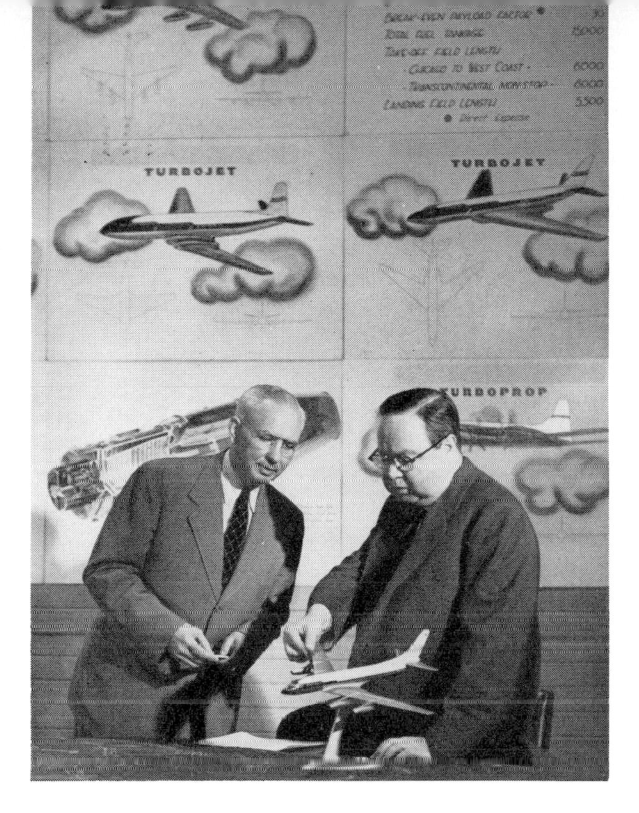

United's long-range preparations for the Jet Age began in 1950, almost 10 years before the company placed jetliners in service. In 1952, a "Paper Jet" project was conducted in which imaginary, theoretical jets were flown cross-country daily. Among others participating in the jet planning were R. D. Kelly, director of technical development (left), and J. A. Herlihy, senior vice-president—engineering and maintenance.

First climax to all the jet planning came in November, 1955, when President W. A. Patterson of United and Donald Douglas, head of Douglas Aircraft, signed papers whereby United ordered thirty DC-8 jets at a total cost of $175 million. Commitment, soon upped to forty, kicked off a flurry of jet orders by other domestic U.S. airlines.

The Douglas DC-8, introduced to the airways by United in September, 1959, serves the Main Line's long-haul routes. Powered by four Pratt & Whitney J-57 or J-75 engines, it carries from 105–119 first-class and coach passengers, has a cargo capacity of 6¼ tons and cruises at 550–575 miles per hour.

EQUIPPED FOR

The Boeing 720, which went into service on United in July, 1960, is used for medium-range operations. Powered by four Pratt & Whitney J-57 lightweight engines, its first-class-coach passenger capacity is 99–105; cargo capacity, 5¼ tons; cruising speed, 550–600 miles per hour.

The twin-engine French Caravelle joined United's jet fleet in July, 1961, on short-to-medium-haul routes. It has two rear-mounted Rolls-Royce engines, carries 64 first-class passengers and approximately 2¼ tons of cargo, has a cruising speed of 500–530 miles an hour.

THE JET AGE

Still to come is the short-to-medium-range Boeing 727, of which United has ordered forty for delivery late in 1963. It will have three Pratt & Whitney turbofan engines mounted at the rear. Passenger capacity will be 70–114; cruising speed, 550–600 miles per hour.

To introduce its Jet Mainliners to the public in 1959–60, United conceived JETARAMA —largest exhibition ever staged by any airline. Three circus-type tents housed a variety of displays. Behind them, a jet itself was on exhibition. JETARAMA attracted more than one million people in twelve major cities.

Typical of the air-minded who flocked to JETARAMA was this group at Portland, listening to an explanation of the DC-8's sound suppressor system.

CHAPTER XVI

Era of Expansion

United's thirty-fifth anniversary year—1961—found the airline in the throes of its most spectacular era of growth. The switch-over to jetliners was rapidly trebling the capacity to move both passengers and cargo and the speed of the jet Mainliners had shrunk the Main Line, timewise, to half its size in the days of propeller-driven planes. Addition of new airways through consolidation had brought the Mainliners winging into almost all of the important traffic centers in the United States. United was once more the country's largest airline—in airway mileage, volume of traffic, gross revenues, size of fleet, and number of employes. United's merger with Capital Airlines joined the second largest airways system with the sixth largest. The union created an air transport giant with 18,000 route miles serving 116 cities. Overnight the United family increased to more than 30,000. The Mainliner fleet jumped to 264 planes.

These impressive figures give little idea of the impact of the merger on the United system and on the domestic air transportation picture. It brought the United shield for the first time into forty-eight cities scattered from Minnesota to Florida, enabling United to fan out to a spread of Eastern terminals as it had long served the West Coast. It removed the wraps from restricted United service to a dozen or more cities previously served by both airlines. The merger also saved Capital from bankruptcy and disintegration and pointed the way to restoring the country's airlines to financial health by eliminating excessive and debilitating competition fomented by the CAB's open-handed extension of route certificates in 1955.

The story behind the merger includes another of the romances of air transport. Capital's beginnings dated back almost as far as United's. The airline was launched on April 27, 1927, one year after United's predecessors began flying the mail in the Far West. The founder, owner, and pilot was Cliff Ball, a barnstormer who took off from a cow pasture airstrip at Bettis Field, Pittsburgh, in a fabric-covered open-cockpit Waco biplane for the 127-mile flight to Cleveland. Ball had captured a Post Office air-mail contract for his embryo airline, which he imaginatively called "The Path of the Eagle." The only passenger brave enough to ride in Ball's bobbing mail planes that first year was Will Rogers, cushioned by mail bags. One day two passengers appeared at the field and asked the fare to Washington, D.C. To discourage them, Ball asked $100 apiece. The passengers accepted and were bumped over the mountains to Hoover Field, on the present site of the Pentagon. Thus, Capital's valid claim to one of its many "firsts" in the airline business—first airline to carry passengers over the Alleghenies.

In 1929 Ball's struggling airline was taken over by Pittsburgh Aviation Industries Corporation, organized by capitalists Frederick Crawford, C. Bedell Munro, and George R. Hann, who changed the name to Pennsylvania Airlines and added a Pittsburgh-Washington flight. (Munro and Hann were still directors when Capital was absorbed into the United system.) The airline made a living and the outlook was rosy until 1934, when F.D.R. canceled all air-mail contracts. Suddenly deprived of its meal ticket, the airline faced starvation. But its backers decided to stay in business and go after passenger traffic. They bought a Fairchild two-passenger cabin plane, then a tri-motored Ford, which had room for twelve fares, if that many fares could be induced to leave terra firma.

When the air-mail contracts were restored, they were less profitable. Pennsylvania Airlines had to lure more passengers into the air or go broke. So did a lusty young competitor, Central Airlines, which sprang up in Pittsburgh to fly passengers over Pennsylvania's routes, extended to include Grand Rapids, Detroit, Milwaukee. Central Airlines underbid Pennsylvania and captured the Pittsburgh-Cleveland air-mail contract. Pennsylvania fought back by purchasing a fleet of faster twin-engine Boeing 247s from United, and by buying Kohler Aviation Corporation, which had the Detroit-Milwaukee air-mail contract. Central met the challenge with a fleet of Stinsons, and by cutting fares. The two airlines operated identical schedules, and the first plane to reach an airport usually flew off with the passengers. In 1936 the Pennsylvania Airlines directors decided to sell to United Air Lines, in a transaction that would have given stockholders a share of United for each share of Pennsylvania stock, instead of the one-for-seven exchange of 1961. When the ICC blocked this merger, the Pennsylvania and Central owners were forced to consolidate to survive. The combined airline was known as Pennsylvania Central Airlines until 1948, when the company moved its headquarters to Washington, D.C., and changed its corporate name to Capital Airlines.

As Pennsylvania Central and later Capital Airlines, the company grew by leaps, extending its service across northern Michigan from Detroit and Chicago to Buffalo, and south to Baltimore, Washington, Norfolk, and Richmond. Later Knoxville, Memphis, Atlanta, Birmingham became Capital terminals. At its Pittsburgh headquarters, the company operated a flight training school, a central dispatch office, and a maintenance base. The fleet consisted of profitable DC-3s until after the war, during which Capital trained Army and Navy pilots at Roanoke, Virginia, and flew military personnel and cargo on contract. After the war, the ambitious Capital management was the first to put DC-4 airliners in service. These were augmented by Constellations, which for a time gave Capital the speediest Chicago–New York service.

The airline grew too fast for its financial health. To serve new population centers it needed new planes, and was always deeply in debt to pay for them. To meet the competition of better-heeled competitors, Capital pioneered in 1948 the first scheduled air coach flights. The low-fare flights attracted the passengers, but many of them were fares from Capital's own first-class planes. Rival airlines soon added coach flights and Capital no longer enjoyed an advantage. Though it had grown with an impressive record of "firsts" to be the nation's sixth largest airline, Capital was always on the brink of financial trouble.

In 1954, under the prodding of a swashbuckling old-time pilot, J. H. "Slim" Carmichael, who had been made president to put the airline over the top, the directors decided to go all out for a fleet of fifty-six British turbo-prop Viscounts, for which Capital made a modest down payment and gave notes for most of the $68,000,000 commitment. Thus Capital added another "first" to its record—first airline in the U.S. to offer jet-powered service. The Viscounts' 350-mile-per-hour speed exceeded that of competitors' DC-6s, Constellations, and Convairs, and equaled that of the then-new DC-7s. Although they used propellers as well as jets for propulsion, the forty-six passenger Viscounts were the last word in airliner luxury in 1955. Capital looked like the pace-setter among the domestic airlines. American, Eastern, Western, and several other lines followed Capital's lead, ordering American-built turbo-prop Lockheed Electras. But United's management, after a hard look at the turbo-props, decided to make the big leap to straight jetliners.

After 1958, when competitors' straight jets went into service, Capital's Viscounts were no match for them, particularly on the heavy traffic Chicago–New York, Chicago-Washington, and Pittsburgh–New York runs. By that time, the burden of the debt incurred to buy the Viscounts was crushing Capital. The airline still owed Vickers-Armstrongs, Ltd., $34,000,000 on the fleet. The Capital management found it impossible to raise both the millions to pay for the Viscounts and still more millions to finance the purchase of a new fleet of jetliners to meet competition.

In an effort to bolster the ailing airline, the CAB hastily added new routes to the Capital system, among them Chicago-Minneapolis, Great Lakes–Florida, New York–Atlanta, and Washington-Atlanta-New Orleans. Unfortunately, it was too little and too late. Capital had no means of financing acquisition of a 550-mile jetliner fleet to keep apace of rivals. In the desperate effort to hold customers, Capital's pilots flew the Viscounts at top speed. Cost of maintenance zoomed. Passengers still preferred the faster straight jets. Thus the long-haul flights which the CAB had granted to pull Capital out of the hole became a burden instead of a boon. In May, 1960, after Vickers-Armstrongs, Ltd., had filed a foreclosure suit on Capital's Viscount fleet, the directors made merger expert Thomas S. Neelands, Jr., of New York, chairman of the board to find an answer in a hurry to the dilemma.

The merger was negotiated in something of a whodunit mystery atmosphere. The plot flashed back to 1955, when Capital and Northwest Airlines flirted briefly with the idea of union. When this romance fizzled out, Capital's President Carmichael sounded out Patterson on possible merger with United. The two presidents agreed upon an informal meeting of several United and Capital directors—with the presidents absent.

"Let's let them decide who'll be president if we merge," said Patterson.

By the time the directors assembled in New York, with Curtis Barkes as United's spokesman, the Capital management had cooled to the merger idea. Capital had its first Viscounts in service and they were pulling passengers off United, American, and TWA planes on the high-density New York–Chicago route. With more Viscounts on the way, Capital looked as though it was off to the races. A short time later, when Patterson encountered Carmichael, the latter said, "The best thing that ever happened was that we didn't merge." Capital Airlines stock had soared on the New York Stock Exchange.

Three years later, the rosy picture had dimmed. Capital was in deep financial trouble. General David P. Baker, who had succeeded Carmichael as president, had emissaries sound out United again on merger. Patterson sent word back that he wasn't interested. Next a spokesman for Vickers-Armstrongs, Ltd., which was trying to collect the $34,000,000 already overdue from Capital, made feelers. Patterson still wasn't interested. The next approach was from a New York emissary of Neelands, who had by this time taken over for Baker in the maneuver to stave off bankruptcy. Patterson and Barkes met secretly with Neelands in New York. Neelands, who had already sounded out other airlines on a merger with no success, pointed out that Capital's only hope was consolidation with United, because no other airline had the financial stamina to shoulder Capital's debts and at the same time provide a 575-mile jet fleet to meet the competition that was strangling Capital. It had to be a fast merger. Time was running out. Capital was already several months behind in payments to Vickers-Armstrongs. Was United interested?

The answer, Patterson replied, was yes, but United didn't choose to enter a contest with other airlines who were eager to divide up Capital's routes. If Neelands wanted a merger, the negotiations had to be carried on without publicity. Neelands heartily concurred. There followed five weeks of intensive negotiations, in which Patterson was only a long-distance participant. United's financial Vice-president Curtis Barkes took over the direct negotiating with Neelands and with the representative of Vickers-Armstrongs, Ltd., who had to be satisfied, since they could foreclose on the airline any time. To throw reporters off the scent, Patterson made a trip to the Pacific Northwest and stayed there during the critical period of negotiations. On July 28, 1960, after the merger papers had been signed, he and Neelands issued a statement at a joint press conference in Washington, D.C., then headquarters of the Capital system.

The merger was a complicated financial deal, with equally involved integration steps to follow, if and when the CAB approved the wedding of the two airlines. Patterson and Neelands had already explained the proposed consolidation to the CAB board members. The two airline heads did all the talking at this session; no member of the regulatory board gave the slightest clue as to the CAB's attitude. But it was obvious that if the merger was disapproved the CAB would have a defunct airline on its hands, one that could be kept afloat only through generous infusions of subsidy.

The intricate consolidation plan evolved included features which had to be acceptable to Vickers-Armstrongs, Capital debenture and stock holders, all subject to approval by the CAB. The cost in cash to United, for purchase of Capital's routes, such planes as it owned, and facilities in various cities, was zero. But the cost in newly issued United shares and warrants was approximately $33,000,000 at the market value of UAL securities on February 1, when the CAB formally approved the merger. The holders of $12,000,000 of Capital Airlines subordinated debentures were to receive 20 shares of United common stock for each $1000 par value of debentures. As of the date of United's offer, Capital debentures were quoted on the market at $570 per $1000 bond. United common was quoted at $31 per share. Thus, Capital debenture holders were offered $620 of stock for $570 of bonds. Capital stockholders were to receive one share of United common and a warrant to purchase 1½ shares of United common at $40 per share for each 7 shares of Capital stock. The market value of Capital stock on the day of United's offer was 8¼, even though the company was faced with bankruptcy which would completely wipe out the equity, and the value of the United stock and warrants offered for each share of Capital was estimated at $6.50. When the merger was first broached, it was thought that United might benefit substantially from a Capital tax carry-over credit. Subsequent exploration proved this to be a will-o'-the-wisp. United received only insignificant tax benefits from the merger.

Vickers agreed to take back fifteen of the Capital fleet of fifty-six Viscounts, reducing the turbo-prop fleet inherited by United to forty-one. United also fell heir to ten Lockheed Constellations, ten DC-4s, and 17 DC-3s. United's operations staff planned to use the Viscounts on short flights as far west as Omaha until they could be replaced by short-range turbo-jets. The balance of the Capital fleet had the "For Sale" sign on it. To help Capital stay in the running on key north-south runs, such as New York–Washington–Atlanta, and Pittsburgh-Miami, Patterson leased Capital two Boeing 720s in January, 1961.

Announcement of the merger agreement sparked a hot competition in Washington, D.C., before CAB officials. Eastern Air Lines, Delta, National, Northwest, and Allegheny vigorously opposed the consolidation. Capital's rivals urged the CAB to lop off large chunks of the Capital network and give or sell them to airlines already operating over these routes. They argued that allowing United to take over Capital's routes would create another airline behemoth, then asked that they themselves be granted virtual monopolies on chosen Capital runs. United had reserved the right to cancel out on the merger if the Capital system was dissected, or if the CAB failed to okay the merger by February 1, 1961, because the lifeblood of ailing Capital was draining away.

In the hearings before the CAB, it was pointed out that the consolidation promised better service for passengers, preservation of jobs for Capital's 7840 employes, salvage of a major airline that was on the brink of disaster. Objecting airlines had their say, as did seven unions that asked for the right to be heard. Only TWA and American Airlines, among United's competitors in the Eastern half of the country, remained neutral. The Vickers-Armstrongs representatives delayed action on their foreclosure suit against Capital, pending the outcome of the hearings.

In September the Board made it clear to five hopeful rival airlines that it would not consider dismembering the Capital airways system, although a group of CAB attorneys had urged doing just that. On December 30 the CAB examiner hearing the case recommended approval of the merger. On January 31, 1961, the CAB issued a press announcement giving the Board's blessing to the consolidation, although the final order remained to be issued. On April 4, 1961, the CAB formally approved the United merger plan, with only minor changes. On June 1, Capital's assets became an integral part of the United Air Lines structure, and United assumed what remained of Capital's liabilities. Important among these assets were over 7000 Capital employes who pinned on United insignia. Patterson welcomed them into the United family, saying, "The Capital employes are an excellent group and I haven't encountered a single Capital Airlines employe I'm not glad to have with us."

Many of the ex-Capital workers were apprehensive over how they would fare when absorbed into the larger United fold. They soon found out. Many of them found raises in their pay envelopes to bring wages up to UAL standards. Every Capital employe was guaranteed a job with United, with the exception of officers and directors, and some of the former were transferred to the United payroll. The United pension blanket was stretched to cover all former Capital employes at a cost of $800,000. United earmarked over $300,000 to train Capital ground workers in United methods.

Seven hundred Capital crew members were scheduled for refreshers and jet training at the United "University of the Air" in Denver. Capital employes moved to other stations on the Main Line were protected against loss if they had to sell homes. Surplus Capital employes in cities where both airlines had maintained facilities were guaranteed jobs elsewhere, or else generous severance pay. The integration of the Capital people into United was worked out in advance by the United-Capital Merger Planning Committee, set up six months before the take-over occurred. The melding of the employe groups proceeded smoothly from the day the United shield replaced the Capital insigne over ticket offices, stations, and shops.

Meshing the intricate traffic patterns of the two airways systems was more difficult. The timetable issued July 1, 1961, with a new section devoted to United's Atlantic Coast schedules northbound and southbound, told the story. To bolster service on the longer flights inherited from Capital, United used newly delivered Boeing 720s. The first weeks after the merger became known as "the month of torture." Service all over the system deteriorated to something less than United's vaunted Extra Care performance. By the end of 1961, flights and service were back to par.

Organizationally speaking, the United-Capital merger also sparked some wide-reaching changes. As early as January, 1961, veteran UALer Curtis Barkes was elevated to executive vice-president—finance and property. A. M. de Voursney, who had started with United in Chicago Reservations in 1940 and risen to vice-president and treasurer, was named executive vice-president—administration with responsibility in the areas of company costs and certain related activities. R. E. Bruno was promoted from comptroller to vice-president and treasurer and G. R. Harms, formerly administrative assistant to Barkes, was named comptroller.

After the merger became effective on June 1, a number of management changes in the operating areas also took place. Transportation Services was split into two divisions—East, with headquarters at Pittsburgh; West, with headquarters at Denver.

Regional headquarters for Ground Services, Passenger Service, Sales, and Personnel also were expanded to take care of the added cities on the old Capital system.

As a result of the merger, Patterson decided the time had come to bring almost all of his top-level officers back under the same roof and announced that the senior vice-presidents of transportation services and flight operations and their staffs would move from Denver to Chicago when United's new Executive Office building was completed northwest of the city. That left Jack Herlihy, senior vice-president—engineering and maintenance at San Francisco, the only non-Chicago man on the General Staff.

In October, 1961, experience in operating the merged system dictated still further reorganization. George E. Keck, former vice-president—base maintenance at San Francisco, was elected executive vice-president—operations and a member of the Board of Directors, as was A. M. de Voursney. Reporting to Keck and through him to Patterson were all operating administrations—flight, transportation services, engineering and maintenance, line maintenance. P. A. Wood, former assistant vice-president—engineering and maintenance, became vice-president—base maintenance to succeed Keck.

At the same time, D. F. Magarrell, senior vice-president—transportation services, announced plans to take an early retirement as of March, 1962. To succeed him, F. A. Brown was elected to the senior vice-presidency, moving up from head of the transportation services east division. That job then went to C. E. Haneline, former regional manager—ground services for the Great Lakes Region, who was elected a vice-president to balance O. T. Larson, who was vice-president—transportation services west. W. E. Alberts, former vice-president and assistant to the president, was named vice-president—management services and controls.

Having acquired the losing Capital airways system, which was fast going downhill, Patterson's immediate problem was to make it pay. At the press conference announcing the merger, reporters asked him how United could do it when the Capital management had failed to accomplish the feat. His answer revealed the challenge. Pointing out that Capital Airlines took in $108,000,000 in

1959, compared to United's gross of $330,000,000, he said: "Put that much additional revenue into United Air Lines and if we can't make a profit out of it, we shouldn't be in the business."

United was peculiarly positioned to make the former Capital routes profitable after the difficult initial period of integration. The merger lifted restrictions the CAB had placed earlier on United service between several teeming centers of population, restrictions aimed at giving distressed Capital Airlines an advantage on these routes. Among them were Chicago-Detroit, Chicago-Washington, Pittsburgh-Philadelphia, Pittsburgh–New York, Detroit-Cleveland. Now, for the first time, United could offer a balanced schedule pattern between these important traffic centers. On the longer-range former Capital routes over which the Viscounts had been pushing their engines vainly trying to compete with straight jets, United's jetliners could offer the best of service. These included the New York–Atlanta–New Orleans and the Atlanta-Washington-Philadelphia routes, and the flights from Great Lakes population centers, notably Cleveland and Pittsburgh to Florida destinations.

The Florida and Gulf routes gave United a new winter traffic mecca comparable to Hawaii and Southern California. This provided work for Mainliners that would otherwise have been idle part of the winter months. Even more important was the increased utilization of United's jets in transcontinental service. As improved schedules were worked out, many of these jetliners were able to fly extra flights of up to five hours on the north-south Atlantic runs, after completing their daily transcontinental flights. United's statisticians estimated that this extra time flying for the transcontinental jets on both coasts equaled the work of eight new jetliners costing $40,000,000.

The Viscounts pushed off these longer flights by the jetliners came unexpectedly into their own. Diverted to short-haul flights, and operated at reduced speed, 325 miles per hour, they fitted into the system so well that United bought back six of the Viscounts returned to Vickers-Armstrongs in the merger deal. Capital's older propeller-driven planes, the Constellations, DC-4s, and DC-3s, were retired and sold.

After the merger, Patterson was asked how it felt to be head of the country's biggest airline again. He replied, "The merger may make United the nation's largest airline, but to us this is not necessarily a blessing. Size tends to destroy some of the personal relations with customers which have characterized air transportation from the start. What we want to run is not the largest airline, but the best."

CHAPTER XVII

Battle of the Jetliners

On October 25, 1955, in what he has since described as "the most important single decision in United Air Lines history," President Patterson made the great leap forward into the jetliner age. In a contract signed with Donald W. Douglas that day for delivery of thirty DC 8 Mainliners powered by jet engines, he changed the face of air transport not only for United but for the entire domestic airline industry. Twelve days previously President Juan Trippe had done the same for Pan American and rival overseas carriers by ordering the first fleet of Boeing 707 Jetliners. It is doubtful if either airline president realized the extent of the upheaval the jetliners would cause in the decade to come, although Patterson remarked at the time, "The first airline to order a jetliner fleet will either revolutionize the industry or go broke; this time we have to be right."

This comment had a special significance for United. In ordering the Douglas DC-8s, Patterson and the UAL engineering staff had made the most daring "sight-unseen" bet in airline history. They had promised to pay $175,000,000, more than United's entire fleet of 160 propeller-driven Mainliners was worth at the time, for a dream jetliner still on the drawing boards. The nearest thing to a flying DC-8 they had seen was a six-foot plastic model, which the two presidents held admiringly in their arms for the benefit of photographers to celebrate the momentous decision.

The United DC-8 order touched off a tidal wave of jetliner

orders by other airlines. American Airlines, then TWA, ordered fleets of Boeing 707s for transcontinental routes. The Boeing 707 prototype was already flying and the Boeing Company was prepared to make deliveries nearly a year before Douglas could roll out the first DC-8. This meant nearly a year of lopsided competition for United. Rivals would be flying jetliners at 575 miles per hour while the propeller-driven Mainliners would be churning along at a leisurely 375 miles. First to order jetliners, United would be last to put them into the skies. Patterson accepted this calculated disadvantage philosophically.

One reason was that the DC-8 was United's dream, although it bore the Douglas name. It represented ten years of diligent work by United's engineering, operating, and sales staffs. The DC-8 was an airline's jetliner, whereas the 707 evolved out of a military jet tanker. Oddly enough, the end products were almost identical in size, shape, power, and carrying capacity. But on October 25, 1955, when United's jetliner staff chose the DC-8, they looked like quite different airplanes.

The United jetliner had become a gleam in Patterson's eye back in 1947. He and Jack Herlihy, vice president—engineering and maintenance, had just rejected a proposal from an airplane manufacturer to build an eight-engine jet airliner that would carry 40 passengers at 540 miles per hour. British airplane manufacturers were building the Viscount turbo-prop—half jet, half propeller—and had designed the first all-jet Comets. The Russians were pushing jets, too. The four big American airliner builders were toying with ideas for jetliners and hopefully waiting for the airlines or the government to underwrite the building of the first prototype, as United and rivals had underwritten the first four-engine propeller airliner, the DC-4, back in 1936. After rejecting the eight-engine jet plane, Patterson remarked to Herlihy:

"Well, the jet transport day is coming, isn't it?"

"Yes, and it's almost here," agreed Herlihy.

"Let's appoint a group of engineers to make United the best-informed airline on jets," suggested Patterson.

Herlihy agreed. They immediately set up a United Jetliner Committee, headed by Technical Development Superintendent Ray D. Kelly. The members, most of them from the staff of the

San Francisco Maintenance Base, constituted more than a shopping committee to find a good buy in jetliners as manufacturers came up with designs. The committee rounded up every item of information available on jet engines and their performance, then fitted this knowledge to the visionary airliner that gradually took shape to handle United's jet age traffic.

In 1950, Herlihy and Kelly flew to England to ride in the De Haviland Comet and the Vickers Viscount, both already flying on British airways. Although enthusiastic over their smooth jet rides, Herlihy and Kelly found the British jets too short in cruising range for United's transcontinental flights, too small in seating capacity to be money-makers. The United Jetliner Committee knuckled down to write specifications for a jetliner that would carry a profitable load far enough and fast enough to earn a living. By 1952, the dream jetliner had shaken down into a 100-passenger, 550 mile-per-hour turbine-jet airliner that could cross the continent nonstop with fuel to spare to reach alternate airports if the destination terminal were socked in by weather. These specifications were turned over to plane manufacturers.

Meantime, a bugaboo had arisen. Traffic control authorities, and airline operations people, too, were apprehensive over how the 575-mile jets would fit into the slower propeller-plane traffic patterns, particularly around major terminals, such as New York, Chicago, San Francisco. United's Jetliner Committee decided to find out. It launched a simulated "paper jet" service across the country. Daily, simulated jet flights left San Francisco and New York to wing at high elevations across the country. These "paper jets" were constantly watched to see what traffic, weather and other problems they might encounter en route, had they been real jetliners. When weather closed in at terminals, they were diverted to other airports. By the end of a year, this game had provided United with some important answers. The most important one was, the jets would mesh handily with prop-plane traffic.

With this question mark answered, Patterson knew it was just a matter of time until some airline took the plunge into the jet age. He resolved that United would be the airline—at least on the domestic routes. Every department was alerted to familiarize itself with jetliner developments. In spare time, pilots began boning up on jet flying techniques. Mechanical supervisors studied the servicing of jet engines. To help visualize the dilemma of seating and feeding a hundred or more passengers in a single plane, Herlihy and his staff built a full-scale jet fuselage mock-up at the San Francisco Maintenance Base. Stewardesses served a full-scale meal aloft to a mock-up load of live and hungry simulated passengers.

By 1955, conferences with airplane designers had firmed up United's dream jetliner. Starting from scratch with the United specifications, Douglas had designed the jetliner that became the DC-8. Boeing had evolved the 707 from the Boeing K-135 jet tanker which had already flown thousands of hours. When the airlines and the government hesitated to order a prototype, Boeing's President William M. Allen persuaded his directors to gamble $16,000,000 of the company's money building the first Boeing 707. Patterson and United's engineering and sales staffs flew to Seattle to ride in this pioneer jetliner early in October of 1955. They were enthusiastic and in a buying mood.

"Can you change the cabin dimensions?" asked Patterson.

"We can lengthen it, but we can't widen it," the Boeing's engineers told him flatly.

The United jetliner shopping expedition flew south to Santa Monica, where they talked with Douglas engineers. The DC-8, still on the drawing boards, was also still a rubber airliner that could be stretched. Douglas agreed to redesign the cabin, making it two feet wider to accommodate coach seats six abreast. The studies of United's sales staff indicated that a 100-seat jetliner would rarely be filled with first-class passengers only. United wanted a jetliner adaptable to both first-class patrons, sitting four abreast, and coach passengers, sitting six abreast. This extra two feet of width was a major consideration in Patterson's decision to wait an extra year for the DC-8s.

Ironically, the day after he notified President Allen of Boeing of United's decision, the Boeing designers found they could widen the fuselage of the 707, after all. As soon as they did this, American Airlines ordered thirty Boeing jetliners to be delivered in 1958. TWA, Continental and National Airlines followed. This meant that most of United's major competitors on the transcon-

First-class section of a DC-8 Jet Mainliner, looking forward toward the "Red Carpet Room" lounge. Unitized seats contain individual air vents, stewardess call button, reading light, and serving table, whose position is not affected by recline angle of seat ahead.

This is the "Red Carpet Room" lounge for first-class passengers on the Boeing 720 Jet Mainliner. Seats are of the semi-reclining theater type with individual reading lights, ashtrays, etc.

Jet Age ramp look on United is symbolized in this view at San Francisco. Telescoping JETWAY loading ramps link second level of terminal with plane doors, protect boarding and deplaning passengers from the weather and eliminate passenger traffic on the ramp proper. In addition to San Francisco, United now uses the JETWAY at New York (Idlewild) and Seattle-Tacoma; plans additional installations at other major cities.

JETWAY "corridors" can be extended from terminal to aircraft door in less than 60 seconds. Passenger agent in the outboard cab section drives unit on positive-traction wheels to DC 8 doorway. Height is adjusted electromechanically.

This view from the first-class entrance way of a DC-8 shows how passengers are completely protected from the weather when they board via JETWAY.

Dramatic night view of United's $14,500,000 passenger terminal at New York's Idlewild Airport, dedicated in 1960.

Interior of the block-long, two-story structure, which contains 250,000 square feet of space. In foreground are United-developed express check-in counters which speed pre-ticketed passengers from lobby to boarding area in as little time as two minutes.

tinental flights would be in the air well ahead of United, which had kicked off the jetliner revolution on the domestic routes. Only Eastern Airlines' Eddie Rickenbacker, a noncompetitor, decided to wait for the DC-8s, along with Patterson, who upped the United order in 1957 to forty Douglas jetliners. Later, Delta and Northwest Airlines chose DC-8s. United's management reconciled itself to a lean year from the fall of 1958 to September, 1959, when DC-8 service could be inaugurated between New York and California.

Anticipating a reluctance on the part of air travelers to ride on the jets at first, the airlines and the aircraft builders earmarked sizable budgets to educate the public from "prop thinking" to "jet thinking." They couldn't have guessed more wrongly about that unpredictable human, the confirmed air traveler. United's experience in the rugged year 1959 is an illustration. At San Francisco, Los Angeles, Chicago, New York, the jetliners took off loaded to capacity, with scores of "go-shows" at the gates waiting for the seats of "no-shows," who were rare birds. The DC-7s got the leavings. Unfortunately, the jetliners bore the AA and TWA insignia, while the DC-7s were United Mainliners.

To cut losses, United's transcontinental DC-7 flights were discontinued as fast as American and TWA gobbled up the cross-country traffic. The DC-7s were shunted into shorter flight service, such as San Francisco–Denver, New York–Cleveland, where there was no jetliner competition. This gave the Mainliners a decided edge on these runs and business boomed. To everybody's amazement, the Mainliners carried more passengers than in 1957 and turned in a profit, rather than the anticipated loss. Though the uneven competition recalled the losing battle in the Chicago–New York run in 1934 when the same rivals' DC-3s lured the passengers from United's slower Boeing 247s, the transition to the Jet Age turned out to be smooth and painless.

Came the big day, September 18, 1959, when Mrs. W. A. Patterson snipped a rope of carnations at San Francisco Airport to make way for eager passengers to board Flight 800. Five hours, eighteen minutes later, after a 2286-mile hop, Captain J. A. McFadden eased the shining new DC-8 into New York's Idlewild Airport. Simultaneously, Flight 801 carried the first westbound load of passengers from New York to San Francisco. Soon daily Los Angeles–New York and Chicago-California DC-8 flights were luring fickle air travelers back into the United fold in such numbers that the stand-bys were waiting at the United's boarding gates.

Early in 1960, following a smooth but breath-taking New York–San Francisco–Honolulu "DC-8 to the 50th State" press flight, United launched jet service between Hawaii and California. On the return flight, the huge jetliner winged nonstop from Honolulu to Chicago in 7 hours, 52 minutes, setting a new speed record and heralding the day when inland cities would become overseas terminals.

United's DC-8s soon hung up some unbelievable records. One of them whipped from Seattle to San Francisco with a full load in 1 hour, 12 minutes. Another flew from Chicago to New York in 1 hour, 29 minutes. The Los Angeles–Chicago record was cut to 3 hours, 14 minutes; San Francisco–New York to 4 hours, 37 minutes. Captain James N. Going, with an assist from the "jet stream," brought a load of passengers from Honolulu to San Francisco—2450 miles—in 3 hours, 42 minutes. Air travelers ceased to think of distance in terms of miles; the United States was 4½ hours across, 2½ hours from Canada to Mexico.

In their early Jet Age planning, the airlines' prognosticators, United's included, thought the jetliners would handle the long hauls while the DC-7s, DC-6s, and Convairs that were bumped off the transcontinental flights could easily handle the short-haul traffic. Again, they misjudged the whims of the unpredictable air travelers. Passengers quickly became so jet-minded that they griped when they had to board prop planes, even for short hops. Day after day, at Los Angeles International Airport, hundreds milled about the gates hoping to catch a jet for San Francisco, while DC-6s and DC-7s departed with seats to spare. Patterson was one of the first to recognize that an airline could not long exist half jet, half prop. At his urging, United's engineers drew up specifications for a shorter-range jetliner and started shopping again.

This medium-haul jet problem called for another major decision. The airplane manufacturers were alert to the potential of this market. Lockheed's answer was the Electra turbo-prop, which American and Eastern had already put in service. But the 400-mile-per-hour turbo-props were no match in the battle for passengers against 575-mile straight jets. Convair's entry was the 880, a straight jet, which United almost bought, but finally rejected because the original fuselage was too narrow. Douglas had no small jet. Then Boeing scaled down the 707, with lighter-weight engines and landing gear and smaller wings, into the 2500-mile-range 720. After engineers lopped 50,000 pounds out of the jetliner's weight, Patterson ordered twenty-eight Boeing 720s for flights such as Chicago–New York, Denver–San Francisco, and between major cities of the West Coast.

Paradoxically, after ruling out the turbo-props, Patterson inherited a fleet of forty-one prop-jet-propelled Viscounts in 1961 in the United–Capital Airlines merger. On their longer flights, notably between Chicago and New York or Washington, the Viscounts had been fighting a losing battle for traffic against the speedier straight jets. After the merger, these odds were quickly evened by the Boeing 720s which United had fortuitously ordered. The Viscounts then picked up the load on the shorter hauls, for which no American plane builder had yet delivered a low-flying, economical, money-making jet without propellers. And propellers were just what the air traveler no longer wanted to see outside his window.

"There's a jet airplane in France, the Caravelle," Patterson told Herlihy late in 1959. "Why don't you go over and look at it?"

At first Herlihy was anything but enthusiastic about buying an airliner built overseas. But after a firsthand look at the craftsmanship of the Sud Aviation plane builders in Toulouse, France, and rides in the Caravelle, he and his staff returned from Europe bursting with enthusiasm for "La Belle Caravelle," a small transport with two jet engines alongside its tail. The clean wings, almost like a glider's, gave it extraordinary maneuverability. It could land and take off easily from short landing strips. The windows were triangular for better vision. Herlihy described the Caravelle ride as the quietest he had ever made. Several European airlines were already using Caravelles. After specifying a few modifications, United ordered twenty Caravelles for delivery in 1961.

The Mainliner all-jet fleet was rapidly shaping up. Patterson could foresee the day when propeller-driven planes would disappear from the Mainliner fleet entirely. There was still one gap, the short-to-medium-range flights, typified by such runs as Chicago-Toledo or Pittsburgh-Washington. Late in 1960 the quest for a jet plane to serve this short-haul market ended at the Boeing plant in Seattle. The answer was a radical new jetliner, the Boeing 727, powered by three jet engines clustered around the tail. Cruising at 550 miles at medium altitudes, the 727 was designed to carry up to 100 passengers and to operate from mile-long airstrips. On December 5, 1960, United ordered forty Boeing 727s for delivery in 1963.

This brought United's potential jetliner fleet in five fantastic years from the ordering of the first jetliner to 40 DC-8s, 28 Boeing 720s, 20 Caravelles, 40 Boeing 727s, 47 Viscounts. Even without spare parts, they were valued at more than $650,000,000, double the net worth of the entire airline when the Jet Age dawned. An additional $90,000,000 had to be spent on ground equipment and facilities to load and unload the jetliners. In the brief span of five years, United had exploded from a little big business into a transportation giant.

How Executive Vice-president—Finance and Property Curtis Barkes found the dollars to pay for the jetliner fleet and the costly array of terminal equipment to berth the jets and handle their passengers and cargo is a piece of financial legerdemain. As forecast, the jetliners were great revenue producers, once in service. The DC-8s and Boeing 720s began paying back part of their cost long before the Caravelles were delivered in 1961, and the Boeing 727s would join the fleet in 1963. Paying for the forty DC-8s was a $230,000,000 financial high hurdle. The twenty-eight Boeing 720s called for an additional $112,000,000. The twenty Caravelles cost $65,000,000. The forty Boeing 727 short-range jets were a $160,000,000 commitment. But the fleet of 128 jetliners was easily able to carry 50 per cent more passengers twice as far as the 1958 fleet of 186 propeller-driven Mainliners.

This was only part of the high price of admission into the Jet Age. Almost every facility along the Main Line had to be enlarged or built anew. During 1958, before a single jetliner had been delivered, the capital outlay for jet service was $75,000,000. In 1959, it rose to $113,000,000. By 1964, the turning point in the vast outlay for the jet age, United's debt for the jet revolution was projected at a staggering $350,000,000.

Where did all the dollars come from? Three big insurance companies—Metropolitan Life, Prudential, and Mutual Life of New York—made the DC-8 order possible by joining in the purchase of $120,000,000 worth of United Air Lines debentures, in addition to $40,000,000 which United had already borrowed from the three sources. This was augmented by a $130,000,000 credit, later increased to $165,000,000 to be drawn upon as needed, established by thirty banks in cities along the Main Line. Barkes managed to earmark more millions out of earnings and sales of planes to pay for the Jet Age debut. Dividends were cut from $1.50 to 50 cents per share in 1957 to conserve cash, but shareholders received regular stock dividends to make up for the reduction. In 1960, United offered $25,000,000 worth of convertible subordinated debentures. Investors responded by oversubscribing the issue; within a year, the debentures were selling for $140, reflecting the public's confidence in United Air Lines.

The jetliners proved to be workhorses of the airways, with far less time out for servicing than their propeller-powered forerunners. In the air ten hours per day, they made money with 60 per cent load factors. There was a surprising angle to their earning power. The money-making part of the jetliner turned out to be the rear cabin, where the coach passengers sat six abreast. Thousands of new passengers were lured into the air by speed, comfort, and low fares. Thousands of "firsts" switched to coach to save one-third. Many companies ordered their people traveling by jetliner to go coach. The partitions on jetliners separating the coach from the first-class luxury passengers gradually moved forward, squeezing out more firsts, squeezing in more coach travelers. Luckily, the jetliners earned as much per square foot of cabin space from the coach areas as from the first-class section.

To help convert air travelers from "prop thinking" to jet-mindedness, United's Senior Vice-president—Sales and Advertising Robert E. Johnson and staff in 1959 dreamed up "the greatest airline show on Earth," Jetarama. The company's salesmen-showmen toured the Main Line for six months with a Jet Age road show in three huge and colorful tents, set up at major terminals along the United system. The star of the show was either a DC-8 Mainliner or Boeing 720 in front of the three tent pavilions. After learning about jet power in flight, with the aid of cut-away jet engines, reversers, landing gear, and communications equipment in a Dependability Pavilion, visitors toured the plane, debarked into the Safety Pavilion to see how crews were trained, then wound up in the Extra Care Pavilion, where a mock-up DC-8 interior demonstrated food galleys, the seating arrangements, and other items of jetliner comforts. Before Jetarama concluded its year-long run, more than a million prospective United passengers had enjoyed its varied exhibits.

Jetarama gave passengers a preview of United's $17,000,000 Instamatic reservations system, which would be installed in 1961. Instamatic was triggered by the warning of Reservations Manager Maury Perry back in 1953 that a faster reservations system than any yet conceived was a must to handle the Main Line's pyramiding traffic. As a stopgap, the IBM Ramac system was installed. Meantime, a committee of UAL reservations and engineering experts collaborated in drawing up specifications for an electronic brain that could instantly record and then remember a million or more reservations. Nothing like it had been built, so the brainstorm was handed to a team of electronics wizards from Stanford Research Institute of Menlo Park, California. These imagineers concluded that the "brain" could be built. The Teleregister Corporation of Stamford, Connecticut, assisted by the Philips Electric Company of Holland built it, a two-story electronics maze at Denver with nerves extending to 827 sales agent sets in United offices scattered from coast to coast.

Instamatic utilizes three data processors known as "Telefiles," which record and remember well over a million items of information. It reports within two seconds whether a seat is available on any of United's 960 daily flights for a year in advance. It sells seats right up to the time of the plane's departure. With lightning speed it keeps track of seat turnover during the last two hours before flight time, when some flights formerly had lost up to one-third of their passengers while other travelers eager for seats were being turned away because ticket agents didn't know holders had cancelled.

Everything connected with the jetliner age became a multi-million-dollar item. Training jetliner crews was one example. United's "University of the Air" at Denver burgeoned. The seven jet simulators ordered to train crews cost as much as two new jetliners. The seven-week intensive training course for flight crews began a year before the first DC-8 was delivered. Drawing full salaries while they studied in classrooms or flew "jetliners" that never left the ground, the pilots, first officers, and second officers became so familiar with flying characteristics of jets that they were veterans before they put foot in their first jetliner cockpits. These amazingly realistic machines not only changed pilots in seven weeks from "propeller thinking" to "jet thinking." They also screened out about 10 per cent of the old-timers who found the transition too difficult to make. These veterans "went back to props" or switched to ground duties.

Under the rigorous jet schooling curriculum set up by "Professor" Jay G. Brown, the veteran pilot who headed the flight training school, the "students" entered the DC-8 simulator cockpits as full crews, to learn jet flying as they would be doing it shortly in actual flight. The instrument panels were duplicates of those in jetliners. Even the simulated flight atmosphere seemed real. Radio contact was made with a traffic control tower. Records provided the same engine sounds as in flight. Speed, altitude, and other gauges responded as though the plane were in the air. When the flying technique called for ascending, descending, banking or turning, the cockpit pivoted on hydraulic cylinders. Most important of all was the "trouble console" panel behind the flyers, where the instructor could set up any emergency problem without warning to the crew to see how well they handled the situation. This was experience crews seldom had opportunity to gain while training in real planes.

"Even with equivalent training in the jetliner itself, our crews would not be as well trained as they are when they graduate from the simulator," declared D. R. Petty, senior vice-president—flight operations.

United's jet training program was an $8,000,000 investment that paid off not only in top-flight jet crews but in another unexpected way. A dozen airlines, both domestic and foreign, the Air Force, and a score of companies operating their own aircraft enrolled pilots in the Denver airmen's university for training by Jay Brown and his staff of 109 instructors and technicians, all veterans in their lines. Even the faculty learned from the teaching.

"I've learned more about flying from three years of simulator instructing than I did in a dozen years of flying," one veteran instructor remarked.

Though pilot training was the most expensive item, costing United about $75,000 per crew, the training and updating of the 3200 United flying officers (plus 600 more from the Capital system following the merger) was only part of the United educational program, which cost $11,000,000 per year. Mechanical and scientific technicians studied in classrooms in a dozen cities along the Main Line. Stewardesses were trained at Cheyenne until late in 1961 when a new education center opened on the executive grounds near Chicago's O'Hare Airport. This training center was the equivalent of a sizable technical school with a score of classrooms, laboratories, and living accommodations for 176 students. In addition, executives were sent to Stanford and Harvard Business Schools for refreshers or special training. To see that any United employe who wanted to study and broaden his knowledge (roughly one out of every five) had a chance to do so with guidance, David S. Ritner was named Vice-president in Charge of Employee Development in January, 1961.

In the United Jet Age pattern, even as in the piston-engine era, employes were even more valuable than the planes and the other equipment they used. The company's philosophy had been epitomized by Patterson some years earlier in a talk before the annual Stanford Business Conference.

"When I think of employes (including management people), I think of how we in business treat an expensive machine, the high value we place on it, the care with which we use and maintain it or shift it to another part of the plant, and the preparations we make before we retire it from service.

"That machine shows up in the balance sheet at the end of every month, along with other assets, and there is a dollar value attached to it which we know we want to preserve. It's unfortunate that the balance sheet doesn't indicate the value of the employes with whom we work every day. If we could just put down something about '20,000 employes, value $80 million,' maybe we'd be considerably more conscious of their worth."

Among the costly phenomena of the jetliner transition were the spectacular terminals in the major cities of the Main Line. Airports were no longer burdens to the taxpayer that cities had to provide to keep up with each other and to satisfy civic pride. In the Jet Age, terminals became vast business complexes in which the landing strips and boarding facilities were magnets to bring trade to restaurants, hotels, stores, banks, factories, and many other tenants besides airlines.

At New York, to handle increased traffic at Jet Age speed, the larger airlines designed individual terminals, which the airport authorities built and leased to the users at rentals adequate to amortize the cost in a few years. Thus, United's terminal at Idlewild International was a $14,500,000 investment in in-motion efficiency which United will pay for in twenty years in rentals. Built on three levels, it featured automatic check-in stations to handle passengers as fast as they could pass through the gates, after which they moved upstairs to the waiting rooms and boarding concourses on the level of the jetliners' doors. Rivers of luggage flowed via a maze of belts in the basement to planes. More belts delivered luggage to incoming passengers as quickly as they could walk from their planes. At Chicago's O'Hare and Los Angeles' International the terminal designers built new decentralized Jet Age airports from scratch. At San Francisco and Seattle, whose centralized terminals were the last word in airports a decade previous, long wings housing double-deck concourses spread the traffic and separated each major airline's operations.

The ground equipment required at each major terminal to service a jetliner and load or unload 120 passengers and their luggage, added up to a fantastic array of mobile vehicles—forty-one, in the case of a DC-8, including a mechanical giraffe with a neck forty feet high to check the airliner's lofty tail lights. These vehicles included turbine starters, window washers, vacuum cleaners, water tanks, air conditioners, cabin supply and food service trucks, luggage-container carts, to mention only a few.

Most ingenious of these jet support vehicles was the Jetway, the telescopic covered gangplank that stretched itself from the waiting room of the boarding concourse like a monstrous caterpillar on wheels, to the door of the jetliner, then drew itself back when the embarking or debarking was completed. Each jetliner was served by two Jetways, through which a hundred or more passengers walked in a matter of minutes, without stepping up or down a single stair, between the plane and the second story of the concourse. The Jetways completely separated the streams of passengers on the upper level from the hustling service crews on the ground below. Each Jetway was a $65,000 investment. At San Francisco Airport United had ten of them, at New York thirteen, at Chicago sixteen, at Los Angeles sixteen, at Seattle four.

Even the maintenance crews found their work revolutionized. When air travelers discovered that jetliner speed enabled them to fly anywhere in the country in time to sleep in a bed, night flying tapered off. The jetliners could fly across the country and back to home base or to Honolulu and back to San Francisco easily in a day. Maintenance work became a job for the night-shift owls, not only at the main maintenance base in San Francisco, but at other ends of the line as well. The "bugs" in the jetliners were remarkably few, and mainly in the luxuries such as the flush toilets, the plush seats, the tricky reading lights, but not the jet power plants.

"The jet engines have exceeded our fondest expectations," declared Jack Herlihy. "They're ten times better than any power plant we've ever had before."

The one serious malfunction was in the hydraulic system, the marvelous mechanical muscles by which pilots controlled the landing gear, the ailerons, rudder, wing flaps, and other movable components for maneuvering the huge, heavy jetliners. In temperatures ranging from 120 degrees on the ground at tropical airports to 40 below at cruising altitude, these muscles were put to new strains. Following a hydraulic failure, a DC-8 landed under emergency at Denver Airport on July 11, 1961, then veered into an abutment, hit a utility truck and burned with a loss of seventeen lives. United promptly detailed a DC-8 to Edwards Air Force Base in the Mojave Desert where UAL, Douglas, and FAA engineers flew it in a series of rigorous tests to simulate every strain hydraulic muscles might encounter in flight, landing, or take-off. Following these tests, all of United's DC-8s and Boeing 720s were outfitted with more powerful hydraulic pumps. This, plus new techniques for pilots in applying their mechanical muscles, soon reduced the malfunctions.

For United, as for all of the major airlines, a knotty question was what to do with the outmoded propeller-driven planes. The original idea was to use them for short-haul flights and for cargo service. Some of United's DC-7s were modified for cargo. The capacious Sevens were well suited for this use. But the jetliners' bellies were also capacious, and they moved freight almost twice as fast as the DC-7s. All over the country manufacturers began reducing inventories in district warehouses or closing the district depots entirely, relying on fast jet cargo to supply their customers. This new look in air cargo was only one surprising phase of the jetliner revolution. To sort and load, or unload and unscramble the flood of cargo, United engineers completed in 1961 at San Francisco Airport a Jet Age air freight terminal whose belt and roller conveyors sorted, weighed, consigned, and loaded up to 100,000 pounds of air cargo daily. The new cargo facility set the standard for similar installations at major terminals.

Among the magicians of the Jet Age was a new electronic flight computer in the Operations control office in Denver. By feeding into this sophisticated electronic system the information that enabled a pilot or first officer to work out his flight plan in an hour of calculation, this amazing mechanism delivered a flight plan in eighteen seconds for any flight between any two points on the United network. The jet planes had revolutionized dispatching, too. Every flight was controlled from Denver, where dispatchers, picking up a phone, could talk with any pilot in any Mainliner over the continental United States.

As it winged six miles above the earth, and usually above storms as well, each jetliner was encased theoretically in a box of space, maintained by the radar eyes of the FAA. This box was usually 100 miles long, 10 miles wide, and 2000 feet in depth—until the jetliner neared its destination. There local electronic eyes took over, cut down the size of the box of space, monitored the jetliner to its landing.

Unfortunately, the FAA, short of funds, had to control a Jet Age airways system with radar eyes made for propeller plane speeds. The limitations in the use of these controls indirectly led to the first disastrous jet accident, the tragic collision on December 16, 1960, of United Flight 826, which crossed paths at the wrong split-second with a TWA Constellation over Brooklyn. To cope with the sky traffic problems generated by jetliners' speed, the FAA established at Atlantic City, New Jersey, a National Aviation Facilities Experimental Center. Here traffic-control experts tested the new radar "eyes" evolved by instrument makers to enable jetliner crews to see through fog and storm. Other experts worked on "brains" to calculate the jetliners' positions instantly. Out of simulated catastrophe conditions evolved a new technique of positive traffic control that made repetition of the Brooklyn disaster virtually impossible.

The Jet Age quickly opened fabulous new horizons to travelers. Soaring at double the speed of the prop plane and with almost double the seat capacity, each jetliner enabled nearly four times as many passengers to reach destinations with speed and luxury as had the airliner it replaced. By Jet Mainliner, the New Yorker could leave snow and sleet behind him at breakfast time and dip in the Hawaii surf before dinner. Motorists could leave their cars in the garage at Chicago and pick up a rent-a-car four hours later in sunny Southern California. Clevelanders could week-end in Florida as effortlessly as they had formerly vacationed on the shores of the Great Lakes. Almost overnight, the jetliners had emancipated mankind from time, distance, and geography.

EPILOGUE

Still Higher Horizons

At the end of the first edition of this history published in 1951 to celebrate United Air Lines' twenty-fifth anniversary, we looked into the crystal ball along with United's dreamers, and had this to say:

"Most amazing of all, the daring young men who first dreamed in the twenties of flying passengers and cargo, as well as mail, from coast to coast in a single day and night, and who made that dream come true, were still the young executives running the airlines of the fifties. This was especially true of the United system. They were still dreamers, too, eagerly scanning the higher horizons of tomorrow, when jetliners promised to shrink the globe as much in a decade as conventional airliners had shrunk it in a quarter of a century.

"The still higher horizons were realistic as well as figurative. Jetliners promised to lift them from the 20,000- to the 40,000-foot altitude, where weather was constant and speeds were so fantastic that the New Yorker might catch a plane in the morning, deliver his speech at a luncheon in San Francisco, and return home that night. In the crystal ball, jetliners spelled a new revolution for air traffic; speeds so fast that one of tomorrow's planes could deliver the load of two of today's; fares so low that planes might become everybody's transportation coast-to-coast or country-to-country; and finally, the annihilation of time and space and sectionalism."

As this edition goes to press in United's thirty-fifth anniversary year, many of these daydreams, which seemed about as far ahead as men could see in 1951, have come true in one decade without much fanfare. The jetliners have shrunk the globe and revolutionized both transportation and men's thinking. Many of the same young dreamers are running the airlines and they are still looking into crystal balls. Some of them see supersonic airliners in these crystal balls as clearly as they saw jetliners a decade ago. All of them agree that the supersonic airliner will be a more fantastic leap ahead from the jetliner than the jetliner was from propeller propulsion. The jetliners are pushing the sound barrier. The next leap ahead must crash through it to twice the jetliner's speed. The first supersonic airliner will cost a half billion dollars or more; the first fleet will cost twenty millions per airplane. These windowless airliners, resembling rockets, will span the continent or fly to Hawaii in two hours. Flying west, passengers will get to their destinations before they started, clockwise. Fortunately in W. A. Patterson's crystal ball, which has been one of the most reliable, supersonic jetliners are a long way off in the future. Long enough for us to acclimate to the small world of the jetliners.

Chronology

PRE-1926

March 3, 1919 Eddie Hubbard, in partnership with W. E. Boeing, launches 80-mile Seattle-Victoria flying boat air mail service.

Sept. 8–11, 1920 Inauguration of coast-to-coast air mail service, New York–Chicago–San Francisco. Mail flown by day, trained at night; time, 82 hours.

Feb. 22, 1921 First through day-and-night air mail flight from coast to coast. Impressed by this demonstration, Congress appropriates $1,250,-000 for continuing and expanding air mail service and lighting the airways.

1923 Henry and Edsel Ford back William B. Stout in Stout Metal Airplane Company to develop Ford Tri-motor plane.

July 1, 1924 Inauguration of regular day-and-night air mail service, coast-to-coast; time, 32 hours.

Feb. 2, 1925 Kelly Bill authorizes Post Office to award air mail contracts to private companies.

April 3, 1925 Ford Motor Company inaugurates own air cargo operations between Dearborn, Mich., factory, Cleveland, and Chicago; wins air mail contract in January, 1926.

May 21, 1925 National Air Transport organizes to bid for Chicago–New York air mail contract.

July, 1925 Frederick B. Rentschler organizes Pratt & Whitney Aircraft Co. to design and build Wasp air-cooled radial engines.

Oct. 7, 1925 Walter Varney awarded Elko-Pasco air mail contract.

Nov. 7, 1925 National Air Transport wins Dallas–Kansas City–Chicago air mail contract.

1926

Jan. 8 Vern Gorst organizes Pacific Air Transport.

Jan. 27 Gorst wins contract to fly air mail, Seattle–Los Angeles.

Feb. 15 Ford line flies first contract air mail between Dearborn, Mich., Cleveland, and Chicago.

April 6 Varney Air Lines flies first mail over 460-mile Pasco-Boise-Elko route; suspends service for 60 days on April 8.

May 12 National Air Transport begins air mail service over 995-mile Chicago–Kansas City–Dallas route.

June 6 Varney resumes Pasco-Elko flights; southeastern terminus subsequently changed to Salt Lake City.

July 31 Stout Air Services wins air mail contract for CAM-14, Detroit to Grand Rapids.

Sept. 15 Pacific Air Transport starts air mail service, Seattle–Los Angeles.

1927

Jan. 29 Boeing Airplane Company and Edward Hubbard win 1918-mile Chicago–San Francisco air mail route; contract turned over to Boeing Air Transport on March 28, 1927.

April 2 National Air Transport wins Chicago–New York air mail contract.

July 1 Boeing Air Transport starts San Francisco–Chicago service with 25 Wasp-powered Boeing 40s.

July 22 Stout announces intention to cancel Detroit–Grand Rapids air mail contract, effective in 45 days.

Sept. 1 National Air Transport inaugurates service over Chicago–New York route as Post Office Department retires from air mail flying.

Sept. 1 Stout begins carrying passengers between Detroit and Cleveland; follows with Detroit-Chicago service on Nov. 1, 1928.

Sept. 1 Air express service launched by airlines and Railway Express Agency.

1928

Jan. 1 Boeing Air Transport acquires control of Pacific Air Transport.

July Ford discontinues air mail operations between Dearborn, Cleveland, and Chicago.

Oct. 30 Boeing Airplane & Transport Corporation formed as holding company for Boeing Airplane Company, Boeing Air Transport, and Pacific Air Transport.

Trimotored Boeing 80s introduced by Boeing Air Transport on Chicago–San Francisco run; were followed in 1929 by Boeing 80-As.

1929

Feb. 1 United Aircraft & Transport Corporation formed as holding company for Boeing Airplane Company, Boeing Air Transport, Pacific Air Transport, and Pratt & Whitney.

April 15 W. A. Patterson resigns from Wells Fargo Bank, San Francisco, to become assistant to P. G. Johnson at Boeing.

President Patterson of United (right) and T. D. Neelands, Jr., chairman of the board of Capital Airlines, are shown at Washington, D.C., on July 28, 1960, just after press conference announcing merger plans. (*Washington Post photo.*)

United/Capital Merger Planning Committee, which worked out myriad details for a smooth transition from two companies to one while formal Civil Aeronautics Board approval was awaited.

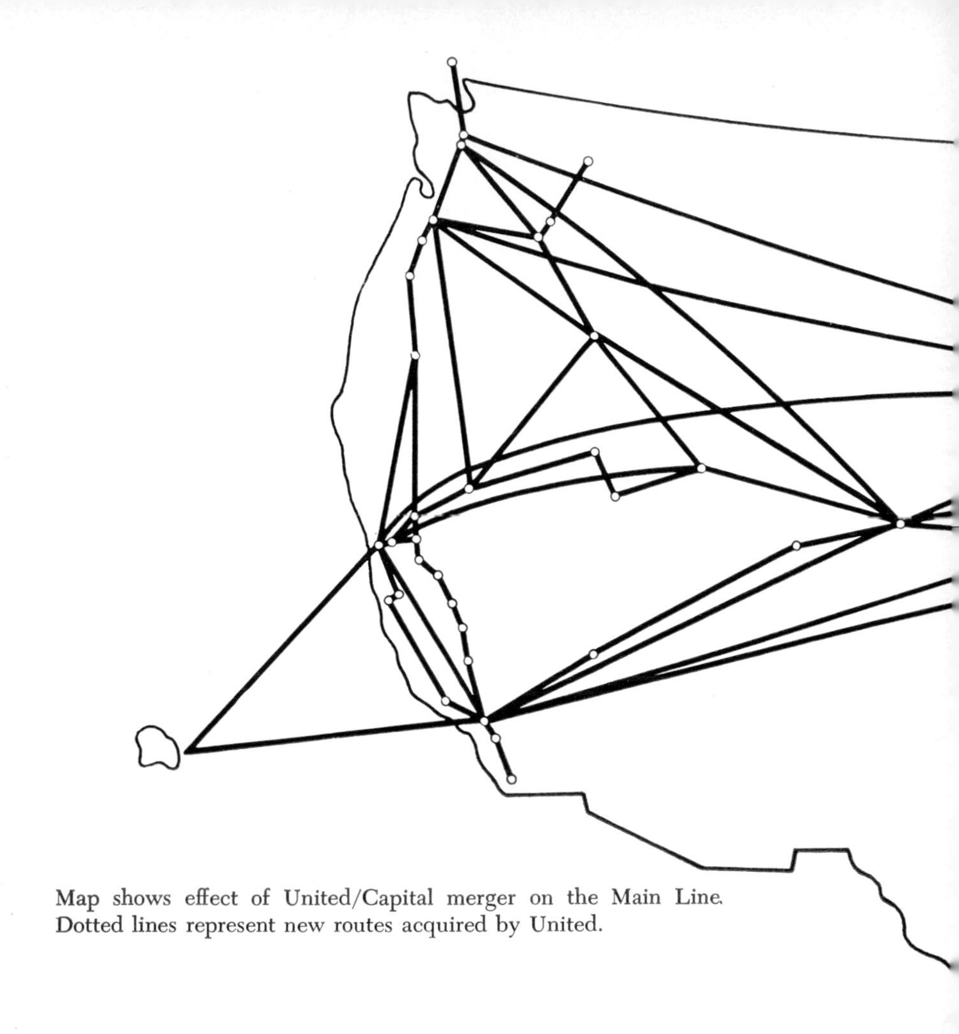

Map shows effect of United/Capital merger on the Main Line. Dotted lines represent new routes acquired by United.

First tangible evidence of merger was placement of United identification on former Capital public contact facilities, as here at the Willard Hotel ticket office in Washington, D.C.

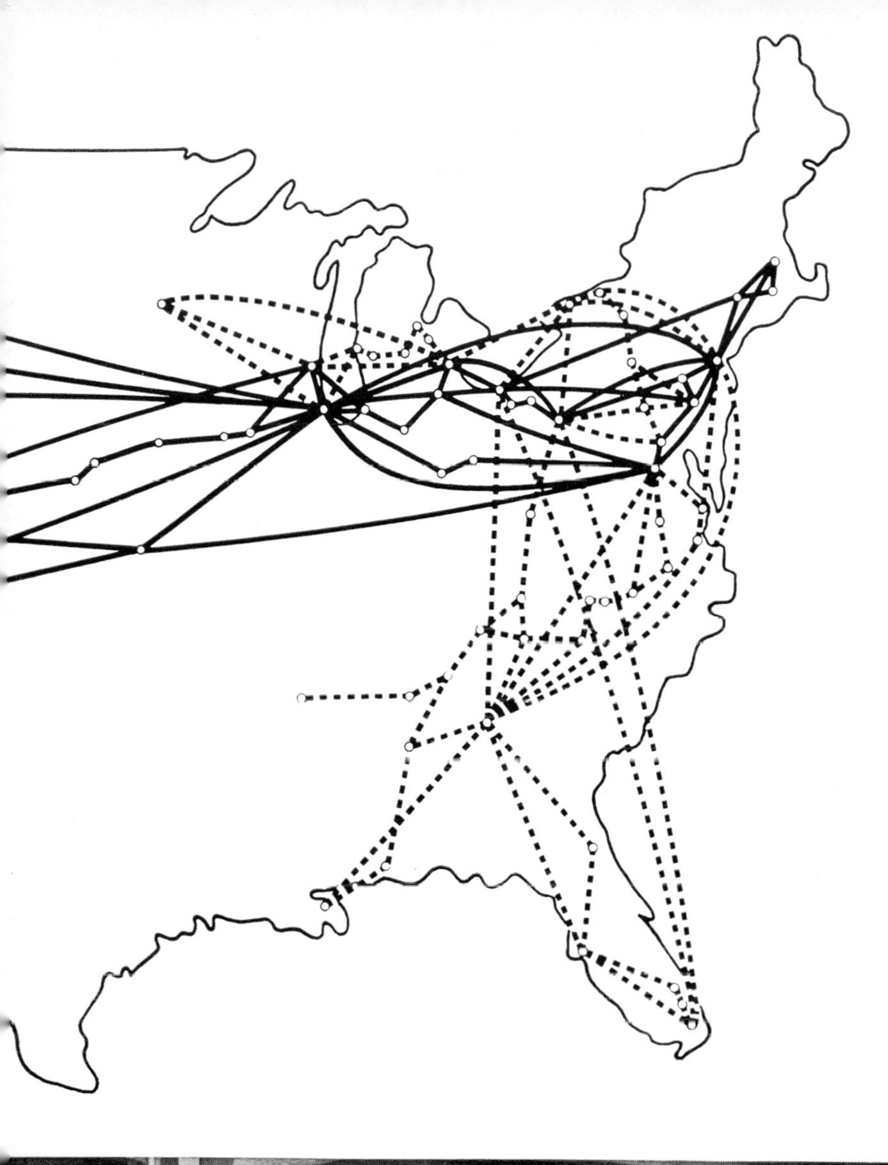

UNITED AIR LINES

With merger, United acquired a second large maintenance base—this one at Washington, D.C., where the Viscount fleet is given regular overhaul. It contains 150,000 square feet of space and encompasses three and a half complete hangars.

The first Viscount to be repainted with United's colors after merger rolls out of the Washington Maintenance Base. Others in the 41-plane Viscount fleet acquired by United received similar new paint jobs as they underwent regular periodic overhaul.

June 30 Stout Air Services, country's most experienced passenger line, bought by United Aircraft & Transport and later merged into National Air Transport.

Sept. 16 Boeing School of Aeronautics established at Oakland to train pilots and ground crews.

Sept. 23 Varney Air Lines extends operations from Pasco to Spokane, Portland, and Seattle.

1930

March 31 United Aircraft & Transport captures National Air Transport after exciting stock and proxy battle, merging San Francisco–Chicago–New York Main Line into one operation.

April 29 Congress passes McNary-Watres Act which encourages further airline growth including operation of larger passenger planes.

May 15 World's first airline stewardesses employed by Boeing Air Transport on San Francisco–Chicago route.

May 19 Postmaster General Walter Folger Brown summons airline operators to so-called "spoils conferences," sets up three competitive transcontinental rivals for United.

June 30 United Aircraft & Transport buys Varney Air Lines.

Nov. 30 National Air Transport abandons Stout's former Chicago–Detroit–Cleveland route.

1931

July 1 United Air Lines organized as management company for Boeing Air Transport, Pacific Air Transport, National Air Transport, and Varney Air Lines.

1932

Jan. 16 Omaha-Watertown extension forced on Boeing Air Transport.

June Construction starts on Boeing 247, first all-metal, low-wing transport.

1933

March 3 Postmaster General Brown era ends with 27,062 miles of airways in operation; United system handles 40 per cent of all traffic.

March 30 First Boeing 247 delivered to United Air Lines.

June Boeing 247s placed in service, reducing coast-to-coast time to 19½ hours.

July W. A. Patterson becomes president of Boeing Air Transport, Pacific Air Transport, National Air Transport, and Varney Air Lines; continues as vice-president of United Air Lines.

September Senate committee headed by Hugo Black launches investigation of alleged collusion in air mail contracts.

Sept. 30 Boeing Air Transport absorbs Varney system.

1934

Feb. 9 Air mail contracts canceled by Postmaster General Farley.

Feb. 18 First DC-2 sets coast-to-coast record of 13 hours, 4 minutes.

Feb. 20 Army pilots take over air mail service, flying military planes; United continues operating regular schedules without mail.

March 10 President Roosevelt cancels all air mail flying because of epidemic of Army plane crashes.

March 17 Army air mail flying resumes in daytime only.

March 30 Government advertises for new bids for air mail routes.

April 13 Presidential decree purges all airline executives summoned to Postmaster Brown's so-called "spoils conference." W. A. Patterson becomes head of reorganized United Air Lines.

May 1 United Air Lines, Inc., becomes operating company.

May 4 United Air Lines receives contracts covering all segments of its coast-to-coast and Pacific Coast system but loses Chicago-Dallas route.

June 12 Congress passes new Air Mail Act, forbidding airlines and manufacturers to be affiliated.

July 20 United Aircraft & Transport holding company divided into three separate companies—United Air Lines Transport Corporation, United Aircraft Corporation, and Boeing Airplane Company. Separate identities of National Air Transport, Boeing Air Transport, Pacific Air Transport, and Varney Air Lines finally dropped.

August 23 United contracts with Railway Express Agency to handle air express; other airlines set up General Air Express.

1935

June 4 United files "Long Suit" in U.S. Court of Claims for damages from air mail cancellation and to clear executives of collusion charges.

1936

February General Air Express folds; other airlines join United in Railway Express contract.

March United Air Lines, in collaboration with Transcontinental & Western Airlines, Pan American Airways, Eastern Air Lines, and American Airlines places order for experimental Douglas DC-4.

December Douglas DC-3 service inaugurated by United Air Lines, cutting coast-to-coast time to 15 hours 57 minutes.

December First airline flight kitchen opens at United's Oakland station.

1937

January 19 "Skylounge" luxury service opens between New York and Chicago.

July 1 United buys Cheyenne-Denver operation of Wyoming Air Services.

July Overnight sleeper service inaugurated, coast-to-coast.

1938

August 22 Civil Aeronautics Act becomes effective, establishing Civil Aeronautics Board and emancipating airlines from Post Office Department control.

1939

May First DC-4 demonstration flights made cross-country by United Air Lines.

1940

Airlines become increasingly important in movement of national defense passenger and cargo traffic.

June 19 Civil Aeronautics Board denies merger of United and Western Air Express; approves interchange of equipment for through sleeper service between New York and Los Angeles.

October Boeing School of Aeronautics begins training military personnel.

1941

Jan. 1 First airline pension program established by United Air Lines.

February Airlines release all DC-4s on order from Douglas Aircraft to government.

Under Edgar S. Gorrell, airlines lay plans for pooling resources to form global war transport system, thus avoiding being taken over by government.

Dec. 7 Pearl Harbor—and airlines "go to war."

1942

Jan. 9 United Air Lines' overhaul base at Cheyenne becomes modification center for bombers.

May Airline operations to Alaska begin under Army contract.

Sept. 23 Pacific operations begun by United Air Lines under Army contract.

1943

March 1 "Long Suit" settled—United Air Lines awarded withheld air mail pay for all former subsidiary lines.

June 7 Civil Aeronautics Board awards Toledo-Washington route to United.

Sept. 27 United acquires 75 per cent of capital stock of Lineas Aereas Mexicanas, S.A.

Oct. 15 Cargoliner service begun coast-to-coast.

1944

April United applies for routes from San Francisco and Los Angeles to Honolulu.

July Civil Aeronautics Board awards Cleveland-Hartford-Boston route to United.

Nov. 15 United concludes 2½ years of military flying in Alaska for Air Transport Command.

Dec. 21 Civil Aeronautics Board okays United service to Detroit.

1945

January United Air Lines receives special National Safety Council award for three years and more than one billion passenger miles of accident-free operations.

July 31 Bomber modification ends at Cheyenne after 5500 Flying Fortresses have been prepared for combat.

Nov. 10 Training of more than 7000 military personnel completed at Oakland training center.

1946

Jan 1 Forty-hour work week pioneered for industry.

March 1 Converted Army C-54s take to airways to relieve traffic congestion. Postwar confusion on airways with airlines unable to handle pent-up flood of priority-free traffic.

July 2 Civil Aeronautics Board awards San Francisco–Honolulu route to United.

1947

Confusion on airways gradually ends as airlines get back equipment and experienced personnel from armed services.

March 6 United acquires Los Angeles–Denver route from Western Air Lines, thereby gaining direct entry from East into Southern California.

April 27 First postwar airliner, five-mile-a-minute, pressurized cabin DC-6, goes into coast-to-coast service, cutting transcontinental time to less than 10 hours.

May 1 United opens San Francisco–Honolulu service.

1948

January Operations hub opened by United at Denver to set new pattern for centralized control of airline activities.

April 28 All maintenance work centralized by United at new San Francisco "push button" overhaul base.

July 8 United carries 10,000,000th passenger and flies five billionth passenger mile.

Use of "best weather" routes and expanded system of electronic aids, including ILS and surveillance radar, bring new dependability to airline operations.

Family air travel plan proves popular.

1949

Airline dependability shows continued increases with United, for example, completing 98 per cent of all scheduled miles.

May Air coach services expand but economic justification debated.

1950

Scheduled airlines of U.S. achieve record traffic highs and net earnings and move to sound economic level. In year, domestic and U.S. international airlines carried 19 million passengers more than 20 billion miles.

Jan. 15 Boeing Stratocruiser service introduced by United on San Francisco–Honolulu route.

July New war clouds—and airlines begin participation in Korean airlift.

Aug. 4 Civil Aeronautics Board grants Los Angeles–Honolulu route to United; service inaugurated October 9.

1951

Jan. 31 United completes 10,000th crossing between California and Hawaii in more than eight years of trans-Pacific operations, both commercial and military.

Feb. 20 Order placed by United for 30 new-type, twin-engined Convair-Liner 340s, to cost $16,500,000. Order subsequently increased to fifty-five.

April 6 United Air Lines and commercial air transportation round out first quarter century of service.

Sept. 30 Coast-to-coast air coach service inaugurated by United, using four-engined, 66-passenger DC-4 Mainliners.

1952

June $56,000,000 plane purchase program announced by United, to include 25 four-engined DC-7s.

July Operations of United Air Lines' subsidiary, Lineas Aereas Mexicanas, S.A., sold to new Mexican company, Lineas Asociadas Mexicanas, S.A.

Sept. 11 UAL service temporarily suspended at Santa Barbara, Monterey, Eureka-Arcata, Red Bluff and Rock Springs, in compliance with Civil Aeronautics Board order.

Nov. 16 Mainliner Convair service introduced to provide improved service to intermediate cities across Main Line.

1953

February United Air Lines and Radio Corporation of America launch program to develop airborne radar unit for weather mapping on commercial transports.

March 22 DC-6 air coach flights inaugurated by United between California and Hawaii, then extended in April to United's mainland routes.

July Employe stock-purchase plan introduced by United for three-year period. Company adds 15 per cent to each participating employe's investment.

July 16 United Air Lines opens new Denver Operating Base, representing latest in centralized control of airline operations.

September Through one-plane service between the Pacific Northwest and Southwest provided through interchange operations of United Air Lines, Braniff International Airways, and Continental Air Lines.

Oct. 3 More than three years of flying troops and supplies in Tokyo airlift concluded. During 39 months of contract operations, United completed approximately 1000 round trips between San Francisco and Tokyo, carrying 25,000 troops and large quantities of military and medical supplies.

Oct. 6 Post Office Department and four U.S. scheduled airlines—American, Capital, TWA, and United—begin experiment in carrying first-class mail by air between Chicago and both New York–Newark and Washington, D.C.

Dec. 17 Nation observes 50th anniversary of powered flight—from the Wright Brothers' first flight at Kitty Hawk, N.C., to the Douglas DC-7.

1954

April 1 U.S. government reduces Federal transportation tax from 15 to 10 per cent, representing annual saving of $40,000,000 to nation's travelers.

May 24 United conducts first dawn-to-dusk flight from New York to Honolulu. New DC-7 Mainliners span 5000-mile route, stopping only at San Francisco, in 16 hours, 51 minutes elapsed time.

June United completes installation of four electronic flight simulators at its Chicago and Denver flight training centers to provide advanced and improved pilot training.

June 1 DC-7 Mainliner nonstop, coast-to-coast service opened between San Francisco and New York. Eastbound nonstop time, 7½ hours; westbound, with one stop, 9½ hours.

July United announces sale of its six Boeing Stratocruisers to British Overseas Airways.

Aug. 1 United reaches all-time high of 300,000 miles of flying daily.

August United Air Lines' Board of Directors votes expenditure of $21,000,000 for new aircraft; $4,000,000 for installation of airborne radar on company's fleet.

October United begins experiments with model Airdock at Denver.

Nov. 16 United carries its 30-millionth passenger.

Dec. 31 U.S. scheduled airlines complete year with best safety record in history. Carrying nearly 35 million passengers over 20 billion passenger miles, they establish passenger safety rate of 0.07 fatalities per hundred million passenger miles.

During the year, airlines organize Civil Reserve Air Fleet, earmarking several hundred four-engine aircraft for military airlift in emergency. Airliners are modified to make them adaptable for military use—with airline crews—on 48 hours' notice.

Passenger helicopter service begun in New York and Los Angeles areas by two scheduled operators.

1955

Jan. 1 DC-7 Mainliner service inaugurated by United between Hawaii and California.

Feb. 16 United receives permanent authorization to operate between Los Angeles and Honolulu.

April 1 Civil Aeronautics Board reduces subsidy-free air mail rates paid to 13 trunk-line operators. New rates range from 35.8 to 86.6 cents a ton-mile.

May 6 First nonstop flights between New York and San Francisco, requiring only 8¾ hours for the 3000-mile trip, launched by United.

May 15 Twenty-fifth anniversary of airline stewardess service, pioneered by Boeing Air Transport, United forerunner.

June Civil Aeronautics Board grants permanent certificates to 13 local service carriers.

June Three additional electronic flight simulators ordered, making United the largest airline user of such equipment in the world.

July United completes first installation of C-band weather-mapping radar.

Sept. 16 Airline "Big Three"—United, American, and TWA—institute 30-day excursion rates on coast-to-coast air coach flights—$160 round trip between designated East and West Coast cities.

Sept. Civil Aeronautics Board removes restrictions on United nonstop flights between Pacific Northwest and Chicago. Service launched Oct. 31, 1955.

Oct. 25 United is first domestic airline to order jetliners—30 Douglas DC-8s costing $175,000,000.

Nov. Civil Aeronautics Board authorizes United service to Pittsburgh and Kansas City. Flights subsequently inaugurated at Pittsburgh on Jan. 22, 1956; at Kansas City, March 1, 1956.

Dec. 28 Largest single airline-financing program in history completed by United—$150,000,000 over five years for expansion into jet age.

1956

Jan. 4 Service resumed to Santa Barbara and Monterey after three-year suspension.

April 6 United's 30th anniversary. In first three decades, UAL carried 38 million passengers nearly 25 billion passenger miles.

April 24 United completes 20,000th crossing on California–Hawaii route, representing some 50,000,000 miles of military contract and commercial flying since September, 1942.

April 30 United inaugurates DC-6A Cargoliner service between New York, Chicago, and San Francisco. Huge "flying freight car" carries 30,000 pounds of air mail, express, and freight.

July Six domestic trunk airlines—American, Eastern, National, Northwest, TWA, and United—agree on service of alcoholic beverages in flight—no drink served aloft to contain more than 1.6 ounces of any alcoholic beverage and no more than two drinks to any customer—in line with United's already established policy.

August Civil Aeronautics Board approves Boston–Washington, D.C., route for United, closing former East Coast gap.

Employe stock-purchase plan extended for second three-year period.

Oct. 1 Government eliminates 10 per cent federal transportation tax on international or overseas travel. Airlines press for complete elimination of tax, originally adopted as wartime measure to discourage nonessential travel.

Oct. 28 United "retires" last DC-3s from fleet. In 20 years of service, twin-engined planes flew nearly 400,000,000 revenue airplane miles and carried approximately 12,700,000 passengers.

December 20th anniversary of airline flight kitchens, pioneered by United at Oakland in 1936.

1957

March United and six other domestic airlines apply to Civil Aeronautics Board for 6 per cent fare increase to provide partial relief from narrowing profit margins pending final decision in General Passenger Fare Investigation.

April United's employe total passes 20,000 mark.

DC-7 Custom Coach service inaugurated by United.

Sept. Domestic airlines adopt $3 penalty charge for reservations not canceled and not used in effort to solve "no show" problem. Minimum Time Limit on ticket pick-up and reconfirmation on return and stopover reservations also part of program.

November United orders 11 Boeing 720 intermediate-range jetliners plus 10 additional DC-8s.

1958

January Top management of United broadened—in anticipation of complexities of jet age—to include seven senior vice-presidents and 18 vice-presidents.

February RAMAC, electronic reservations system, placed in full service on United's Main Line.

June United carries 50,000,000th passenger.

July $16,000,000 order placed by United with Teleregister Corp. for new electronic reservations system needed to meet Jet Age challenge.

September United begins jet flight crew training at Denver with first DC-8 electronic simulator in airline history.

October Airlines discontinue round-trip and certain other discount fares and cut family-plan discount from 50 to 33⅓ per cent.

1959

January Federal Aviation Agency, created by Congress in August, 1958, becomes fully operative, replacing previous Civil Aeronautics Administration and Airways Modernization Board.

January Dayton and Columbus added to United's Main Line.

April United sets industry record when all 16 American and National League baseball teams sign for charter flights—nine of them on an exclusive basis.

June First Douglas DC-8 Jet Mainliner delivered to United.

June Order signed for 11 more Boeing 720 jets, bringing total to 18.

September United inaugurates DC-8 service between San Francisco and New York.

September Jetarama, unique tent show created by United to introduce general public to the Jet Age, begins cross-country tour.

December By year's end, United terminates service at Scottsbluff, Grand Island, North Platte, Iowa City, Bend-Redmond, Klamath Falls, Bellingham, Twin Falls, and Ogden in accordance with decisions by the Civil Aeronautics Board in various local service cases.

1960

Feb. 18–22—"DC-8-to-the-Fiftieth State" introductory flight. New York–San Francisco–Honolulu, 9 hours, 53 minutes; Honolulu-Chicago nonstop, 7 hours, 52 minutes.

February United orders 20 medium-range Caravelle jetliners from Sud Aviation of France, for delivery in 1961.

April First Boeing 720 jetliner delivered to United.

May United's new $14,500,000 passenger terminal at New York International Airport dedicated, marking full completion although it had been in use since previous September.

June DC-7A Cargoliners placed in service by United.

June Ground broken for new UAL Executive Office and Training Center buildings near Chicago.

July Boeing 720 service inaugurated by United.

July Plans announced for merger of Capital Airlines into United Air Lines, subject to approval of the Civil Aeronautics Board and shareholders of both companies.

August UAL service at Cheyenne suspended following CAB order.

September United completes first full year of jet service, having carried 1,300,000 passengers more than 1,800,000,000 revenue passenger miles.

September Jetarama concludes its one-year tour, during which time it was seen by 1,090,000 people in 12 cities.

October Stockholders of both United Air Lines and Capital Airlines approve plan to merge Capital into United. Hearings in the merger case held before CAB Chief Examiner Thomas Wrenn.

1961

April 35th anniversary of United Air Lines.
CAB formally approves United/Capital merger.

May New Instamatic reservations system placed in use by United—the largest interconnected electronic data-processing facility ever built for business use.

June Legal merger of United and Capital takes place on June 1.
First Caravelle jetliner delivered to United from France.

July Caravelle service inaugurated between Chicago and New York.

October United's new $2,000,000 Training Center opened at Chicago.

December New Executive Office Building opened at Chicago.

INDEX

UNITED
UNITED
UNITED
1960 · BOEING 720
United
United
1950 · BOEING STRATOCRUISER
United
United
1946 · DOUGLAS DC-4
United Air Lines
1937 · DOUGLAS DC
1933 · BOEING 247
1930 · FORD TRI-MOTOR
1928 · BOEING 80-A